Life at Southern Living

Life at Southern Living®

A SORT OF MEMOIR

JOHN LOGUE &
GARY McCALLA

LOUISIANA STATE UNIVERSITY PRESS
Baton Rouge
MM

10 09 08 07 06 05 04 03 02 01 00

5 4 3 2 1

Designer: Amanda McDonald Scallan
Typeface: Sabon
Typesetter: Coghill Composition
Printer and binder: Thomson-Shore, Inc.

Library of Congress Cataloging-in-Publication Data

Logue, John, 1933–
    Life at Southern Living : a sort of memoir / John Logue & Gary McCalla.
        p.   cm.
    Includes index.
    ISBN 0-8071-2561-X (cloth : alk. paper)
    1. Southern living—History.   2. Logue, John, 1933–   3. McCalla, Gary.   4.
Journalists—Southern States—Biography.   5. Periodicals, Publishing of—Southern
States—History—20th century.   6. Corporate culture—Southern States—History—
20th century.   7. Southern States—Social life and customs—20th century.   I.
McCalla, Gary.   II. Title.

F206.S855 L64 2000
975'.043'092—dc21
[B]   00-037066

All photographs are reproduced courtesy of *Southern Living*.

Let this book be a toast, lifted to those editors and photographers and designers who have made Southern Living *the South's best-loved magazine, and also to those men and women in circulation and advertising sales who have spread the love where it would do the most good.*

Contents

Illustrations

Life at Southern Living

The thirty-foot-high windows set in native stone glowed in the trees like The Diamond as Big as the Ritz. A waterfall spilled down from the stone and ran like a trout stream through the floor of a three-story atrium which connected to a second building of steel and glass which burned in the dark like a sister gem. The captive stream in the atrium seemed to tumble with the lights of Christmas into the deep ravine, joining a second stream below the two buildings, making three round, descending pools which flowed on into a one-acre pond unseen in the outer darkness.

In reality the waterfall, the stream in the floor of the atrium, the water from the two streams roiling among rocks and ferns into the ravine, the water in the round ponds was captured by separate, hidden hydraulic systems and recycled like nature domesticated.

Automobiles pulled into the parking decks which hung like concrete terraces, themselves dotted and softened with trees. The people stepping out of the cars were dressed to wound. Heels if you wore them, diamonds if you had them, the older men stuffed into their best suits and ties, the younger men in a variety of more contemporary costume.

Women met and hugged as if they'd changed identities with their finery. To watch them, to hear them, you would not think they had seen each other all day every working day of the year. Most of the men were husbands or lovers or friends of the women who worked here. The men who were not husbands or lovers or friends but who actually worked here took on the same shine of enthusiasm as the women. The occasional men who came with men, and women who came with women, did so casually and nobody paid a damn bit of attention.

Towering over the comings and goings of the evening in the main lobby was a twenty-one-foot-tall sculpture by Texas artist Doug McLean, curving steel into an abstract landscape capturing the low mountain and thick trees and the living promise of growth outside the glass windows. The raw power of the sculpture was accepted by the party-goers as casually as if it were a low vase of cut flowers. All through the two buildings were original paintings and craft pieces in clay, glass, wood, metal, fiber collected from leading artists throughout the South. It was difficult to look away from one's work and not see into the imagination of some artist.

In the lobby, at the seafood station, were whole salmon poached in white wine, and fresh Gulf shrimp on ice with cocktail sauce. There was basil cheese terrine and sun-dried tomatoes. Spring rolls with peanut dipping sauce. Vidalia onion strudel. Parmesan cheese puffs with spinach cream filling. Soft drinks, "beer and wine until 10 P.M."

In the original employees' lounge was a carving station, serving hickory-grilled tenderloin of beef, roasted pork tenderloins with apricot salsa, honey-cured ham in Rosemary buns.

In the corporate dining room were desserts: old-fashioned ginger cookies, bounty of celestial brownies, and a variety of fruits and dessert cheeses, with coffee, hot spiced cider, cranberry fizz, and, of course, eggnog.

In the atrium between the two buildings, in the new employees' lounge that was ready now for the 1995 party, was a pasta station, with an assortment of ravioli and grilled vegetables, wild mushrooms, spinach walnuts. Also a pizza station, with Mediterranean pizzas and focaccia.

In the new auditorium were soft drinks and mineral water.

On the mezzanine of the main building, photographs of families and/or lovers were being taken by the company's highly skilled photography staff as a record of the evening.

There would be dancing in the atrium, around the "trout stream" meandering through the floor, "from 8 P.M. until 11 P.M.," when much of the decorum would be blasted into the night by a local disc jockey, with couples getting down to "Everybody Dance" by C&C Music Factory, or "Start Me Up" by, who else, the Rolling Stones, or maybe some slow dancing to Natalie Cole singing "Unforgettable," as the night eased toward the midnight hour, this annual dance having yet to break up at 11 P.M.

The night was not a command performance. It was the annual Christmas party. And it was a true, ding-a-ling party. Not so many companies can pull that off. But the company in Birmingham, Alabama, that publishes *Southern Living* has managed to do it for years.

Gyrating around the food tables were 1,200 employees of Southern Progress Corporation and their families and guests. Fuel for the party came from the astonishingly profitable *Southern Living* and its first cousin, Oxmoor House, the book division, as well as the upscale magazine of deathless interiors, *Southern Accents*; the nation's largest food magazine, *Cooking Light*; and the parent magazine of them all, *Progressive Farmer*, which has survived since 1886 and is yet the dominant farm magazine in America. *Weight Watchers* magazine was to join the publishing lineup within the year as a cash acquisition, and a new magazine, *Coastal Living*, was to be launched in the spring of 1997 and become a remarkable success.

Southern Living serves over three million subscribers and commands the affection of *fourteen million* readers each month. This magazine of travel and gardens and homes and food and Southern people contributing to the good life enjoys the most astonishingly loyal audience in all of magazine publishing. Together the company's magazines and books account for an annual profit of over $200 million, all now flowing to Time-Warner, owners since buying Southern Progress for $480 million in 1985, one of the best buys in American publishing history.

Careless of the company's financial history, the party raged on. The tall, thin young man called "Tom" each time he stopped to shake a hand was the new president, Tom Angelillo, a career employee and a Washington and Lee man, very much the gentleman, just as were the gentlemen who started the company over a hundred years ago. He was consecutively popular with the crowd under the great sculpture. He couldn't get to the carving station for the sea of hands he had to shake. (The seafood station was there, all right, but his colleagues knew that this man would sooner eat a live wolf than a dead fish.) His wife, Rosey, was as beautiful as she was tiny, in a velvet jacket with a sequined bodice and a brief chiffon skirt, all black and glittering like the night.

Coming through the jangle of glad noise was a short, thick-in-the-chest older man, somewhat lost in the crowd, his once-dark hair shot through with gray. You would have to look at him very carefully to notice his American Indian heritage and to see the lingering aspects of the once-young man who had climbed in the boxing ring uncounted times to take on all amateur comers, be they Golden Glove or college fighters. His name was McCalla. Gary McCalla from Amber, Oklahoma, and now Birmingham, Alabama. Before he retired he had defined and edited *Southern Living* for twenty-two years.

Shaking his hand was another older guy, not tall, not so skinny as he once was, with an Irish flush on his face and some wise-ass mischief not far from his lips. His name was Logue. John Logue. Before he retired he had been Creative Director of the company and editor-in-chief of Oxmoor House.

"McCalla, who are these people?" said Logue.

"Godamighty, don't ask me," said McCalla.

The Christmas issue, 1995, of *Southern Living* listed 123 individuals on its editorial staff.

"Remember our first editorial meeting at Callaway Gardens?" said Logue. "Seven of us in one van? That was it, the *Southern Living* staff."

"Yep. And not one damn idea where we were going."

"Who would've guessed this was where we were headed?"

McCalla laughed his growl of a laugh, his voice having dropped an octave deeper about every ten years. "It's good to see the damn kids running things," he said. "None of 'em ever saw the inside of a magazine until they got here."

"Well, it wasn't exactly *here*," said Logue.

"No," McCalla said, "not hardly." The contrast with the aspect of the old building at 821 North 19th Street made the two of them laugh. They remembered the dark awnings and the unwashed windows and the black water tank on top with the proud logo: *Progressive Farmer* painted on the side, and the exposed pipes running under the high ceilings, including the sewer pipe which once cracked into a ghastly mess and had to be temporarily propped up with a two-by-four.

"We are gonna write the bloody book: *How to Commit Journalism*," said Logue. "We're gonna quit talking about it and write it."

"I'm game," said McCalla, who had finished building his two barns and his thirty acres of wooden fences with his own hands and had finally been persuaded by his accountant to get the hell out of thoroughbred horse racing and had some time on his hands. Logue had finished writing the two mystery novels he owed Dell Books, and he had time on his hands, too.

"Remember your old philosophy for the magazine," said Logue, " 'simple, square, and straightforward' . . . the *exact opposite* of the people who wrote it, designed it, photographed it, and sold it."

"True," said McCalla, "but the only real scandal we ever had was me."

"Oh, yeah? Strangers might believe that, but nobody else would. Listen, we won't tell everything that happened. But everything we do write, did happen. I'm calling you Monday," said Logue, who then eased off to the carving table, hoping to get to the 150 pounds of beef and the 100 pounds of pork tenderloin before the Washington and Lee man broke away from the crowd and ate it all up.

Moving toward McCalla, a head above the crowd, was an older man with a tall face and a square jaw who would remind you of the long ago cowboy star Randolph Scott. His name was Cunningham. Emory Cunningham. He had joined The Progressive Farmer Company in 1948 and ultimately became its president and chairman. The idea for starting *Southern Living* in those post–World War II years had been his obsession, and very likely his most memorable contribution had been to convince the elderly men who owned the company to risk it all on the idea of this new magazine for the New South. Just what this new magazine should include was a matter for much debate among those men, most of whom had been born in the nineteenth century, and the result had damn near sunk the entire enterprise.

Decades later, at the end of his career, Cunningham had convinced the owners—facing ruinous inheritance taxes—that it was time to sell the company. And he convinced them to sell it to Time, Inc. There was much concern among employees that graduates of the Harvard Business School would soon be publishing *Southern Living*. On the day the company was sold, Cunningham said to the department heads: "We may wind up influencing them more than they influence us."

Funny thing. Sitting today in the corner office on the thirty-fourth floor of the Time-Life Building is Don Logan, president and CEO of Time, Inc. Its world-wide magazine and book publishing operation reports directly to him. Like Cunningham, a child of North Alabama, Logan came to The Progressive Farmer Company to run its computer fulfillment service, stayed on to save Oxmoor House from oblivion, and succeeded Emory as a very popular president and CEO of Southern Progress. "They didn't swallow us. We swallowed them," was the gleeful response at Southern Progress to Logan's move to New York.

Cunningham and McCalla shook hands, even while shaking their heads at the building, the two-story sculpture, the glad rags and the glad noise, the everywhere Christmas prosperity in the room.

"These young people have no idea where we came from," said Cunningham, turning, looking across the happy chaos of employees and their families.

"No," McCalla said, "they couldn't imagine." While he had Cunningham captive, McCalla said, "Emory, do you remember the memo Logue and I wrote to you in the early days, saying what we believed had to be done to save *Southern Living*?"

Emory thought about it, shook his head, "No. I don't remember that."

McCalla didn't press it. Some months later Emory said that he had looked in his files and found the memo, but he did not comment on it other than to say he found it.

McCalla himself pressed forward to the carving table, being a red meat man . . . "as rare as you can make it . . ." The twenty-three years of feasting in the test kitchens at *Southern Living* had honed his palate for every good Southern thing that a man might eat.

The glass in the thirty-foot-high windows continued to shine into the night, joining the thin vibrations of Michael Jackson singing "History."

1

A Visit to 19th Street

1965. Gary McCalla whipped his new Mustang down Highway 79 from Huntsville, Alabama, headed for a job interview in Birmingham with The Progressive Farmer Company. (The same original Mustang sits in the driveway of his farm today, a family heirloom, gathering value with each passing year.)

McCalla had been running an operation called Tech Productions. It built traveling exhibits that NASA used to tell its space exploration story across the country, hoping to keep the program popular with the American taxpayers.

"We had about one hundred of the best graphic artists in the country," remembered McCalla. "We were just a little ol' operation, but we were about a fourth the size of The Progressive Farmer Company in business volume. We'd lost our latest contract in Huntsville, but we'd gotten one in Houston. I liked Houston. But I didn't want to get back in the game. I wanted out. Preparing a bid for a NASA contract was hell. Once I came in on a Saturday afternoon and only left my desk on Wednesday for two hours to sleep in my bed. The rest of the week I just slept sitting at my desk until the bid was in the next Saturday."

Not that there hadn't been some good times in Huntsville. McCalla had met Werner Von Braun and several of the other rocket scientists that he brought with him from Germany after the war to help America put a man on the moon.

McCalla got to be real friends with Von Braun's trigger man on all his rocket firings, Albert Zieler. "I met Zieler at a party. We used to go out drinking in the private clubs around Huntsville. He taught me to water ski. We were at a party one night after Albert had fired all those rocket shots out in the Pacific. He was a big, tall, rangy, good-looking guy. I said, 'Albert, how many space shots have you fired?' He thought a minute, 'Oh, about six hundred and ninety-two.' I said, 'Damn, I didn't know we'd fired that many.' He said, 'You must remember . . . the first six hundred were V-2s.' He had a sense of humor," remembered McCalla, "not that there was anything funny about the V-2s themselves. Albert loved the United States. All the German scientists I met did. They chose Huntsville to live in because the low mountains reminded them of Germany."

A telephone conversation with an old friend had put McCalla on the road to Birmingham. "I called an old army buddy of mine, Paul Cook. We'd served in France together. In fact, he introduced me to my first wife, who was from Paris. I said, 'Cook, I got to get back to civilization.' "

Cook, in 1965, was director of tourism in South Carolina. He'd heard that The Progressive Farmer Company was starting a new magazine, and that it was supposed to include travel editorial. Cook knew that McCalla, after getting out of the Army and leaving a job with Dresser Industries, had spent a year on the street trying to find investors to back a travel magazine he'd dreamed up and named *Passport*. He only got as far as a very slick dummy prototype. In truth, it put to shame the brochure Progressive Farmer had created to help sell advertising into the first issues of the yet-to-be-published *Southern Living*.

McCalla was definitely interested in this new magazine. Cook could tell him little about its direction, other than it was going to circulate in the South. McCalla was about to learn that Cook was standing at the end of a long line of those who didn't know what exact direction the magazine was about to take, including the editor.

Progressive Farmer magazine was no mystery to McCalla. He'd grown up on a farm in Oklahoma reading it. Before he hit the road for Birmingham, he'd gotten a phone call through to Red Youngsteadt, who had recently been named editor of the formative *Southern Living*. Youngsteadt's first name was Norman, but he preferred to be called Red. He didn't have a job opening at the moment, but he said he'd be willing to talk to McCalla about future employment. He said *Southern Living* was going to be a magazine for the New South.

"Red, are you gonna try to do what *Sunset* has done in California?" asked McCalla, as prophetic a question as there has ever been in the history of the magazine business. Red had never heard of *Sunset*. McCalla had picked it up on the newsstand a time or two in Texas. It was a regional magazine of travel, food, home, and gardens and was owned by the Lane family in Menlo Park, California.

McCalla, who has a remarkable sense of direction, perhaps from his Choctaw ancestors, lost his way in north Birmingham. In those days, the city had no system of signs to guide travelers through town. And mighty few people were looking to stop and live in Birmingham, which had been at the epicenter of the ongoing racial conflicts in America. The images of Bull Connor, police dogs, fire hoses, and Martin Luther King writing his famous letter from the Birmingham jail were fresh in the minds and fears of Americans. McCalla had told his father he was interviewing for a job in Birmingham. His reaction had been, "Why the hell would anybody want to live in Birmingham?"

McCalla found his way past Boutwell Auditorium, which had been built when Enrico Caruso was barely in his grave. Reluctantly he parked his new Mustang in the uneven, unpaved lot across 19th Street from the Progressive Farmer building. The three-story concrete pile loomed like something from the early Industrial Revolution. He crossed 19th Street, which ran on between low, failed, often boarded-up buildings and an occasional cheap dive, past an historic but neglected cemetery—one long avenue of dreams gone sour, not an optimistic address for a new magazine of the modern South.

Beside the low entrance was the proud bronze plate: THE PROGRESSIVE FARMER, the only aspect of the outside building cleaned and shined, as if a good name could conquer all. Even the vintage building did not prepare McCalla for the telephone switchboard inside. A woman with earphones over her head like a pioneer telegrapher sat connecting and disconnecting conversations as she plugged and unplugged black umbilical cords into a switchboard such as you could not find outside of an AT&T museum. He was to learn her name was Joyce Black. No more pleasant, efficient employee ever worked for a publisher. God knows she had to be the last of her line at that switchboard. She directed McCalla up the stairs to the office of Red Youngsteadt.

A few years later, Joyce advised an applicant for an editorial assistant's job with this same Mr. McCalla, saying: "You are a very brave young woman." Joyce didn't know how brave. Barbara, for years, dominated the job as executive assistant of *Southern Living*, and in retirement has had the more arduous role of Mrs. McCalla.

McCalla stepped into the long, dark concrete corridor of the old Progressive Farmer building, which gave him pause. "I swear, it reminded me of Verdun, France, and the underground fortress called the Citadel, built in the 1870s. You could look down the concrete corridor of the Citadel for five hundred yards." Adding to the gloom at Verdun for McCalla was the silence of the one million men killed there during World War I.

The Progressive Farmer building was the first concrete-reinforced structure in Birmingham, built by American Transfer. It was for a long time the home of the *Birmingham Post*, which in pre–World War II years shared space with *Progressive Farmer*. In 1965 the building was still stocked with canned food and water as an official city bomb shelter of the Cold War. It would have taken a direct hit to bring down the twelve-inch walls, which, when the phone company drilled to install new lines, routinely ate steel bits. McCalla, staring down the corridor with thoughts of Verdun, knew nothing of the hot wars raging inside the building over the editorial content of the unborn magazine, *Southern Living*.

Red Youngsteadt proved to be a quiet little man, with a high, freckled forehead, a thatch of fading red hair, and a jumpy little mustache. He looked for the world like a bureaucrat out of Africa, which in fact he had recently been. He was rather solemn, more than quiet, and had none of the energy necessary for the job of running a magazine. Most of the energy in his office was supplied by Editorial Assistant Beth Carlson, whose rapid words and quick steps and overwhelming warmth were for years to dominate the *Southern Living* offices, along with her petite blonde pal, Dixie Snell, who later managed to keep McCalla and Logue almost on the straight and narrow while turning out an amazing amount of editorial material as a part-time employee.

Joining the staff, shortly after McCalla, was a smart, beautiful editorial assistant, Carey Hinds, a senior at Birmingham Southern, who was to have a brief but critical role in the destiny of the magazine.

Carlson, not long before her unexpected death, remembered that in the summer of 1965 Youngsteadt sat behind his large desk "looking at his thumbnails," rarely so much as taking a telephone call from the outside world. He only jumped at the inside voice of Dr. Alexander Nunn, who ran all editorial of The Progressive Farmer Company, including that of the unborn *Southern Living*, with the iron conviction of a man in love with the nineteenth century. Dr. Nunn, aiming his bald bullet head and staring through his prescription glasses, was known to advise young employees, including the future President Emory Cunningham, that: "We are mighty hard on whiskey here at *The Progressive Farmer*." (After seeing cases of booze disappear up into the hotel suite of his first *P.F.* advertising sales meeting, Cunningham as an apprentice salesman understood that "hard on whiskey" had separate meanings within the organization.)

Dixie Snell was born with that delightful name despite the suspicions of incredulous subscribers and advertisers. She remembered that Red Youngsteadt was a particularly "humorless man." She said, "He was not much to look at, but wasn't much to talk to either. He never did smile. He was such a deadpan. You know me, I went in his office one day and said, 'Red, why don't you smile sometimes?' Uh-oh, he didn't like that. I was glad he wasn't on the magazine when they called me back to work in August. That's terrible to say. I hope he doesn't read this."

Dixie was assured that Red, in fact, was dead and exempt from embarrassment, his strange career at an end. Youngsteadt studied art at the University of North Carolina. He came to *Progressive Farmer* in 1955 as visual arts editor. He left five years later as information advisor to the Sudanese government, working in Ethiopia, Nigeria, Algeria, and, of all places, Paris. He'd come back to *P.F.* as associate managing editor, meaning he helped place the ads in the farm magazine's confusing number of editions. He'd never been so much as a regional editor.

In a bizarre power play, Dr. Nunn named Red Youngsteadt editor of *Southern Living* in May of 1965. The first issue was due to be published in February of 1966, and when McCalla entered the building on June 25, the clock on the wall was ticking.

The more contemporary thinkers within the company had wanted a national search made and an editor selected with consumer magazine experience. The Old Guard within the farm magazine would not hear of it, though Dr. Nunn did interview at least one outside candidate for editor of *Southern Living*. That was Jim Autry, the young managing editor of *Better Homes & Gardens*. They flew him from Des Moines, Iowa, to Birmingham in early 1965 to be interviewed.

"I really wanted the job," Autry told his longtime friend Gary McCalla these thirty years later. "I was a Southern boy, from Mississippi, and I thought, 'This job, building a Southern magazine, is for me.' " Autry's father had been named by *Progressive Farmer* as "Rural Minister of the Year" in 1964. His father also wrote fiction, and one year he wrote ten of the twelve short stories that appeared in *Progressive Farmer*. Coming from a religious father known to *P.F.* for his writing, Jim Autry was a serious candidate to edit the long-anticipated *Southern Living*.

Autry told McCalla, "I met with Dr. Nunn, Mr. Butler, and several others. They wanted to take non-farm circulation from *Progressive Farmer* and publish a magazine for those readers using the *P.F.* editorial staff. There was no other plan. I knew the demographics of that excess *P.F.* circulation was probably not ideal. And the *P.F.* staff's ideas for food photography were awful." Autry cited the infamous "Thanksgiving from Outer Space" as typical of the story ideas the *P.F.* staff had dreamed up for the *Southern Living* food section.

"I wrote a long letter to Dr. Nunn, outlining what I thought was a good plan for the new magazine," said Autry. "I outlined exactly how I would go about executing the plan. I heard later that Dr. Nunn thought my letter was 'arrogant and impertinent.' I also heard later that my letter was used as a sort of guide to producing *Southern Living*."

It was very likely that Autry got his later information from Paul Plawin, who ultimately left *Southern Living* for *Better Homes & Gardens*. McCalla, who joined the *Southern Living* staff in the summer of 1965, never saw Autry's letter, or even knew that it existed. Not to say Dr. Nunn didn't use elements of it in his own planning. Autry obviously incurred Nunn's wrath with his very logical argument that outside talent would have to be brought in to create a successful consumer magazine.

But that wasn't the last time Jim Autry was contacted by The Progressive Farmer Company. He left *Better Homes & Gardens*, temporarily, and was editing *New Orleans Magazine* in 1968, when *P.F.*'s new president, Emory Cunningham, was interviewing outside talent to come in and take over a faltering *Southern Living*.

"Roger McGuire knew I was leaving New Orleans and going back to *BH&G*," said Autry. "He called me and said, 'Before you go back, come talk with us.' I didn't because I'd already told Bob Barnett that I was returning to *BH&G*."

Neither McGuire nor Cunningham offered Autry the editor's job in 1968, but he would have been a serious candidate. McCalla (who was to get the job) and Logue kidded McGuire about it for years after *Southern Living* had achieved significant success. "No telling how much money we would be making," they would say, "if we had a real editor." McGuire would only grin and deny nothing.

In 1965, McCalla visited briefly with Youngsteadt, who was even more vague in person than he had been on the telephone as to the direction of *Southern Living*. He said it was to be "a magazine edited by Southerners for Southerners," a cliché phrase that didn't explain anything. Red quoted Eugene Butler of Dallas, Texas, principal owner and president of the company and nearing his fiftieth year on the editorial staff, as believing *Southern Living* "could help heal the breach between rural and city people in the South."

McCalla, who had grown up on an Oklahoma farm, "had no idea what the hell that meant. 'What breach?' " he wondered, but kept his counsel, which he will admit has always been his strength when it comes to company politics. In twenty-two years of editing *Southern Living* he wrote two memos. "Hell, they can't hang you for what you don't put in writing" was a favorite McCalla saying.

He came away from his conversation with Youngsteadt with the belief that the new magazine would be whatever editorial beast Dr. Alexander Nunn commanded it to be. And God help the disbelievers.

McCalla met the staff's two new all-purpose writers, Brad Byers and Paul Plawin. "Byers was a serious, uptight sort of guy," remembered McCalla. "He worked for the Dow Chemical magazine, *Dow Corral*, in Boulder, Colorado, when The Progressive Farmer Company contacted him. And he'd edited the *Texas Presbyterian* magazine. And maybe that's why Dr. Nunn hired him. He wouldn't dazzle you as a writer. He was no big hit with the girls, either, but he had an eye for them."

Byers said years later that he and Jim Autry were interviewed at the same time in Dallas, Texas, by Eugene Butler, Dr. Alexander Nunn, and *P.F.* Texas Edition Editor Charlie Scruggs. Autry was up for editor of *Southern Living* and Byers for associate editor. Byers had been recommended by the chairman of the University of Texas Journalism Department, DeWitt Reddick.

Byers said Autry wanted to know who at the company would have the authority "to kick ass." And that Dr. Nunn said that at The Progressive Farmer Company they didn't "kick ass." Byers said the *P.F.* men told him they had "one million dollars to spend on *Southern Living* over the next five years."

Byers said he felt Red Youngsteadt never had the full confidence of the "hierarchy" at *P.F.*, or confidence in himself as editor of *Southern Living*.

He said, "I felt his downfall was when—probably in response to all our criticism about the backwoods attitude—he proposed doing a piece on Martin Luther King in the first issue." That would have done it with Dr. Nunn.

Gary McCalla does not remember Red proposing a story on King. "He could have done it, but it got by me," he said.

Dixie Snell remembered that Byers could be severe in his criticism. "We didn't exactly hit it off," she said. "He was a loner, didn't fraternize with the rest of the staff. I was designated to do his typing and filing, which was okay with me, but if you made one little mistake he blasted you. He should have been a professor. He thought he knew everything. Now is *he* living? Are you going to send *him* one of these books?"

"He is. We are," said Logue, cheerfully, as they ate lunch at O'Charlie's. "I've read his stuff. I don't think he could write home for money. Plawin was clearly the better writer."

Dixie made fewer mistakes per typed page than any other editorial assistant imaginable. And she also compiled the Travel Calendar and for years wrote the opening Travel South pages to the magazine by herself.

"Be sure and put that in," said Dixie, "that I did the Calendar and the Travel South by myself. How many people do they have doing it now?" Dixie always loved to stir things up.

"Did Plawin meet your specifications?" asked Logue. "Judging from his photographs, he was not a bad-looking guy."

"Oh, that Plawin could write," said Dixie, admitting that he was not half bad-looking. "He hated it when they cut his stories and changed them all around. He was a nice guy."

"He was a tall, blond, contemporary-looking fellow," said McCalla, "unusual for that staff. He'd worked for the *Ledger-Star* in Norfolk, Virginia. Paul said he'd been recommended by an editor of *Reader's Digest* he'd proposed a couple of stories to, but had never met."

There was a famous incident over one of Plawin's leads in the editorial hall where *Southern Living* hung the galley proofs of upcoming issues. Any one of about twenty editors on *Southern Living*'s or *Progressive Farmer*'s staff could stop by and alter any sentence they pleased. Plawin in his lead described flying down to New Orleans to do a city salute. He had one of the characters on the plane ask another: "What the hell is going on down in New Orleans?" The word *hell* created immediate trauma in the Progressive Farmer building. It was crossed out, and what *in the heck* was inserted. That was crossed out and what *in the devil* was inserted, and that was crossed out and what *in heaven's name* was inserted, and finally, three or four other words were crossed out and, in bold handwriting, what *in the fuck* was inserted, as bold as sin and damnation. The entire population of the building sneaked by, one at a time, to see the word on the page, as if the sexual act itself was illustrated in full living color.

"You can't blame me," said Logue. "Plawin and Byers hadn't quit, and I hadn't even been interviewed." But there was a wistful look in his eye. He turned to McCalla, "There has never been anybody in journalism with handwriting to equal yours. I'd love to have seen that word. I'd have known who wrote it."

McCalla denied everything, admitting he wished *to heck* he had written it. (Plawin's sentence finally ran: "What the *zilch* is going on down in New Orleans?")

Southern Living had taken the first step in its ill-fated efforts to attract fashion advertising by hiring Fashion Editor Bonnie Jean Carr from the local Loveman's Department Store. She was bright and every bit as beautiful as her name, which sang like a Scottish ballad. She also had talent. But the magazine's advertising staff was never to lay a white glove on the fashion industry.

McCalla was introduced to the nervous, rail-thin art director, Bob Simmons. He had been art director of the *Fort Lauderdale News* and then of the failed *Atlanta Times*. Any port in a storm, and Simmons needed a place to park his swipe file.

"Simmons had this huge collection of layouts from other magazines," remembered McCalla. "When he picked up a story and its photographs, he rummaged through his swipe file to find some layout that appealed to him. Then he used that typeface and that design. That's why one spread in the early *Southern Living* would look like *Better Homes & Gardens*, and the next spread would look like *McCall's*, and the next would look like *Field & Stream*." And Simmons was in love with borders. He would have put a border around the Mona Lisa if he could have gotten his hands on it.

Simmons was also famous among the staff for showing Afghan hounds. He'd throw two of them in his car and drive three hundred miles one way to a dog show over the weekend.

Without question it was Simmons who a couple of years later made the most astonishing hire of an assistant in the nearly one-hundred-year history of the company. He interviewed only one candidate, a young girl who came roaring up on the back of a motorcycle. (This was in a primitive era when McCalla and Logue had yet to be taught by the company's now vice-president, Jeanetta Keller, not to say *girl* for young woman.) She jumped off the motorcycle in a skirt so short it would have been cheap if it cost one hundred dollars an inch. Her hair was a catastrophe, not from the wind but from not having been washed since Woodstock. In fact, the entire young beast hadn't seen the inside of a shower since the last presidential election. We don't mean to say she wasn't cute. Just a tad rank.

Simmons put it this way: we hire her, or I walk. If McCalla had been sitting in the editor's chair, the next sound heard would have been Simmons's thin tailbone hitting 19th Street. She came to work.

"I remember," said Karen Lingo, who appears in these pages in due time, "she brought all of her wedding gifts one day, and held a garage sale . . . at the office. I still have some things that I bought from her."

"The first morning she let all the editorial assistants know that she didn't wear underpants," said Dixie, unable to stop laughing. Actually, she let the city of Birmingham know; Sharon Stone must have met this girl.

McCalla stepped into Logue's cubicle, puffing on his pipe. "There are only four words I can't stand to hear a woman say," complained McCalla. "That girl has been here one hour, and she's said all four of 'em." Logue loved it. He introduced her, elaborately, to everybody who came in the office. But her design work was not as original as she was. When Simmons went, she went. "It was a loss to journalism," remembered Logue, "and the city water rates went up, too."

As far from a hippie as one could get was *Southern Living* Foods Editor Lena Sturges, reporting not to the editor, Youngsteadt, but to Oris Cantrell of *Progressive Farmer*. (Who reported to whom on the early *Southern Living* staff is something right out of a nightmare by Kafka, which we will be interpreting shortly.)

McCalla knew a formidable, wide-bodied ranch woman when he met one, and believe it, he met one in Lena Sturges from Kerrville, Texas. To be fair, you would have to admit that Lena's editorial assistant rarely wept before 10 A.M. "Sturges fired more assistants, or they ran crying for the door, than all the rest of our editors put together," said McCalla.

Lena had studied at the feet of the even more formidable Sallie Hill, first woman vice-president of the company. Miss Hill, as Homes Editor, never reported to the editor of *Progressive Farmer* but only to the president of the company. She retired with a quantity of company stock which was worth millions when the company was sold in 1985.

Make no mistake, Lena Sturges's bite was worse than her bark. But she loved the magazine to her very death. And few have faced off against Mr. Death with more courage. For all of her iron-plated bluster there was a country charm about Sturges that was impossible to resist—unless you happened to be typing her manuscripts or answering her telephone. Jean Wickstrom (later Liles) was the first young editor to join *Southern Living* with the stuff to tame the savage beast in Sturges. Jean also created a Foods Department on which The Progressive Farmer Company built an empire. Ironically, Jean was never made a vice-president. But her story comes later.

Two horticulture writers on the *Progressive Farmer* staff were going to do the gardening and landscaping copy for *Southern Living*. One eventually slipped into a year-long writer's block and was unable to produce a line of copy for either magazine. The company in its benevolence kept him on the payroll until he found another job outside of publishing. The other horticulture editor was less helpful. He actually produced gardening material, and it was technically okay, but he was knee-deep in Bermuda grass when it came to garden design. All these years later, McCalla and Logue can look on a photograph of one of Hank's autumn flower arrangements in a football helmet and be lost for words to describe it. He eventually found his way back into the academic world.

You would figure a farm magazine would know about gardening. And it did. It was an understanding of garden design that was missing. The garden section would prove to be a years-long nemesis until Dr. John Floyd came on the scene to make that section the visual glory of the magazine.

Which brings us to photographers. McCalla kept up a quarter-century-long love/hate relationship with photographers. Maybe it was because, at heart, he was one of them. He helped pay his way through the University of Oklahoma, after he gave up boxing, by photographing their great football teams. He could have made a living as a photographer, even shooting two covers of *Southern Living* the first two years, one a mock setup of Mardi Gras in New Orleans and the other a fall foliage scene in the Smoky Mountains, "both excellent," said Logue. And, of course, he was just as stubborn as the rest of the photographic breed. "Maybe that's why I had so much trouble managing them," admitted McCalla.

But McCalla had never seen the equal of Long John McKinney, photographic editor of *Progressive Farmer* and the early *Southern Living*. McKinney affected a big safari hat and a great load of equipment and worked with a big view-finder camera. He always carried a red jacket he could throw on a dowdy farmer and a bucket of red paint he could use on his gate if it needed it. That it might have been a green gate didn't bother McKinney at all. He worked very much like the old nineteenth-century pioneers who used glass plates. His stuff was absolutely composed. The people might have been stuffed. But the effect of his landscape shots was undeniably beautiful, even powerful.

"John would make eighty-five shots of the same scene, leaving the editor one pose and no alternatives," said McCalla, "but the old boy was pretty good." Logue thinks some museum should round up McKinney's landscape shots of farms in the American South for an exhibit. He can hear the scholars arguing over the popularity of red fences among the old farmers.

Bob Lancaster was a veteran photographer who was about to be let go by *P.F.*, but McCalla, when he became *S.L.* editor, took him on his staff and the homes section of the magazine was the beneficiary. Philip Morris will have to tell about Lancaster, the never-changing rituals of his work and his undying appetite for lunch.

There was one other skinny young man on the farm magazine's staff, hoping to become a photographer. McCalla also took a liking to him: Gerald Crawford, from outside of Dothan, Alabama. He later became chief photographer of *Southern Living*. Crawford had come to work in the company mail room, and one of his jobs was to put the flag on top of the building, right up there with the water tank.

"One day we got a call from the Birmingham police department," remembered Beth Carlson. "They asked, 'Are you in distress?' I answered, 'I think we might well be. We're not sure just what to put in the magazine, and I'm afraid we're losing an awful lot of the company's money.' The policeman said, 'Well, you ought to know your flag is flying upside down on your building.' "

Those were the days.

Youngsteadt invited McCalla out to his house before they were to go to dinner with the stoic, iron-fisted Dr. Nunn and Miss Cantrell, who was to be in overall charge of all homes and food and fashion and entertaining stories in the new magazine, though Oris's entire life experience had been with farm families.

McCalla remembered that Youngsteadt said, "We'll get a drink up at the house, because we're not going to be drinking later." Nothing stronger than sweetened iced tea.

What McCalla remembered most about dinner was that he said very little—"for which he had a very great talent," said Logue. Most of the conversation was social. "My wife was pregnant with our third child," said McCalla, "the talk was of families. Nothing was said to indicate the direction of the new magazine." Dr. Nunn did tell McCalla that *Southern Living* had no permanent openings, but if he wanted to come down and try out on a temporary basis they'd give him a chance. He'd obviously been impressed with the professional look of the dummy of McCalla's never-published magazine *Passport*. And Gary was careful not to look thirsty for a bourbon and water during the entire dinner. As soon as he got back to Huntsville, McCalla took Dr. Nunn up on the offer.

"Nobody ever told me I was no longer temporary," said McCalla. "I guess I edited the magazine twenty-two years without a permanent job."

Asked if he was willing to take the chance because he sensed the power vacuum on the new magazine, McCalla said, "Probably. I didn't come to that kind of cold-blooded decision. But it was probably in the back of my mind that someday somebody was going to have to make some hard decisions. I'd made plenty of hard decisions at Tech Productions. They sent me up there to straighten it out, and I had to let about half the staff go. To be honest, working on the first issue of *Southern Living* was like a vacation to me. I'd been putting in fifteen-hour days for too long. I was ready to get back to civilization."

The particular civilization, *Southern Living*, in 1965, was only slightly less chaotic than a Groucho Marx movie.

June 25, 1965. McCalla reported to work. The big open space on the second floor that *Southern Living* was occupying had not been divided into individual offices. So on his first day on the job, McCalla found himself holed up in the long, unprivate conference room. He grew tired of this arrangement, and a bit later advised the company if it would have some wallboard delivered, he would himself build individual cubicles for the magazine staff. Which he did.

Other things were moving even more slowly, as the February 1 publication date moved ever closer.

"Red showed me an outline for the first issue," said McCalla, "and it never changed." Little thought and less energy were going into all the subsequent issues of 1966. And no thought at all was given to the years beyond 1966. It was as if *Southern Living* was to be a one-issue phenomenon, which—the way things were headed—was not beyond the realm of possibility.

Morale on the staff was lower than the energy level. The week before McCalla reported to work, Dr. Alexander Nunn flexed his muscle with a memorandum to Red Youngsteadt. In minutes it was copied and circulated to the *Southern Living* staff, which felt mightily put down. The memo read:

June 17, 1965

I hope that everybody now understands that the position of Editor of *Southern Living* is comparable to and on an equivalent basis with "Edition Editor" of *Progressive Farmer.* This automatically carries with it, so far as the Company is concerned, the same broad working relationships among individuals, sections, or divisions as obtains with *Progressive Farmer*'s edition editors and their relationships with others within the Company. I had felt that this was clearly understood by all of us, but apparently this is not quite so . . .

Dr. Nunn obviously felt an unwelcome breeze of independence blowing up the *Southern Living* hallway, God knows from which direction, and wanted to put the lad Youngsteadt in his place. And be certain he understood that he had no more authority than the five regional editors of *Progressive Farmer*, who, of course, all bowed down to Dr. Nunn.

Things got even more heavy-handed in Nunn's tortured memo. He made it clear that the art director of *Southern Living* reported not to the editor, Youngsteadt, but to the *Progressive Farmer* Art Department. That the Food and Homes and Fashion Departments of *Southern Living* reported not to the editor but to Oris Cantrell of *Progressive Farmer.* That the garden editors of *Southern Living* reported to the executive editor of *Progressive Farmer*, Dr. Nunn. That the chief photographer of *Southern Living* was John McKinney, who reported to Dr. Nunn. That the managing editor of *Southern Living*, who made up the advertising and editorial pages, reported to *Progressive Farmer.* All this leaving *Southern Living* Editor Red Youngsteadt in absolute charge of Paul Plawin, Brad Byers, and the yet-to-report-to-work Gary McCalla.

Logue, marveling at the memo these years later, said, "I would like to have seen Henry Luce of *Time*, Harold Ross of *The New Yorker*, and Herb Mayes of *McCall's* all come down in one limousine and edit a successful new magazine with those same lines of responsibility."

Gary McCalla kept his peace and bided his time.

"The next big argument that ran through the building," he remembered, "involved the story on Houston that Paul Plawin was writing. We were going to publish a 'city salute' and a 'state salute' in alternate issues. Dr. Nunn *didn't want the writer to use the name of the city*, which, as I said, was Houston. It was *Progressive Farmer*'s style to refer only to the *county* a city was in. Dr. Nunn wanted Byers to use Harris County rather than Houston in his *city* salute." McCalla shook his head, still amazed. "Now this was a lunatic idea if I ever heard one, for *the magazine of the modern South*."

Finally, Dr. Nunn gave in and let the magazine use Houston in its story on that city. "But when the first issue was published," said McCalla, "Dr. Nunn marked the story all to pieces for not including an analysis of Houston's waterworks and its garbage disposal system, for not documenting how many Boy Scout troops there were in the city, and all manner of encyclopedia-type stuff that no subscriber wanted to read.

"It was pretty grim," said McCalla, grinning. "There wasn't any direction as far as I could see." They were listing him as "Mid-South Editor." But there was no editorial plan for him or anyone else.

"We didn't even have a Travel Editor listed on the masthead in the first issue," said McCalla. "Don Cunningham, our advertising man in Atlanta, raised Cain about that, and I took over the Travel Editor's job immediately and got the title by the fifth issue." No one had imagined that travel was going to be the dominant advertising category that first year and the top advertising category every year since.

McCalla hadn't been on the magazine staff a month when he and Paul Plawin and Brad Byers got together one night at Byers's house. They agreed, "Hell, Red's in trouble. We've got to find a way to help him." They were not alone in their thoughts.

The next Monday Beth Carlson handed McCalla his copy of a memo from Dr. Nunn, directing the *Southern Living* staff to gather in the conference room, where Gary was already holed up with his skimpy files. "I said to myself, 'Uh-oh, that's it for Red,'" remembered McCalla.

Dr. Nunn stepped into the room of anxious faces, trailing his longtime assistant behind him, Dr. O. B. Copeland, whom he then introduced as the new editor of *Southern Living*.

Which makes this an appropriate moment to pause in our narrative and take a quick look back into the past, in order to understand the forces that brought *Southern Living* into being, and those same forces that had left it in such a mess before the first issue was even published.

2

Where It Came From and How

If we are going to step into the past, we might as well step all the way back into 1886, when *Progressive Farmer* had its beginning. Leonidas L. Polk had survived the battles of Kinston and New Bern and Gettysburg. *Leonidas L. Polk*—now there is a name right out of Faulkner, by way of the Civil War. He came out of the war a colonel and dead broke, his farm in Anson County, North Carolina, in ruins.

When he'd gotten body and soul back together, Colonel Polk took up a new fight, to establish an effective agriculture department in North Carolina, as well as a state agricultural college.

Colonel Polk armed himself with the written word. He published the first issue of *Progressive Farmer* on February 10, 1886, as a weekly newspaper. He wrote: "The Industrial and Educational Interests of our People paramount to All Other Considerations of State Policy is the motto of *Progressive Farmer*, and upon this platform shall it rise or fall. Serving no master, ruled by no faction, circumscribed by no selfish or narrow policy, its aim will be to foster and promote the best interests of the whole people of the state."

The colonel gave the publication a feisty start, and it has kept its stinger all these years. He quickly accomplished what he set out to do.

The North Carolina Department of Agriculture was reorganized immediately to better help farmers. And North Carolina State University was founded in 1887. In the meantime, *Progressive Farmer* had attracted 11,760 subscribers and was off to a lively start.

Colonel Polk died in 1892, just when he was getting set to run for president of the United States on the Populist ticket.

But a seventeen-year-old boy had joined the *P.F.* staff in 1887. His name was Clarence Poe. He became editor in 1889. He became friends with five presidents of the United States, wrote a book every few years, was awarded more than a dozen honorary degrees, and ran the magazine until 1953.

Employment at *Progressive Farmer* has not been for the faint of heart. Eugene Butler joined the company in 1916. He far eclipsed Poe's sixty-seven-year employment record. Gene Butler was president of the company from 1953 until 1968, but he never stopped reporting to his editorial desk in Dallas, Texas, until the last, failing months of his life, and he lived to be well over a hundred.

"McCalla, you were a short-timer," said Logue. "You only edited *Southern Living* for twenty-two years."

Progressive Farmer bought out fifteen other farm magazines over the years, most importantly *Southern Farm Gazette*, owned by Dr. Tait Butler. Dr. Butler, and then his son Gene, became primary owners of the company. In 1911, The Progressive Farmer moved the company headquarters from Raleigh, North Carolina, to Birmingham, Alabama, a transportation center then intersected by seven railroads.

Progressive Farmer introduced regional editions to American publishing. It concerned itself with family life as well as farm life. Colonel Polk's daughter became the first Home Department editor in 1898, and was known over the years to readers as "Aunt Jenny." In 1932, in the heart of the Depression, the magazine published its first four-color cover. Paintings by N. C. Wyeth and other important illustrators appeared in *P.F.*, as did short fiction.

Emory Cunningham said, "I think the greatest thing *Progressive Farmer* did was give farm people something to read." T. Harry Williams pointed out in his definitive biography of Huey Long that the future governor of Louisiana grew up in a farm home that offered only the Bible and *Progressive Farmer* as reading material. Perhaps without *Progressive Farmer* we would never have had *All the King's Men*, or even "The Kingfish" himself.

No doubt the magazine had much farm and family and even political influence, with its one million subscribers by 1930. But in terms of profitability, it was never more than a modest family business. Dr. Alexander Nunn said that Clarence Poe told him when he was hired, "Now Alec, you can never expect to make more than four thousand dollars in a year if you work for *Progressive Farmer*. But you will influence for the better the lives of thousands of families."

This sense of mission, of duty, of living life as a crusade permeated the professional careers of the nineteenth-century men and women who ran The Progressive Farmer Company. There is a wonderful photograph (see first illustration) of members of the original *Progressive Farmer* staff reared back in chairs, looking as revolutionary and as dangerous as the Jesse James Gang. This may be compared with a photo of the company officers a few years later (see second illustration), having taken on suits and collars and neckties and looking as prosperous as Republicans. To crusade was a characteristic to be admired, but one that damn near sunk *Southern Living*.

Smith Moseley, as a young man, came to know Clarence Poe well, and Eugene Butler, and Dr. Alexander Nunn, and John S. Pearson, treasurer and general manager, men who shared a fervor for *Progressive Farmer*. Smith has lived in Birmingham in the same house for fifty years. He's a man of great formality, with a voice out of Ecclesiastes. At eighty-four, he still drives himself to the Fifth Quarter, off the Green Springs Highway, where he is known and welcomed. Smith's routine is to travel to Las Vegas three times each year, where he is also known and welcomed at Caesar's Palace; to read and write and teach poetry each summer at St. Simons Island, Georgia; and to attend the annual reunion of the 559th Bomber Squadron wherever it might be meeting.

In an interview at the Fifth Quarter, McCalla and Logue tipped their glasses against Moseley's ration of brandy. "This was not originally a gesture of friendship," said Smith. "The ancient kings tipped their cups together, spilling a bit into each other's cup, so they could be sure they were not being poisoned. Okay, I know a lot of stuff," said Smith. Which was why we had him seated there.

Smith had left the *Birmingham Post* in October, 1941, during a long strike against that newspaper. He joined The Progressive Farmer Company, which at the time shared the same building at 821 North 19th Street. He came over to sell classified advertising. He'd been interviewed by Advertising Manager Fowler Dugger, who years later was to interview the young Jim DeVira. In 1941, Dugger had already lost his voice box to cancer.

"He conducted our interview with notes, in that classic handwriting of his," said Smith.

"That sounds like something out of Dickens," said Logue.

"Which reminds me that Dickens in his youth was one of the world's great shorthand experts," said Smith, "transcribing his notes from Parliament with a quill pen, sharpened with a knife, while dashing from place to place in a rough-riding carriage."

Set back on the trail, Smith said, "*The Progressive Farmer* in 1941 was grossing probably less than one million dollars a year. I was knocking 'em dead. I was making forty-five dollars a week."

J. S. Pearson was general manager of *P.F.* when Smith signed on. "An important fact in the history of the company is that Pearson personally saved it from bankruptcy by his standing with the bank, which supplied it with money to keep operating during the Depression," Smith said.

"Pearson was a tall, slim man, never overweight, distinguished in a plain, modest sort of way. He used to come up on Saturdays when I would be working and ask for a postage stamp. I would fish one out of the stamp box, and he would go into his pocket and count out the exact change and put it in the box. Baptist integrity."

Smith remembers Clarence Poe as if he were sitting in the next booth of the Fifth Quarter. "Oh, I would say he was a tremendously able man, and highly egotistical," said Smith. "He spoke with a sort of twang. I can hear him now . . . Somewhere in a speech he would say, 'Back in 1923, I wrote in the *Progressive Farmer*, . . .' and he would read off a paragraph he had written. He quoted from himself in the big to-do in Raleigh over the fiftieth anniversary of his editorship of the magazine.

"Alec Nunn was master of ceremonies of the big event," Smith said, "and he got off one of the best rejoinders. A congressman spoke, supposedly a friend of Poe's and Nunn's and the company's. Alec introduced him elaborately. The congressman corrected him, saying, 'I didn't fly in from Alaska, I flew in from Puerto Rico.' He was not chairman of *this* committee, he said, but chairman of *that* committee. And so on. Nunn introduced him again, briefly, later in the program, and the congressman did the same thing, correcting tiny misstatements. After the congressman sat down the second time, Alec said, 'I hope our good friend the congressman is taking as complete advantage of the big mistakes being made in

Washington today as he is of the little mistakes being made here to-night.' "

More about that historic evening later.

"You know Dr. Poe had two full columns in *Who's Who*," Smith said. "There is an anecdote I love to tell about him. It happened long before my time.

"Theodore Roosevelt came to Raleigh. All the politicos and bigwigs in the community were there to hear him. Way in the back of the room was a skinny little guy with his pants cuffs halfway up his legs. The Great Man finished his speech and was down in the audience shaking hands when he suddenly jumped back on the platform. He asked, 'Is there a man named Clarence Poe in the hall?'

"Way in the back, Poe stumbled to his feet, adjusted his britches, and walked up the aisle. While the big figures in Raleigh fumed and fretted, Roosevelt chatted forty-five minutes with young Clarence Poe: 'I've been reading your articles . . . and I agree with you on so-and-so.' "

Poe must have loved it. As Smith said, he "was never a man to underestimate himself."

Poe and the other men who ran The Progressive Farmer Company had crusaded for better schools, better roads, rural electricity, and better lives for farm families. Asked about their belief that the magazine shaped the very lives of its readers, Smith said, "I sponsor the hypothesis myself, maybe defensively.

"I once wrote in a speech that '*Progressive Farmer* is greater than the sum total of all the human effort that has gone into its production.' And that it 'has made a greater contribution to the education of the American farmer than many of the great universities.' I said, in truth, 'It was the University of the South.' "

Small wonder that such men, with such beliefs, wanted to invest the future *Southern Living* with the same crusading quality.

After December 7, 1941, there was a desperate pause in the careers of men who were to help invent *Southern Living*. The eventual prime inventor, Emory Cunningham, left college to fly planes for the Navy in the South Pacific. His cousin Don Cunningham flew B-29s for the Army Air Force. Many employees of The Progressive Farmer Company entered the military service, including Smith Moseley.

Smith took his basic training in the Air Force at Miami Beach at the same time as Clark Gable. He later graduated from photographic school and shipped out on the *Queen Mary* with sixteen thousand other soldiers. "I found a little kiosk I could slip into and be by myself and read," said Smith. "An attendant had used it to hand out towels by the swimming pool, which now, of course, was filled in. I found his log book. One of the bathers had been the actress Deanna Durbin. I could imagine her in her suit by the swimming pool. Years later, someone asked me if I knew of the actress Deanna Durbin. I said, 'Sure, we once went to Europe together.' "

By then an officer, Smith was assigned to the 559th Bomber Squadron. He specified which plane would be fitted with a camera on each flight. The camera would automatically record the damage, or lack of it, when the bombs were released. After the pilots were debriefed, Smith would examine the photographs and write up the results of the strike.

"I was thirty-three when I waded ashore at Utah Beach in the invasion of Normandy," said Smith. "We actually hit the wrong beach. General Theodore Roosevelt, the president's son, made the decision to press on. A few days later he died of a heart attack." Smith lost many friends in the squadron, which flew the two-engine B-26. "Yes, and we are still losing them, of course," he said. "I'm the senior citizen of the squadron."

The war ended. There was once a popular song which went something like this: "How ya gonna keep 'em happy down on the farm, after they've seen Paree?" The answer was, you weren't. Not for long. But those post–World War II years were to be the greatest in *Progressive Farmer* history. Its circulation reached as high as 1.4 million, and its advertising pages set new records.

Two young men joined the advertising sales staff after the war, Emory Cunningham and Roger McGuire. Emory was in his late twenties and McGuire in his early twenties. They were very like older and younger brothers, and quickly came to feel that way about one another. Emory was a native of the little town of Kansas, in North Alabama. McGuire grew up outside of Des Moines, Iowa.

Emory almost joined *Progressive Farmer*'s editorial staff. In fact, he was offered a job. But Fowler Dugger convinced him there was a bigger future selling advertising for the magazine. After a training period he was sent to Chicago to work under Oscar Dugger, Fowler's brother.

This was 1949. Clarence Poe was still running *Progressive Farmer*. He was the last of the men who bought the magazine in 1908 from Colonel Polk's son-in-law. Tait Butler had died in 1939. His son Eugene was still an editor in the Dallas office. He became president of the company in 1953, when his by-then rival Clarence Poe retired to chairman of the board. Poe and Butler would take opposite ends of the argument over whether to start *Southern Living*.

Oscar Dugger, in an interview late in his life, described the Cunningham of 1949 as "a bachelor, rough-hewn, spoke good English, but naive in the social niceties. He had never had a deck of cards in his hands. However, he was solid, honest, had good common sense, and was determined to improve himself." Not to say that "social niceties" in Chicago, 1949, required a man to be able to deal a hand of draw poker. But maybe they did.

"I didn't know diddly-squat," said Cunningham, laughing at his own naiveté. "Not even enough to buy a heavy overcoat. I liked to have frozen to death. I'd lean on Red Norman. His name was Gavin. We called him Red. His office was next to mine. He knew people, and he was selling a lot of business. I'd stop by his office and pick his brain."

Cunningham worked at, and had a gift for, selling advertising. He reminisced about those years sitting in the upstairs study of his Mountain Brook townhouse, which married the contemporary with the traditional in the best *Southern Accents* manner, from bleached wood floors to eight thousand books on floor-to-ceiling shelves. (*Southern Accents* is the upscale first cousin to *Southern Living*.) A couple of years later, the townhouse, with all its books and memorabilia, was to burn to the ground. Thankfully, with no loss of life.

"When I first went to Chicago," said Cunningham, "*Progressive Farmer* ranked fifth, and sometimes sixth, among the six major farm magazines: *Farm Journal*, *Country Farmer*, *Country Gentleman*, *Successful Farming*, *Southern Agriculturist*, and us. We lost a very good salesman in Chicago, Mack Morris, to *This Week* magazine [the Sunday newspaper supplement]. We lost a lot of good salesmen because of low salaries. The company would have been more profitable if it had paid better. We wouldn't have lost so many top people. We were locked in a battle with Alec Nunn and his editors, and with Gene Butler. They didn't want advertising salesmen in Chicago and New York to be paid more than somebody in Loachapoka [a tiny hamlet outside Auburn, Alabama, from which Dr. Nunn commuted to Birmingham]. We couldn't get them to understand the difference in cost of living.

"Anyway," said Cunningham, "Mack learned that *This Week* had published a map showing the coverage of national magazines. He sent me a copy, saying we might be able to use it, as it showed a weakness of national magazine coverage in the South. We never knew that. Some of us may have, but we didn't have anything to show it. This was also the first time I ever heard of 'A,' 'B,' 'C,' and 'D' counties ['A' counties representing the biggest population centers]. *This Week* was far ahead of us in planning and using this material. I showed the coverage map to Paul Huey, our advertising manager, and he said we couldn't afford to print a map like that. And that was the end of it.

"Roger McGuire joined the company about that time in Chicago. He was one of the most creative people we ever had in the Advertising Department," said Emory. "He took over a lot of territory from me, and we traveled a lot and got real, real close. When I showed him all this stuff from *This Week*, he studied it and said, 'I'm going to make a presentation, a "one farm book presentation." ' It was a very simple, but original idea: Whether you buy any other farm magazine or not, you need *Progressive Farmer* because it's the only thing available to fill this gap of magazine coverage in the South. And Roger presented the plan at a company sales meeting in North Carolina."

Cunningham said, "After Roger's presentation, I remember getting on the elevator with Red Norman, one of the greatest people who ever lived. Red had a habit of spitting when he got mad. He sort of spit and said, 'That's the silliest thing I ever heard of. Selling *Progressive Farmer* as the first farm magazine.' You see, at sales meetings, we had always made presentations showing how *Progressive Farmer* should be the second or third magazine advertisers bought to cover the farm market.

"We began to develop this idea of the national media's weakness in the South. I had real good luck with it," said Emory. "I began talking with advertisers about buying *LIFE* magazine and adding *Progressive Farmer* to cover the South." He ignored Oscar Dugger's advice not to waste his time on the tony Elgin watch company, which had never advertised in *P.F.* "Elgin at that time was a prestige thing, like a Mercedes today," said Emory. He sold them five four-color pages.

The Chicago office for the first time sold one million dollars in advertising, and then in successive years it sold two million and then three million, much of it consumer advertising as well as traditional farm equipment advertising.

"From fifth or sixth among farm magazines, we climbed up to first," said Emory. "By 1955, when I moved to Birmingham, we knew how to sell the Southern market. We had a crackerjack sales force. We needed more headroom to grow."

And the South was changing. Farm populations were declining. It was time to fish or cut bait for The Progressive Farmer Company. Among the Old Guard there were about as many bait cutters as fishermen.

Paul Huey died in 1959 while on vacation in Barbados. Cunningham succeeded him as advertising manager, and in 1960 joined *P.F.*'s board of directors. Emory saw to it that the company knew he'd been offered a job by another publisher, and that didn't hurt his chances to move up the ladder of ambition.

The two words *Southern Living* made their first official Progressive Farmer appearance in the board of directors' notes of May 22, 1963. (Emory blew off the importance of other members of the Diversification Committee. "It was mainly Gene Butler and I talking to each other over the telephone," he said.)

Cunningham gave a nine-page report to the board as the chairman of the Diversification Committee. He asked the board this essential question: "Is our long range goal to grow much bigger than we are, with the risk and increased effort and responsibilities such growth demands, or would we rather take less risk, be more sure of profits every year, and accept less potential for long range growth in profit, service, and opportunity for our employees?"

What Emory was really asking was: *Does the Old Guard intend to publish only a farm magazine, as it has since 1886? Or will we roll the dice on a new magazine for the newly prosperous South? If not, gentlemen, I and the other young lions will be moving on to happier hunting grounds.* This, of course, was only implied and not threatened. "We could not have stayed," admitted Emory.

Cunningham recommended: "Effective with October, 1963, issue, change the name of 'The Progressive Home' [*P.F.*'s home section] to 'Southern Living' and begin to position as many as possible of our general and home type advertisements in this section." The sentence was rather convoluted, but the intent was clear: prepare the Homes Department of *Progressive Farmer* to become a free-standing magazine called: *Southern Living.*

He said, "I believe the *Southern Living* idea deserves our most serious consideration as a way to give us more 'headroom' to grow by putting us in line for more consumer advertising." He pointed out that special interest magazines were growing in popularity, and that regional buys were one reason certain national magazines were also growing.

Other national magazines were going down the tube, victims of the twin beasts of television and postal costs. *Coronet, Look, LIFE, The Sat-*

urday Evening Post, and others were struggling or going out of business. This fact did not go unnoticed among the dissenting Old Guard at The Progressive Farmer Company.

Cunningham proposed that one hundred thousand non–farm family subscriptions be switched from *Progressive Farmer* to *Southern Living*, which would publish home and general interest articles. His idea was that the new magazine would include the *Southern Living* pages from *P.F.*, plus "additional editorial pages to make *Southern Living* acceptable to subscribers and advertisers."

He made no mention of the dated, awkwardly written, poorly illustrated, clumsily designed homes material then appearing in *Progressive Farmer*, or the faint appeal it would have to more sophisticated readers.

In raising the combustible question of where the talent would come from to reinvent this weak editorial mix, Emory was careful. Any idea of hiring outside editors was sure to inflame Dr. Nunn and his editorial staff, as it ultimately did. Emory merely asked, "Do we have, or can we, or are we willing to get the people needed to make *Southern Living* a success?" He also asked, "Are we mentally ready to produce the different editorial concept required to serve the audience we visualize for *Southern Living*?"

The honest, unspoken answer would have been a flat *no* to all of the above. And that answer also would have come close to sinking the magazine before it was launched. Fortunately no vote was taken.

Emory, in 1963, did not raise the idea of selling the new magazine through direct mail, a plan he knew would enrage the Circulation Department, which had a history as long as the century of "giving" the farm magazine away through a band of roving *sheetwriters*, many of them rough carnival workers, who sold subscriptions directly to farmers and kept the modest fees, or car batteries, or live chickens they collected. And Emory himself, at that time, had very little knowledge of how direct mail worked.

Later on, when the decision to launch *Southern Living* was made, how it would be sold, and for how much, became volatile subjects. "Oh, my, we had some awful arguments about it," said Emory, "and I took a lot of abuse, personal abuse, from the sheetwriters. I went to the Southeastern Poultry and Egg Show in Atlanta, and these fellows jumped on me about selling the magazine in the mail. They said, 'We built *Progressive Farmer* selling it farm-to-farm, and you couldn't have done it without us, and now you've forsaken us.' I actually got a little bit concerned with them crowded around. They were aggressive, unusual people.

"One of the worst mistakes we made was setting the subscription price at one dollar a year. I remember very well a time I'd been arguing with the board about two things: direct mail and higher subscription prices. It took us a long time to get over selling the magazine for one dollar.

"We had argued about the subscription price for about an hour, and Mr. Butler turned to me, and said, 'Emory, what you say makes a lot of sense. But I have to go along with my circulation director, don't I?' I was walking down the hall afterward with Pop Rogers, our circulation director. And he was really ribbing me about what Mr. Butler said. Pop was a gentle person. For him to get upset and jump on somebody was very out of character for him. But he gave me a hard time. Harold Dobson [his assistant] did also."

Cunningham, in 1963, took care not to raise the question of just what the "general interest articles" in the new magazine would contain. He imagined articles on positive aspects of the South, but he knew too well the crusading inclination of President Gene Butler and Editorial Director Alexander Nunn and the other edition editors of *Progressive Farmer*.

Why was Cunningham so sure that a magazine for the South would be successful? Not to avoid the obvious, it didn't have one, other than highly specialized magazines such as *Progressive Farmer*. National magazines had weak penetration in the South. Because the South was *different*. Its climate. Its history. Its long struggle after losing the Civil War. Someone said, "Writers are forged in the crucible of injustice." So are civilizations.

The same sense of place, of home, of the land, of family, of dispossession, of lost promise that gave distinctive literary voices to Faulkner and Wolfe and Welty and Agee and O'Connor and Penn Warren and Ellison could be found in the lives of Southerners, rich and poor, black and white. Few Southerners were more than one generation from the farm. Blacks in the South were more openly, more cruelly, even legally, until very recently, disenfranchised, creating a deeper pain across the old slave-holding states. (*Southern Living* represents the "good life" and does not go out of its way to appeal to any political or racial group, yet it is believed to have some five hundred thousand black readers.)

"Everybody was running down the South," said Cunningham. "In every movie, if they had a pot-bellied sheriff, he had a Southern accent. I felt that keenly, and a lot of other Southern people did, too, people with their hardships going all the way back to the Civil War. The Depression hit us harder. Everybody up North thought that racial unrest was an Alabama and a George Wallace problem only. It hadn't hit Watts in Los Angeles and Chicago. Southern people were thirsting for something to make them feel good about themselves, along with giving them good practical information."

Some years after the magazine became a success, Cunningham said, "We Southerners would be an insensitive bunch of people if we didn't feel something tying us together." For fourteen million readers each month, part of that *something* these days is the magazine *Southern Living*.

And where did the suggested name, *Southern Living*, come from? This was a question McCalla and Logue had wondered about since coming on the scene three decades ago.

"I think I know," said Emory, sitting in his den all these years later. "I sold advertising in Chicago for six years. Our offices were in the old *Chicago Daily* newspaper building. *Sunset* magazine's sales offices were in the same building. Frank Kelly was a *Sunset* rep. He was probably the best advertising salesman in the Midwest. Frank and I traveled the same areas. We even timed trips to Minneapolis so we could have dinner together. When *Sunset* had a new advertising presentation, he'd show it to me. We developed a lot of ideas together.

"One day I was in Frank's office," said Emory. "I said, 'Frank. When they named your magazine *Sunset*, "The Magazine of Western Living," they should have called it simply: *Western Living*. There wasn't any concept of "Western living" when *Sunset* started. *Sunset* created it.' "

Cunningham added, "I thought to myself, if we started a magazine called *Southern Living*, we wouldn't have to chip away any excess words."

So, the *Southern Living–Sunset* connection goes back even before Cunningham ever proposed a new magazine for the South, a reality that has often left him somewhat defensive. *Sunset*'s formula of travel, homes, food, and gardening no doubt preceded by decades *Southern Living*'s present-day, similar formula. Emory was quick to say, "They learned as much from us as we learned from them." He cited *Progressive Farmer*'s pioneering efforts in regional editions.

What he might well have cited are those things *Sunset* never learned from *Southern Living*, principally how to sell subscriptions in direct mail for enormous profits, rather than give their own magazine away through department stores. Also, *Southern Living* wound the lives of Southerners throughout its editorial pages, giving it an emotional punch that the cool, project-driven pages of *Sunset* did not have. But one thing is for certain: if there hadn't been a *Sunset*, there would not be a *Southern Living* as we know it. It's entirely ironic that today *Sunset* reports to the president of Southern Progress—Time, Inc., having acquired it for one-half of the $480 million it paid for *Southern Living* in 1985. If Time, Inc., were buying Southern Progress today at the same price/earnings multiple, it would have to pay two billion dollars.

Both parties often denied it, but there was always a chins-out rivalry between *Sunset* President Bill Lane and *Southern Living* President Emory Cunningham. Lane's parents owned *Sunset*. He was born with a "silver magazine" in his mouth. Emory's father was a hard-working coal miner–farmer and his mother a much-loved schoolteacher. He worked his way up to the presidency. Lane did not hesitate to refer to *Southern Living* as a pale imitation of *Sunset*. Cunningham in turn pointed out *Southern Living*'s superior magazine and vastly superior bottom line.

Former *Southern Living* Circulation Director Bill Capps said, "I remember Emory passed me one day in the hall, and he said, 'Oh, be sure and let me know when we pass *Sunset* in circulation.' I said, 'Emory, we did that about six months ago.' I mean we passed them without fanfare. It just happened. He said, 'We did?' I said, 'Yeah.' He said, 'Well, congratulations.' And he wrote me a note of congratulations."

Cunningham was voted Co-Publisher of the Year in 1976 by the Magazine Publishers Association, sharing the honor with Richard Babcock of *Farm Journal*. He became the first Southern publisher to win or share the award. Lane, from California, had won it some years earlier. And in the ultimate one-upmanship, Lane was appointed by President Ronald Reagan as ambassador to Australia. Emory would tell you he would rather be fishing with his children and grandchildren on his farm than be ambassador to anywhere, and there would be truth in that. Still, ambassador to Australia was impressive.

The final touch in all of this long-running competition is that McCalla and Logue, in July, 1968, composed a White Paper to Cunningham, stating what they believed had to be done to save the *Southern Living* ship. At that time neither of them had any idea Emory had drawn on *Sunset* as his original inspiration for the very title of the new magazine he proposed, or that he would react favorably to an adaptation of the *Sunset* formula. This narrative will come to that critical moment in due time.

Back to the board meeting in 1963. Cunningham concluded his remarks to The Progressive Farmer board, saying, with the launching of *Southern Living*, "Our destiny would be linked with the future of the total South, as well as the farm South, and The Progressive Farmer Company would be flexible enough to take advantage of all the rapid changes we are sure to see in the years ahead, and these changes may come even faster than we imagine. The problem, of course, is getting from where we are to this point."

An even more pressing problem was: did the company want to risk the trip at all?

The company did what it had done since 1886. It appointed a committee. "They used to meet for a week discussing secretaries' salaries," said Cunningham.

His boss, Oscar Dugger, headed up a *Southern Living* Task Force. Included were Emory, Circulation Manager J. L. Rogers, Assistant Secretary Vernon Owens, and Dr. Nunn's assistant, O. B. Copeland.

"It's interesting," said McCalla, "that no women were on the committee, not even the formidable Sallie Hill. And *Southern Living* was going to be a magazine that revolved around the home."

"My one real involvement," said Vernon Owens, "was to research the name *Southern Living*. I found one garden supply shop using the trademark. It was no problem to clear it." After the magazine became famous, Owens spent much time protecting the name from numerous small businesses trying to capitalize on it.

Speaking for the younger executives of 1963, Owens said, "It was necessary for the company to diversify and grow. We had careers. We didn't want to be there and count beans. We had too many committee operations. That was our problem."

The Old Guard thought the problem was closer to reckless ambition among the young lions. Clarence Poe was dead solid set against the new magazine. "If Dr. Poe hadn't retired as chairman of the board [in 1964], *Southern Living* would never have been published," said Cunningham. "He knew these discussions were going on. He was old. He didn't come to meetings. But he had the illusion he was still running the company. He wrote a long letter against the new magazine. His son Charles was very supportive. I don't mean to sound negative on Clarence Poe. I loved him.

I could sit and talk to him all day." Cunningham, however, agreed that humility was not Dr. Poe's strong suit.

With time and age bearing down upon him, Dr. Poe expressed the belief that magazines had a natural life cycle, and when they had completed it, they vanished. Henry Luce, founder of *Time* and *LIFE*, once said a very similar thing, that magazines when they were born had a certain life span and were doomed to extinction. Poe expressed the feeling that a magazine often died with the individual who had put his entire life into it.

On the occasion of the fiftieth anniversary of Dr. Poe's editorship of *Progressive Farmer*, Eugene Butler took spoken exception to this belief. Earlier in this narrative, Smith Moseley spoke of that celebration at North Carolina State University. Gene Butler followed Clarence Poe's long, rambling speech by saying, pithily: "*Progressive Farmer* is not a one-man magazine." He then elaborated on the long years of contribution to the magazine and the company by the Butler family. One can only imagine the look on Clarence Poe's face at this statement made at the banquet in his honor. The great rivalry between Butler and Poe for leadership of the company must have intensified then and there.

Cunningham said, "Dr. Poe wrote these long memorandums about not going into a new magazine. He said he had known so many families, publishing families, that had wasted their resources trying to start other magazines. And he proposed that the younger people who wanted to start this thing, let them find the financing. In other words, don't take it from me." Emory said, "Poe was a very good writer. His thinking wasn't always as good as his writing."

Perhaps a major reason for Poe's reluctance was his own diminished circumstance. He'd lost a good deal of money in a real estate development.

"That's true," said Cunningham. "Dr. Poe had a farm and a real nice home. It was called Longwood. He decided to develop some of that acreage. That's when Sallie Hill got some of his stock in The Progressive Farmer Company. I don't know who else, but she got the most of it."

Poe never did give the new magazine his blessing. He wrote a final letter to the other directors, dated June 16, 1964. He died soon after. The letter was circulated under the heading: "DO PAST EXPERIENCES JUSTIFY HEAVY EXPENDITURES FOR A NEW SOUTHERN MAGAZINE?" He was gravely concerned about a recent study of American family income that showed 40 percent of Southern households with incomes "of less than two thousand, five hundred dollars."

Poe feared "possible exhaustion of our financial reserves in a venture such as seems to have had no success in the past and for which present prospects for success seem no better."

Dr. Poe was not the only reluctant warrior in the company. General Manager Fowler Dugger, an able man, remembered before his death: "To be honest with you, I had some doubts and was not wildly enthusiastic about it."

The critical vote belonged to President Eugene Butler, whose family held the majority interest in Progressive Farmer stock.

Years afterward, *P.F.* Executive Editor Charlie Scruggs remembered the tough call made by Butler. Scruggs, himself a native Texan, was visiting the company's new offices on Lakeshore Drive in Birmingham and talking with President Tom Angelillo. "Mr. Butler pushed the family fortune right out in the middle of the table," said Scruggs. "He bet everything the family had accumulated in seventy years on the new magazine. Everything they owned was tied up in Progressive Farmer stock. And he pushed it right out in the middle of the table."

In an August 12, 1964, memo to Fowler Dugger, Eugene Butler wrote, "I don't believe we have had a consensus as to how much we are willing to risk in this venture. Personally, I have been willing to put $500,000 into the proposed magazine. And then after spending this amount, if the project looked promising, I'd be willing to put in another $500,000 before we reached the break-even point. But beyond that, I have serious doubts that I'd be willing to go. . . . A good general not only plans for success, but also the best way out of a defeat."

There were no mega-millions behind the new magazine. Even with a sound business and editorial start, it would be a very near thing. And the editorial half of the start was to prove awkward indeed.

"The reason we were able to get the magazine started was Mr. Butler's support," Cunningham declared. "He wanted us to grow. He was willing to risk his money, and it didn't bother him. I think he would have spent every penny he had to make it work. He was very supportive of me. He gave me a lot of confidence."

Gene Butler's support, however, stopped short of agreeing with Cunningham on the future editorial direction of *Southern Living*. He was a nineteenth-century man, and in the magazine's formative years, 1963–65, Butler stood with Dr. Nunn in the belief that *Southern Living* should be a crusading voice in the New South, just as its parent magazine had been in the Old South. What they wanted to do was to champion the importance of the rural South and its ways in the rapidly urbanizing South of the 1960s.

"Mr. Butler and Alec Nunn were so eager to explain farmers and farm life to urban people," said Cunningham. "They thought the whole world depended on it. And they were good men and both of them interested in history. And they knew about certain countries failing because agriculture failed, and they were right about that. But they felt in the United States, farmers weren't appreciated and weren't understood.

"I'm quite sure the major factor in their deciding to go ahead with the magazine was the belief they would have the opportunity to write editorials to explain all this to city people," said Cunningham. "I remember one day I mentioned this possibility to Dr. Nunn. I said, 'Alec, you realize you could speak to city people.' This was a big line. But I had to get him over in favor of the magazine, and I mentioned it in a passing kind of way."

Alexander Nunn had a darker concern that Eugene Butler did not apparently share. This concern very nearly made its way into the pages of *Southern Living*, and if it had, the magazine would have been stillborn. Dr. Nunn very nearly destroyed *Southern Living*, and endangered the company he'd loved and worked for all his adult life.

"Another deep emotional interest of Alec Nunn's was segregation," Cunningham said. "He thought two things would ruin the South, or ruin the country: integration and a decline in agriculture, city people not appreciating farmers. He felt those were fundamental problems and were going to ruin the country."

There is no question but that Dr. Nunn offered the first cover of *Southern Living* to Lurleen Wallace, then governor of Alabama and, of course, wife of crusading segregationist George Wallace. Had Lurleen Wallace appeared on the first cover of *Southern Living*, its reactionary direction would have been fixed forever, and that direction would have led to sudden oblivion.

A man can have a terrible flaw and not be a terrible person. Dr. Nunn spent his career promoting a better life for farmers. Most of those years he worked for very little money. He was honest to a fault. He was a total family man. He said only what he believed. When the company voted to accept whiskey ads in *Southern Living*, he declared, "You will sow the wind and reap the whirlwind." But he was also a captive of nineteenth-century racial prejudice, and all his contributions to Southern agriculture couldn't undo that dark reality.

Nunn's beliefs put Emory Cunningham in a deadly crossfire. "I had a great feeling of affection for Alec," said Emory some years later. "He was just dead wrong, and when a fellow is wrong on a subject of that kind, you can't win an argument with him." Dr. Nunn was also on the Executive Committee of the Board of Directors and had President Butler's ear. Emory knew he could not win a "knock-down, drag-out" with the Old Guard. His only choice of action, as regards the editorial direction of *Southern Living*, was no action at all. Any word on who it was that killed the Lurleen Wallace cover idea died with Dr. Nunn and Gene Butler.

On a more antic note, McCalla and Logue remember the time Dr. Nunn took them as his reluctant guests for lunch with the Lions Club. The meeting went along, complete with song, tail twister, and the whole nine yards. Coming back to the old building on 19th Street, Nunn asked them how they had enjoyed it. Logue said, "Dr. Nunn, I'll have to quote Colonel Danforth, longtime sports editor of the *Atlanta Journal*. He once said he 'had no confidence in grown men who stood up in the middle of the day and sang songs, entirely sober.' "

"Well," said McCalla, laughing, "we were never invited back to the Lions Club."

Women's Editor Oris Cantrell presented Oscar Dugger's *Southern Living* Task Force with *sixteen* proposed editorial departments for the magazine. They included: "1. The Family and the Changing South. 2. Beauty and Grooming. 3. Food. 4. Building, Remodeling, and Repairs. 5. Family Fashions. 6. Clothing and Sewing. 7. Landscaping and Gardening. 8. Recreation and Sports (including travel). 9. Hunting, Fishing. 10. Spectator Sports. 11. Home Furnishing. 12. Interior Decorating. 13. Health. 14. Family Relations (including Teenage Problems and Child Development). 15. Humor. 16. Editorials."

"You might make ten magazines out of that lineup," said Logue, "but you would play hell making one. And this list didn't even include 'Politics and Religion,' which were on the drawing board. Remember we actually ran a sermon to the U.S. Senate by Peter Marshall, who was dead at the time. If he'd been alive, that issue might well have done him in."

"All things to all people will get you killed," pronounced McCalla.

It's interesting that the word "travel" appeared as a lowercase afterthought (within a parenthesis) in this crowded list of proposed departments. Travel was only going to be the biggest money maker in the future of the magazine.

Fowler Dugger, who "wasn't wild" about the new magazine, wrote Gene Butler, "I am convinced we just do not have anyone with the sort of experience and know-how in this new magazine field to head up *Southern Living* . . . without taking too big a gamble on putting it over." No more accurate words were ever penned.

His brother Oscar wrote Butler, "Success of *Southern Living* would depend quite heavily on our ability to find a well qualified, top-flight Editor-in-Chief."

Gene Butler's own son Britt wrote his father, "The Editor-in-Chief or Publisher . . . should be someone in whom we all have almost complete faith—enough faith to give him the authority to get the job done." The soundness of this advice would startle McCalla and Logue, all these years later. *Everybody* who ever worked at *Progressive Farmer* or *Southern Living* or Oxmoor House, or any of our divisions, has a Britt Butler story. Britt was a bright fellow, a civil engineer from Texas A&M. Somehow he was stuck in an administrative role in his family's magazine. He was the sort of guy who drove an old, sorry pickup truck and carried his lunch in a paper sack, even after he was worth fifty million dollars, give or take ten or twenty million. He enjoyed the role of volunteer deputy sheriff and on weekends would affect a Sam Browne belt, pistol and all.

One Britt story. Emory and Vernon put him in charge of every sort of miserable detail to save money, and then they stood back innocently when some action by Britt turned into a catastrophe. Britt got an alert from the company health insurer that alarmed him. It had to do with pregnancy and its effect on corporate rates. Britt typed out a memo that went something like this: *Pregnancy under our insurance policy is treated the same as any other disease. Each department head has the responsibility to report immediately to management when an employee is pregnant . . . or thought to be pregnant.*

Logue loved this memorandum. And immediately invaded the lives of women editors and editorial assistants, memo in hand. "Let's see now, do you suffer the *disease* of pregnancy?" he asked to their initial puzzlement. "Could you *possibly* be pregnant? You know it was *a long weekend.* As I remember you had a *long lunch hour* last Friday." He would duck thrown stapling machines and empty trash baskets. Nobody threw a spittoon. Then he would be on his knees laughing while the women read the memorandum.

They were too amazed themselves to be outraged, and then couldn't wait to spring the memo on their buddies and call women employees all over town to howl about it. Today they would be calling their lawyers. But then it was just the ever-vigilant Britt, a sort of rich man's Falstaff, without the girth or the wit, going about casting a little happy chaos into everybody's lives. It is hoped that these small time bombs in this narrative strike your fancy as comically as they stick in the memory.

The good news was that the Board of Directors, under the influence of President Eugene Butler, voted on March 18, 1965, to go ahead with the launch of *Southern Living*. The bad news was it would be under the absolute editorial control of Dr. Alexander Nunn.

Catch the date: *1965*. Exactly one hundred years after the end of the Civil War. But these editorial wars were just heating up.

3

A Stop in Atlanta

Where were we? Oh, yes. Dr. O. B. Copeland had just been introduced as the new editor of *Southern Living*, with the magazine still seven months away from its February, 1966, launch.

"Cope was a good man," said McCalla.

"Cope was a damn good man," said Logue.

Without exception, every person spoken to in researching this collaborative memoir said, "O. B. Copeland was a good man."

"Cope was a really nice guy," said Brad Byers, "a company man who was comfortable with the authority they gave him and committed to doing what the bosses felt needed done.

"All of us hired from outside the company were convinced the only way to succeed was to put out a magazine that clearly catered to urbanites and suburbanites," said Byers. "The *P.F.* staff believed the way to succeed was to put out a magazine that catered to the farm nostalgia of rural people who had moved to town. Naturally, we clashed. Despite my personal liking for Cope, I never felt he should have been made editor of the magazine."

Of course, under the prevailing conditions, Cope should have told Dr. Nunn to take the job as editor of *Southern Living* and stick it where the cotton didn't grow. Has there ever been another magazine, in the history of magazines, on which most of the staff, for God's sake, did not report to the editor?

Finally, in December, 1965, the art director did report to Cope.

Logue estimated he would have lasted nineteen seconds in the job, just long enough to walk back to Dr. Nunn's office and step in his spittoon. McCalla was a far better diplomat. He would have thought about it for fifteen minutes and nineteen seconds and then stepped in Dr. Nunn's spittoon. In fact, somebody on the *Southern Living* staff once accidentally did step in Dr. Nunn's spittoon, making the most godawful mess that delighted every *Southern Living* staffer, but McCalla and Logue can't remember who did it.

In those days, they gave every editor his own brass spittoon. "The one memento I wish I had kept from those years in the old building," said Logue, "was my spittoon. I can't believe I didn't think to steal it when we moved to the new building on Lake Shore Drive."

O. B. Copeland was an average-sized guy, always dressed in a suit as if leaving for church, which he did every Sunday morning. He had a friendly, sort of lopsided smile. And he was a trouper. He took the job as editor of *Southern Living* under those appalling conditions.

Cope had first joined *Progressive Farmer* in the Depression year of 1938, and rejoined the company in 1959, and he was the quintessential company man. Give him a job, any job, and he would commit himself to do the best that he could. He was also a bright guy who loved his alma mater, the University of Georgia. His Ph.D. was earned in agricultural journalism at the University of Wisconsin, not conferred on him as Nunn's had been by Auburn University. He was an excellent public speaker.

Logue said, "I can still hear Cope, giving a talk somewhere and suddenly quoting from Sidney Lanier's 'The Marshes of Glynn': 'By so many roots as the marsh-grass sends in the sod / I will heartily lay me a-hold on the greatness of God.' It would have raised the hair on the back of the neck of an agnostic."

But Copeland wasn't born to be an editor. Quick, often cruel, decisions have to be made in an instant: to discard a cover photograph that doesn't work, despite a great deal of effort and time and money that went into it; or to kill a lead story that doesn't cut it, though the writer hemorrhaged on the page with his effort; or to fire on the spot a color separator who has let you down (which McCalla was to do four times in about that many years).

Cope was not a stern man, and when it came to making decisions, his instinct was to agree with whoever had last spoken with him. He couldn't say no to Dr. Nunn pushing his activist Old South agenda, and he couldn't say no to the principal owner and president, Eugene Butler (whom Cope always addressed as "President Butler"), who wanted to heal the imaginary anger between farm folk and city folk, and he couldn't say no to Emory Cunningham, after he became president, with his opposite vision for *Southern Living* from the old agriculture editors. Cunningham wanted a magazine that celebrated the positive aspects of the good life in the South. Cope dreaded to disappoint any of them. The resulting new magazine disappointed the readers and the advertisers.

"There was one saving grace about those early issues," said Logue, looking over McCalla's shoulder at the bound volumes of 1965. "They were awkward; they were, God knows, dated in design. They were a consecutive confusion, lacking any definite departments or editorial focus. But one thing those early issues weren't. They weren't phony. They didn't come from a phony editor or from a phony company. People will forgive you a lot if you aren't faking it."

McCalla agreed. "The editorial looked like 1938, especially opposite the advertising pages, which looked like 1965."

When Copeland got the job, he set immediately to work. He told the editors to "get out of town" and bring back good, readable material, while he organized himself to edit the magazine.

McCalla was sent to Macon, Georgia, which is a long way from the "mid-South," which was supposed to be his beat. He went to check out a public garden. But it proved to be a dog, which was one of the luckiest things that ever happened to *Southern Living* magazine. Looking for alternate story ideas, McCalla stopped by the Georgia State Capitol building in Atlanta to call on Bill Hardman, whom he had never met. That didn't matter. Hardman will never meet a stranger in this life or probably the next one. He had been appointed by Governor Ernest Vandiver in 1959 as the state's first director of tourism. Hardman built a network of welcome centers on major Georgia highways that still sets the standard among states. Georgia floats won top prizes in the Rose Bowl Parade. The state became the first in the Union to place travel advertising on television. It was no longer true that Georgia was a state you drove through on the way to a vacation in Florida. Twelve years after starting from scratch, Hardman's advertising budget reached one million dollars, a fair share of it spent in *Southern Living*.

McCalla's visit was by no means Hardman's introduction to *S.L.* But his first meeting with Hardman set a critical precedent. The editor and all the sub-editors of *Southern Living* would keep their integrity about them, but they would take the magazine's editorial message to legitimate advertisers. (Which translated to: *McCalla and Logue would hustle the dear bastards every chance they got.*) In truth, this collaboration among the editors and the advertising sales staff has always been a powerful force in the success of the magazine. McCalla's favorite saying was: "The advertising guys are always welcome in my office—as long as they come in on their hands and knees." He really meant, "as long as they pick up the check for lunch."

If anything was shaking in the American South in those years that was worth paying to see (including along Bourbon Street), Hardman and his fellow state travel directors knew which bush to look under. They knew that the average tourist would drive 150 miles out of his way to visit a legitimate historic site—so long as it was visitor-friendly and good food and lodging could be had along the way. *Southern Living* editors would pick and choose the travel destinations they would feature, but they didn't hesitate to pick the willing brains (and advertising pockets) of Hardman and his travel director colleagues. It was a collaboration to benefit the Southern states, the *Southern Living* readers, the "accidental tourists," and the bottom line.

"Those critical first years, Hardman did more for us than anybody," said McCalla. "He was one of the first to put state advertising dollars into our travel section. More important than that, he helped convince the other Southern travel directors, and plenty of private tourism operators, they should be in *Southern Living*. We would never have survived those first years without the advertising of the Southern travel industry."

Hardman reared back at his desk not long ago, his thick hair gone entirely white. He looked out the window of the small house north of Atlanta that has been converted into his office. He might have been looking into the past. "The first time I ever heard the words *Southern Living*, they were spoken by Don Cunningham. And I think I've heard those two words every day since." Nobody laughs as totally as Hardman. "Don came by my old office in the capitol building to tell us they were starting this new magazine, which was going to do a lot for travel in the South.

He was right about that. And we were excited. All we had to advertise in were Yankee publications. It was great to have our own.

"I'm not sure Don got all the credit he deserved for what he did for *Southern Living*. He never missed a major travel meeting, whether it was in America, Europe, or Asia. You couldn't help but like him. You couldn't forget him and his corny jokes. Even today, people ask me, 'When have you seen Don Cunningham?' I rank Don and Pete Johnson of *Holiday* and Jim Summerville of *Better Homes & Gardens* as the three top ad salesmen that came in my office all those years."

Hardman was invited by O. B. Copeland to speak at *Southern Living*'s first sales meeting at Callaway Gardens. "I don't know how much I lied," said Hardman, thinking back on it. "I said, 'You better get out and sell the South.' I used the old Southern Railway slogan: 'The last half of the twentieth century belongs to the South.' And I tell you what, it has."

McCalla's old army buddy Paul Cook had the same job as Hardman in South Carolina. Cook, and then Hardman, urged McCalla to attend the second-ever meeting of the Southern Travel Directors Council (STDC). It was held at the Grove Park Inn in Asheville, North Carolina, in August, 1965. McCalla went up and thereafter never missed a meeting for years. He was finally considered to be an "honorary twelfth member" of the group, and he was the only magazine editor invited to all their meetings.

McCalla sat with Paul Cook on the back deck of Cook's house in 1966, and the two of them laid out a sixteen-page South Carolina advertising section, the first such state section to appear in *Southern Living*. Very soon thereafter, Hardman weighed in with a Georgia advertising section. And Don Cunningham quickly sold Alabama the first advertising section that was also used as a state travel brochure.

Earlier in the same day they reminisced with Hardman about *S.L.*'s early days, Logue and McCalla sat in Don Cunningham's luxurious home on the north side of Atlanta. Don's a big guy, big all over, and always with a huge smile on his face. He remembered, "I was over in Hawaii having a drink with Alabama's travel director, Doug Benton. We were drinking that Japanese drink, saki. I told him I had this great idea for an advertising section that could also be used for a travel brochure. But nobody would buy it.

"Doug said, 'Give me the figures on it.' And he bought it. And then we sold the same idea to Florida. But it turned out Florida couldn't use it for a brochure. State law said the thing had to be printed in the state. But we got the business.

"Roger McGuire was a great guy," said Don, speaking of *Southern Living*'s first advertising director. "He played an important part in our developing the travel business. I told Roger we needed to put a heavy emphasis on travel organizations, such as NATO, National Association of Travel. Later, DATO, Discover America Travel Organization. I told Roger, 'If you will give me some money so we can go to these travel meetings, I think we can really make it work.' Roger said, 'Go. Take off and go. Just get the business.' And we got it."

McCalla and Logue remembered tending bar until the daylight hours in the *Southern Living* hospitality suite at the DATO and NATO meetings. They'd be the only editors within five hundred miles. Time, Inc., editors would have conceded a year's salary before they would have served drinks at an advertising hospitality suite. But if you want to know where the travel business was—and is—just look in the pages of *Southern Living*.

"The other magazines would just shut down," said McCalla, "because everybody was in our suite anyway. Hardman's right. Everybody loved Don. He had ten thousand jokes. Kept 'em in a big file. He was famous for 'em. Most of 'em terrible. When he retired, he just destroyed 'em. I can't believe it. They were so much a part of his life. Don would call you on the phone with *a great idea*, but first he would tell you a new joke."

"The company ought to have him on tape telling The Wide-Mouth Frog Joke," said Logue. "It's as much a part of our history as the *Progressive Farmer* logo, and it made a helluva lot more money. We got to throw a party for this book, McCalla, and the only way Don Cunningham is gonna get in the door is to tell The Wide-Mouth Frog Joke. We'd put it in the book, but you can't write it, you've got to have Don tell it."

"We threw the greatest party ever given at DATO," said Don. "The meeting was coming to Atlanta. I went to Al Kelly, who ran the Hyatt Hotel, and later became the president of the resort end of Hyatt. I said, 'Al, why don't we get together and do this thing right?' We came up with a slogan: 'The Old and the New Atlanta.' We asked everybody to come down the escalator in the Hyatt. We had waitresses in antebellum costumes flown up from Miami. We had a riverboat and a paddle wheel and bales of cotton, and a guy playing the banjo. The delegates thought that was the complete party. Then the guy on the banjo quit playing 'Take Me

Home, Country Roads,' and started tearing it up with rock and roll. We moved everybody into the 'New Atlanta' room, with waitresses in hot pants, ice sculptures of the Southwest, and red hot New Orleans music. Oh, it was a party." And, oh yes, he got the business.

Back to Bill Hardman. He remembered that he once suggested— during a lunch with McCalla and Emory and Don Cunningham at the Marriott Hotel in Atlanta—that the magazine offer a free advertising page with each four pages purchased. "I was the first to buy the four pages," said Hardman, "and then STDC got others to come in and use *Southern Living* as our bible for travel. It really helped build up the magazine's travel pages, which benefited us all."

Early on, Hardman said the travel industry had one concern: that *Southern Living* was being introduced by a farm magazine, and the first few issues even carried on the cover the subtitle: *an edition of The Progressive Farmer*." He said, "We were afraid it would be Old South, old fashioned."

"Well, it looked like 1938," said Logue.

"Yeah," agreed Hardman, with his huge laugh. "But McCalla took it downtown."

In 1982, some years after Hardman left the state tourism job, he assembled some of the "old-timers" from Southern travel at the Atlanta Hilton, run by his friend Bill Utnik. McCalla and Don Cunningham represented *S.L.* Others present were Ed Stone, Opryland; Roger Brashears, Jack Daniel's; Spurgeon Richardson, Six Flags; Jenny Brownlow, Alabama Mountain Lakes; Don Naman, NASCAR; Fred Brinkman, South Carolina; Bill Hensley, North Carolina; Mike Smith, the Biltmore House; Terry Clements, of the Nashville Chamber of Commerce. Dorothy Hardman kept Bill on time, as always. This meeting launched the Southeast Tourism Society, which now has over five hundred members from the private and public sectors of the travel industry from ten states.

Gary and Don convinced Emory Cunningham that *Southern Living* should be the first corporate sponsor of the organization. In 1997, Bill Hardman stepped down as president, after running the organization from the beginning. Bud Flora of *S.L.* became chairman of the board at the same time.

Millions of dollars of travel advertising from those worlds have flowed into the pages of *Southern Living* in the last thirty years. In no small part, *Southern Living* can thank Providence for a failed public garden in Macon, Georgia.

* * *

But the overwhelming reason for the magazine's early survival was its advertising sales staff, which also sold the farm magazine. You can write it down and we hereby do: The Progressive Farmer Company had the best advertising sales staff in American magazine publishing in 1965 and for years afterward. *Southern Living* could not have survived with a lesser group. They kept the advertising cynics and skeptics believing until the formative magazine could find itself. And if you think that was easy, those guys could have sold you preseason tickets to Wrigley Field for the World Series.

If you imagine we editors were characters, you should have done business with Roger McGuire, and Jim DeVira, and Bill Bentley, and Mike ("The Flaming Irishman") Fitzgerald, and Jerry Jehle, and Don ("The Wide-Mouth Frog") Cunningham, and Smith Moseley, and Dick ("The Jap") Olmstead, and Jerry ("AWOL") Latzsky, and Steve Berezney, and Milt Lieberman, and the company's entire advertising mafia. They will have their song sung here in a short while. ("If only we were once again hanging out at the bar in Joe Muir's seafood restaurant in downtown Detroit, waiting on an order of fried smelt," said Logue.)

Hardman, even in his youth, never did talk to you. He surrounded you with conversation. The first words out of his mouth to McCalla in 1965 were: "I've got to get you up to Stone Mountain. That's where the story is."

Soon, McCalla, riding on an outside elevator up the sheer face of Stone Mountain, was asking himself: "What the hell am I doing up here?" Then he was climbing a vertical ladder up onto Robert E. Lee's shoulder and looking straight down four hundred feet. Risky. But not as risky as the magazine business.

McCalla's brief piece, one of the very few additions to Red Youngsteadt's original outline for that first February issue, became the Travel South lead: "Watching Men Carve a Mountain."

"Interesting thing," said Logue, "McCalla instinctively wrote it in the *second* person: 'On weekdays throughout the year *you* can watch the small team of men working some 33 stories above the base of the mountain . . .' "

Logue added, "A few years later when he became editor, the two of us agreed that the tone and voice of *Southern Living* should be very much a *spoken* tone and voice. And that the tone should be gender neutral. Whether we were talking about cooking or fishing, we would assume all our readers, men and women, would be interested. We weren't going to talk down to anybody. We also agreed that, when appropriate, we would continue to use the second person—*you*—to involve the reader in the action. Our readers would be participants, not spectators.

"Of course, the third person, being so unintrusive, remains the most often-used narrative device in articles. The first person—*I*—has been used sparingly, but to good effect when the writer's actions were central to the event. Especially today, under the good tutelage of Executive Editor Michael Carlton, first-person stories have flourished in the magazine. But the idea that you, the reader, are involved in every page of *Southern Living* remains one of its subtle strengths."

McCalla made it down off the mountain in one piece.

In 1972, Logue went up to document the finished carving—but not as far up as Lee's shoulder. George Weiblen had overseen the completion of the work begun by Gutzon Borglum in 1915 and abandoned in 1925. And now Stonewall Jackson, Jefferson Davis, and Robert E. Lee rode into a granite eternity.

Weiblen came from an astonishing family. His father had served in the German army in 1875 and was one of the Kaiser's favorite trapeze artists. He was also a gifted stone carver. He moved to New Orleans and bought one of the city's famous cemeteries. And that's how the family came to lease Stone Mountain for fifty years from the Venable brothers, who owned it. The Weiblens cut granite to build the Royal Bank of Canada, the Cuban capitol, the Colon locks of the Panama Canal, and hundreds of public buildings all over America.

Southern Living for thirty years has uncovered such remarkable families as the Weiblens whom the national media never thought to bring to life.

McCalla cracks up laughing about the letter Logue got from an angry reader when his story was published. He can still quote from it: "You are ghoulishly, gleefully, dancing on the grave of Gutzon Borglum." Weiblen had said, "Borglum's design was so much all out of reason—too big a job ever to be completed." Of course, Borglum, after he gave up on Stone Mountain, made rather a name for himself by directing the carvings we know as Mount Rushmore.

In the Olympic year 1996, the magazine revisited Stone Mountain, not for its historic carving but for the international tennis competition raging below, *Southern Living* being an official sponsor of the Olympic Games. And so new moments pass into time and become woven into the fabric of the South's collective memory.

4

Vol. 1, No. 1

The *Southern Living* staff returned from the farthest reaches of the South to prepare for publication in the year 1966. Progressive Farmer, despite its insistence on an in-house editor for *Southern Living,* was obviously fearful of its in-house limitations. It contracted with two distinguished consultants for the new magazine: Herb Mayes, editor of *McCall's,* and Wilson Hicks, who had retired from a brilliant career as picture editor and vice-president of *LIFE* during its glory years.

Mayes's contract with *McCall's* did not allow him to accept money as a consultant. So the very proper Old Guard at The Progressive Farmer Company slipped him fifteen hundred dollars a day under the table.

"I can remember Beth Carlson running around the office trying to get him a check okayed," said McCalla.

Some years later, McCalla and Logue had a memorable visit with Mayes in his Upper East Side Manhattan apartment. Before he moved to *McCall's,* Mayes had edited *Good Housekeeping.* His version of events the year he published a three-part novella by Hemingway would make provocative reading. You might have seen in A. E. Hotchner's book *Papa Hemingway* his version of how the manuscript that became *Across the River and into the Trees* was nurtured into print in *Good Housekeeping.*

But since libel lawyers never sleep, we best leave Mayes's story of those events, with his supporting papers in his wall safe, unexplored.

Mayes was not reluctant to give his opinion on the prospects for *Southern Living*. He thought it should be a woman's magazine. Of course, he had never edited anything else.

McCalla said, "Mayes believed we should drop the idea of writing about travel. He said, 'After two or three issues, you will have covered the only few interesting places to visit in the South, and then what will you write about?' Mayes had never been south of the Hudson River," McCalla recalled, laughing.

"We could publish readable travel stories for ten years and never get three hundred miles from Birmingham. But Mayes also had some excellent ideas. He believed every magazine should be seriously departmentalized. But that each issue should also include a surprise, something the readers could never have anticipated. A very good idea. Not a good idea to have a surprise on every page, as we did in the early issues of *Southern Living*."

McCalla said, "Mayes also put great stock in the impact of lively headlines and legends for photographs. He said he always paid one person twenty-five thousand dollars a year to write only headlines and legends. Hell, in 1965, the president of The Progressive Farmer Company was only making thirty-three thousand dollars a year."

"So you hired me to write 'em for half that," said Logue. "And one of your most enduring public statements was: 'We don't need Edgar Allan Poe writing for *Southern Living*.' And you always looked straight at me when you said it."

"I was right, too," said McCalla, laughing his gruff laugh.

"Wilson Hicks was an absolute gentleman," he remembered, "but he didn't tolerate fools gladly. The old agricultural editors got their backs up now and then when Hicks spoke his mind plainly."

McCalla broke into laughter and finally got his breath back. "I remember when Big John McKinney laid his Christmas cover for *Progressive Farmer* in front of Hicks. John had a shot of a yearling calf coming out of Santa Claus's backpack, in the primary colors of green and red. Wilson looked at it for a long time, pretty much in amazement. He said, 'John. That is probably the most awful magazine cover of the twentieth century.' "

McCalla enjoyed both Mayes and Hicks at an editorial meeting in the late summer of 1966 at Dauphin Island, near Mobile.

"I was sick of the handout photographic crap we were running from the food industry," said McCalla. "So, on the way to Dauphin Island, Lena Sturges and I met up with free-lance photographer Bill Shrout at Bayou La Batre on Mobile Bay." Shrout had made a name for himself covering the war in the Pacific for *LIFE.* In one of the terrible invasions, he went in with the first wave, crawled into the trees, and photographed the rest of the Marines coming ashore. He said he got a wire from *LIFE,* ordering "no more phony set-up photographs." Shrout was now living on the Fowl River near Mobile and did some good work for the early *Southern Living.*

He and McCalla composed what was really the first classic *Southern Living* food/travel shot. Shrout captured in color a mound of freshly caught shrimp, sitting on a dark net, with the boat and water in softer focus. It ran in May of 1967, and it could run today in the very sophisticated *Southern Living.*

But the story is getting ahead of itself, and will circle back to the Dauphin Island editorial conference in the summer of '66 a bit later. Meanwhile the first issue of *Southern Living* came off the press for the month of February, 1966.

It was *LIFE*-size, that is 10½ inches wide by 13 inches tall. The decision to begin publishing the new magazine that size was a near-ruinous one. Although the readers liked the big format, the cost of paper and the ever-growing cost of postage made it impractical. In July, 1967, the company would reduce *Southern Living* to *Time* size (from 680 lines per page to 429, in printer's parlance). When that happened many subscribers screamed their displeasure and ran for the exit.

"The reason *LIFE* published in the large format," said McCalla, "was to take advantage of their great photography. It was a picture book. We didn't have the photography. And we didn't have design capability to take advantage of the large format."

The first issue of *Southern Living* was very much an amateur effort and looked it. It could live on its cover, which was not bad, a John McKinney Special of a home in Mobile, with azaleas in full bloom, a family dog tied to a chair, and a pair of young girls riding a bicycle-built-for-two. At the time, probably no readers under fifty years old had ever seen a bicycle-built-for-two. But you would have to say the cover worked.

That the engraver could not hold the red-and-white colors of the azaleas was forgiven. In fact, the readers pretty much forgave everything, so proud was much of the South to get its own magazine.

However, many of the one hundred thousand subscribers to *Progressive Farmer* who did not have rural addresses and who had been switched over to *Southern Living* were howling mad, a condition that would take some time to sort itself out. The other subscribers were only risking *one dollar* for a year's magazines, another near-ruinous management decision to underprice the product.

Skeptics in high places in the advertising world saw much in that first issue to confirm their skepticism, which had previously been expressed. In the spring of 1965, *Southern Living* held an advertising sales meeting in the old Heart of Atlanta Motel. Atlanta, now known as the Olympic City, did not have a first-class hotel in 1965. A featured speaker at the meeting was Herb Manloveg, media director of the powerful advertising agency BBD&O, of New York. Manloveg, a longtime friend of The Progressive Farmer Company, frankly cautioned management against starting *Southern Living*. Magazines as powerful as *Look* and *Saturday Evening Post* and *Collier's* and others had gone out of business or were in deep trouble. Television was a fearsome new competitor. He questioned whether management really understood the risk it was taking.

"Manloveg told me he didn't think it would ever go," Don Cunningham remembered. "He said, 'Somebody has made a terrible mistake. Either that, or I'm damn wrong.' "

Manloveg probably didn't think he was wrong when he picked up his copy of that first issue and read President Eugene Butler's opening *message* in the magazine.

Mr. Butler, beginning with his seventh paragraph, wrote: "*Southern Living* will seek to help Southern cities alleviate many of the hazards of crowded living. Dirty air, filthy water, growing crime, traffic jams, noise and tension combine to make life in so many cities a frustrating and sometimes dangerous experience.

"By wise, long-range planning, our most modern Southern cities are side-stepping the obvious mistakes that have blighted so many Northern areas. We will bring to you well documented stories of these modern miracles of planned development."

So. *Southern Living* was going to *document* the solving of all problems in the cities of the American South. America would damn sure be anxious to see *that*. Even today America would like to see it, as New Orleans, Atlanta, Houston, Dallas, Miami, Birmingham, and Washington, D.C., continue to rank right at the top of the murder rates in the country, with white flight as real as 1965. And Manloveg and his advertising peers must have been comforted to be told of the "obvious mistakes that have blighted so many Northern cities" in which they sat reading this first issue of *Southern Living.*

"Manloveg continued to be a powerful force in advertising, at three different huge agencies," said Don Cunningham, "and once we got rolling, *Southern Living* never had a bigger supporter. He put an awful lot of business in the magazine."

Butler, in his strange first-issue essay, also wrote that *Southern Living,* "by reason of its close association with *The Progressive Farmer,* is ideally situated to promote better understanding between urban and rural people . . . often at odds through lack of understanding." He quoted the Bible: "Behold, how good and pleasant it is when brothers dwell in unity! (psalm 133:1)." He continued, "There is urgent need for these brothers to understand each other's problems better that they may work as partners in the South's progress. This then is our opening message to you."

It was a message that confounded editors, readers, and advertisers. This magazine was going to help solve all modern problems of cities while settling some unknown feud between city and country folk? What the hell was going on?

This question was raised by both consultants: Mayes and Hicks. More about that later.

When Volume 1, Number 1, of *Southern Living* rolled off the press, there was no champagne celebration. "We were too overwhelmed by the idea of having to put out another issue for March to do any celebrating," said McCalla.

That first issue could not rise above its dated, random, dreary design. The contemporary ads of Clairol, Pepsi Cola, Oldsmobile, Royal Crown Cola, Chrysler, and Modess shouted *today.* While the editorial photography and typography and page design looked more like the years of the Great Depression.

There was another, equally critical problem. The composition of the magazine was absolutely chaotic. The table of contents listed categories of Travel, General, Homes, Foods and Entertaining, Fashions and Grooming, Outdoor Recreation, Gardening and Landscaping. In truth, stories from these worlds appeared randomly. After the first fourteen pages you might have imagined you had finished the travel section. Then there was a "one-week vacation" in the Yucatan on page 20, followed by SEE ROCK CITY birdhouses, followed by snow skiing in the South, followed by the Travel Calendar. Surely, you had now visited February's complete travel inventory of stories.

Not so. Thirty-five pages later you were confronted with seven photographs and the question: "Where in the SOUTH are you?" A second question might have been asked: "Where in the hell in the magazine are you?" A blank page had opened up for February, and McCalla had thrown these seven photographs together to test the readers' understanding of locations within the South. (The page proved to be extemely popular and was kept on as a regular feature.)

Was the issue's inventory of travel items exhausted? Hardly. After a hilariously serious story beginning: "A woman can't be truly beautiful unless her hands are as lovely as her face"—and after advice on "tipping, streaking, frosting, and tinting your hair," with illustrations of beehive hairdos to inspire the cast of the Grand Ol' Opry—appeared stories on North Carolina's Mattamuskeet, a time for catching big bass, a wild goose refuge, and the sights and sounds of Cape Romain.

In between these stories were runover material from snow skiing, Mardi Gras, and the Houston city story. In later issues, stories would begin in the middle or back of the book and jump forward. God, how McCalla hated those forward jumps and the design chaos they created. Logue, when he got there, loved 'em. He could write long, from here to El Paso, and jump the narrative like a corrupt king on a checkerboard . . . until McCalla got to be editor and kept a big axe in his desk.

Plawin's Houston story wasn't bad, if a tad gushy: " 'Wow!' he said aloud. 'What do you call it?' and then, after a pause to relish his rhetoric, 'New Gotham!' " Beware of all sentences ending in exclamation marks! The one-color photograph of a night view of Houston seemed to have been printed underwater. The black-and-white industrial shots were okay.

Then comes a "Beautiful Kitchen," which proves more efficient than beautiful, but it does have a good-looking woman at the sink. The next photographic spread of "Southern Furniture" is pure, cold-blooded, manufacturer's handout straight from the warehouse. A continued steady diet of this poor imitation *Better Homes & Gardens,* and *Southern Living* would have died a deserved early death.

Then came four how-to-do-it stories: build your own mailbox, build your own putting green, lay your own vinyl tile, and display your own fish trophy, with a hilariously framed fish scene, the artificial plug dangling two inches from the open mouth of the dead bass.

McCalla threw together the putting green short, which, again, proved popular, and we did it some years later in full color. He made one mistake. He suggested that readers *seed* the Tiftdwarf grass. "All those *P. F.* editors read it, and all the advice they had for us, and not one of them caught it; you can't seed Tiftdwarf," groaned McCalla, who had to answer all the complaints. Served him right.

Talented free-lance photographer Gordon Schenck shot "A Home for Six or a Party of 100." Not a bad house in Chapel Hill, North Carolina. Not bad photographs. Not a bad story by a free-lancer. But the layout of the spread looked like it was right out of *Mechanics Illustrated*.

It was followed by plans for sale for a Chromaster-designed house. Similar plans had long appeared in *Progressive Farmer*. They were consistently ghastly. McCalla hated them. And as soon as he could, which took some years, he killed them with a ball-peen hammer.

Now came *another* page of building your own mailbox, as if the subject had not already come up in the magazine. Once again, it was thrown together to fill an unexpected blank page. "We had only been getting ready for this issue for a year," said McCalla.

Then came a detailed discussion of "Air Conditioning," and how much it costs to operate—a subject that spoke of the new urban life in the South, as rare, at the time, was air conditioning in farm homes. This story is followed by a "Kitchen King" male cook, a feature which endured for years, in this case one Carl Reith, president of Colonial supermarkets in ten states. The advertising boys had to be chortling at slipping this one in, considering all the food products they were hustling to get into the magazine.

Now appeared, "Cornbread, the South's Own Creation." Logue loved to say, "If you had to reduce the entire *Southern Living* story to one word, it would be *cornbread*. It's our Southern metaphor for the staff of life." It was a good story by free-lancer William Boddie—but not a single photograph to illustrate cornbread, not even in black and white.

It was followed by a green-tinted color photograph of chicken sufficient to kill the appetite of a starving man. Then by "Winning Ways with Pork," and by "Treats from Kumquats," and by "February Prize Recipes." No photographs, but an illustration of two English toffs in high hats dusting off their hands and patting their stomachs after eating the prize recipes. English toffs? Go figure?

Now came "Beginners with Roses," all pickup shots with dead black backgrounds. Followed by a handout from Hastings on "Shade Trees."

Then came a fertilizer program for the lawn and "Ways to Prune Southern Shrubs." All reasonable information, drearily presented.

Finally, appeared a Dr. Nunn Special: "Southern Junior Colleges, One Answer to the Enrollment Problem." Before solving the cities' crime and traffic and filthy air and general urban blight, Dr. Nunn and Mr. Butler would first solve the more modest education problem in the American South. Of course, the junior college piece was simpleminded and solved absolutely nothing. It carried no by-line.

"I have no idea who wrote it," said McCalla. "These stories just appeared. None of us on the staff ever heard of them until Cope dropped them on us. Looking through the first year's magazines, I'm surprised how many of these 'crusading stories' there were, and how they disrupted the tone and voice and intent of the magazine."

Oh yes, the back editorial page of the February issue closed with a profile of "The Pecan Candy Man, Williamson Stuckey." The advertising boys must have groaned. As a matter of policy, the Stuckey pecan chain placed no advertising in magazines.

If he hadn't grown up to be a swan, the story about the "ugly duckling" would have never endured. The same is true for *Southern Living*. Yet the South was so eager to have its own magazine, it temporarily forgave *Southern Living*'s awkward beginning. Many readers wrote and called to express their instant affection for the magazine. They couldn't be sure what it was, but it was *theirs*.

Even New York advertising salesman Jim DeVira remembered, "We'd all been selling it so hard for so long. . . . When the first issue came out, I opened it, I thought it was the most beautiful thing I'd ever seen." Harsh reaction from the unforgiving world of advertising soon disabused DeVira of his first opinion of the first issue.

But Southerners seemed to understand that something important had been published. Logue remembers going up to Clemson University in South Carolina to interview Frank Howard in the spring of 1969. Frank was about to begin his thirtieth year coaching the Clemson football team. "He trusted us already," said Logue. "He told me he was going to hang it up the next year, but 'Don't go writin' it yet—they'll be tryin' to recruit my own kin out from under me.' Frank called a couple of days after I got back to Birmingham," said Logue. "He had apparently told his wife what magazine had interviewed him.

" 'Boy,' said Frank, 'You can do me a favor.'

" 'Consider it done,' I said.

" 'My wife has got ever' one of them *Southern Living*s there's ever been . . . except the first one,' said Frank, who had been a brilliant student at the University of Alabama, but who had affected the life of a country boy–coach so long that that's what he had become.

" 'She's got it now,' I said. 'I just haven't put it in the mail yet.' "

Logue says, "You must realize Frank Howard was the *king* of Clemson. Anything his wife wanted in the state of South Carolina he could have gotten it for her. A couple of years later, I ran into him in the Atlanta airport. He hadn't forgotten that first edition of the magazine. " 'Boy,' he said, 'I give my wife au-to-mo-biles she didn't love better'n that magazine.' Frank's wife was not alone."

We have examined closely the contents of the first issue so that you could have some idea of the creative problems the early *Southern Living* presented. But do not imagine that it was laughed at in the South. If you have a first edition, get it out carefully. It's rather valuable. And don't you laugh. Remember, Ford started mass production with the Model T.

5

Cracking the Whip

Consider the advertising pages that appeared in *Southern Living*'s first issue: Clairol, Pepsi Cola, Oldsmobile, Royal Crown Cola, Chrysler, Modess. In the ninety-page issue, there were actually thirty-four pages of ads. These advertisements did not materialize in the magazine out of the goodwill of generous American companies. Somebody had to hit them between the eyes with a crowbar, or at least with our editorial and marketing stories.

Which brings us to the 1965 advertising sales staff of The Progressive Farmer Company. We've already identified it as the best in American publishing. They never denied it. Modesty was not one of their strong suits.

Roger McGuire was ultimately advertising director for *Southern Living*. So far you've barely met him. Before this book winds down, we hope you get some idea of what a singular man he was. (Some of these observations Logue wrote to Roger's wife Pat after Roger died, a death none of us was prepared for.) In looks McGuire would remind you, in his coloring, in his bearing, of the actor Van Johnson. He grew up on a farm outside of Des Moines. Knowledge, especially of the English language, was important to the family. It was not easy for editors to argue with McGuire. He had a better command of the language than most of them.

He also had true friends at the absolute top of the advertising world. Dick Anderson comes to mind. When *Southern Living* was launched, Anderson was a top hand at the No. 2 ad agency in America, Young & Rubicam. Jim DeVira will tell us later how McGuire got Anderson to speak at one of our early advertising sales meetings in Texas. It was a watershed moment in the magazine's history.

Robert Ross, maybe McGuire's best friend, also comes to mind. An advertising man and later a novelist, Ross spent many years with Leo Burnett in Chicago, where he met McGuire. The two of them wound up living near Asheville, North Carolina, in later years. Ross loves telling about the time he and McGuire and two other guys commuted to work together in Chicago. They argued about everything. The other two guys ultimately got into an argument that escalated into a shouting match. They wouldn't quit. Finally, McGuire stopped the car and said, "Fellows, the only way to settle it is to fight it out." So, as rush-hour Chicago traffic fled past, two grown men in business suits were going at it, hammer and fists, while McGuire and Ross collapsed with laughter on the side of the expressway.

McGuire had this wicked fun side to him. Each January 1 he would get up a brutal touch football game, with live blocking and no pads. He'd recruit his sons and maybe Emory Cunningham's sons and other vulnerable victims, once including Logue, who remembered: "It was freezing and raining that day. And muddy. McGuire loved it. We went at one another like wild men. The college football bowls were for sissies in plastic helmets. Then we groaned around the office for a week."

McGuire was a talented pitch man. But standing up in front of a large group, saying just the precise thing that ought to be said, cost him a lot. To know it, you would have to see his hands tremble behind the lectern. You had to admire his strength of character, his willingness to suffer the pressure and never speak of it. But his great strength was the trust he had earned with the advertising world and the true friendships he made.

McGuire opened the Detroit advertising office for *Progressive Farmer* and *Southern Living*. He had the great insight to hire Jerry Jehle, a gentleman cut from the same cloth as himself, to follow him, and who in turn was followed by Dick Olmstead and Bud Flora, and Ed Fisher, and Chuck Siebert, and nobody sold the Detroit market more gleefully than Jan Hess-Wahl. It seems *Southern Living* always had stars in the Detroit office, not to mention the New York office and the Chicago office and the Atlanta office and all our advertising offices.

You must remember in 1965 the Detroit automobile guys thought that women only sat in cars and never bought one in their lives. But McGuire and Jehle and Olmstead and Flora and Fisher and Siebert and Hess-Wahl convinced them to put millions of dollars worth of ads in *Southern Living*, which had a predominantly female readership (but a strong minority of male readers). All it took was a crowbar and a lifetime of friendships.

McCalla and Logue and Foods Editor Jean Liles once made fourteen editorial pitches in New York for McGuire in three days. Only Jim De-Vira, grabbing taxi drivers by the throat, got them to the next appointment. DeVira also grabbed the media buyers by the throat to convince them to give time to an upstart magazine.

It was important for advertising executives to hear directly from the editors what the magazine was about. It also helped *S.L.*'s ad salesmen to hear them, so they could later sing the same song in the same key. De-Vira often could get senior ad executives—who were tough to reach—to make time for the editors. In the early years it was equally important that the advertising bigwigs came away with the impression that the *S.L.* editors knew the territory in the American South. That money spent with the magazine would not be squandered by amateurs.

Logue loves to remember the time McGuire took him to lunch with the account executive on Smirnoff vodka. His name was Roger Bumstead. "I can remember going down a flight of stairs into this French restaurant, expensive as hell. McGuire said we'd be a while, but gave no other warning, typical of McGuire. Our man comes in, shakes hands, and by the time we sit down the waiter has brought three double Smirnoffs without being asked. More of the same came three more times before we so much as ordered lunch. I can't remember what I ate. I ate everything I could get my hands on to keep from passing out. The French give you wonderful stuff but not a whole hell of a lot of it. The drinks kept coming during the three-hour lunch. They kept coming afterward," said Logue.

"I cannot remember one word spoken, just another gigantic glass of ice and vodka looming up in front of me like an unpayable debt. Did you ever see the scene in *Our Man from Havana*, when Graham Greene has the old Cuban general and his vacuum cleaner salesman/hero playing a game of chess? And every time one of them takes a piece from the other, he has to knock back a miniature of booze, of great and horrible variety.

That was the way it was in that French restaurant, always we were subduing some gigantic glass of Smirnoff vodka.

"Finally, by God, Bumstead bounces up, entirely sober, looks at his watch, and runs to catch his train. We stagger back to the old Roosevelt Hotel, which was our headquarters in Manhattan in those low-budget days, and we didn't have another drink until dinner. We wasted our lives, McCalla. We could have been advertising men."

And let's not forget the annual advertising sales meetings. But also not to get ahead of ourselves. We were speaking of McGuire. He and his wife, Pat, a newspaperwoman by trade, had a great variety of friends in high and low places. Remember the book *Walking Across America*, by Peter Jenkins? It sold a million copies in hardback. When Jenkins was broke and divorced and had lost his teaching job, he was walking across America with no book contract, looking for either his own soul or the country's. And among nine hundred thousand people in Greater Birmingham, who invited him to rest from the highway and spend the night in their house? The McGuires, of course.

Logue remembered the time he and his wife, Helen, were guests for dinner at the McGuires. A fire was going in the fireplace, and the Rabbi was there from the National Committee of Christians and Jews. A friendly man, the Rabbi, no chip on his shoulder. He told us he enjoyed many Jewish jokes. But the one joke he couldn't tolerate was the one about the Solid Gold Cadillac, from the Six-Day War with the Arabs. A knock on the door. In comes McCalla and his first wife, and it's like six people come in the door, and McCalla is getting a drink (this was during his drinking days), and comes over in a burst of enthusiasm . . . and tells the story about the Solid Gold Cadillac. McGuire and Logue are bursting a gut laughing before the punch line is ever spoken, and the Rabbi is smiling sickly in spite of himself. Nobody ever had a dull time of it at the McGuires.

One other McGuire story, for the moment. *Southern Living* had increased in wisdom and stature by the early 1970s. McGuire hired a local husband-wife team to put together a multiple-projector slide show on the magazine. It was all spring flowers and twittering birds—one lovely, innocent landscape fantasy of the South. McGuire got together the entire Birmingham magazine team: management, editorial, advertising, circulation. Charlie Metcalfe and his wife cranked up the slide show. Which was innocent enough. Except in the eyes of the one man who counted—President Emory Cunningham. The naiveté of it frightened him. McGuire had never anticipated so volatile a response from the head man. Nobody ever said Roger was an acute politician. In fact, you could hardly accuse him of being accomplished in all the technical nuances of print runs, paper costs, circulation madness, accounting vagaries. It was the *soul* of a magazine that McGuire understood, not so much its technical bells and whistles.

When the music ended on the last blooming azalea, and the lights went up in the Birmingham Downtown Club, the place was silent as the grave, waiting only for what Cunningham would say.

Emory was all apprehension. He got up in a barely controlled panic. He talked for nearly fifteen minutes. It seemed like two days. We couldn't take this rather amateurish production to New York. We would be laughed out of town. He told how *Sunset* magazine produced motion pictures of Hollywood quality and served stone crabs and that advertising people cancelled their vacations to come to these presentations. Which, of course, was baloney, especially the part about cancelling their vacations. And, in fact, *Sunset*'s one motion picture of itself that we later saw was pure corn. To be embarrassed in New York . . . Cunningham feared for *Southern Living*. And his fear fed his apprehension. He was not mistaken in that the risk was very real.

More silence. Logue said into that silence, "I think it's sentimental. More than a little naive. And it catches what we are *perfectly*." Remembering that awkward moment, Logue said, "I copped out plenty of times, in the interest of survival. Not this time. It pleases me to remember that McGuire spoke of it more than once in later years."

McCalla, always the more effective politician than McGuire or Logue, said, "Some of the photographs are not good. We can substitute for them, and I think the show will be better." Cunningham could live with that. He just needed support to soften his terrible apprehension. And if it failed, it was McGuire's baby.

Fast-forward to Manhattan. Dead of winter. Cold. Rainy. Nasty. The show went on at presentations all over the city. And the good gray *New York Times* came out and across the top of the business page was the headline: "Cruel and Unusual Punishment." That a small Southern magazine would inflict the beauty of spring and flowers and birds and mindless happiness on a freezing, winter-bound city of ruthless advertisers. It was a smash hit, of course. The magazine's first big-time publicity in the big city. The doubt in the Birmingham Downtown Club was nowhere in evidence.

As Logue wrote Pat McGuire, "All we have had of Roger for a long time in Birmingham is our memory of him. When he left the company, something went out of the air as surely as if the oxygen had been siphoned away. It is not hard to define that absence: his wit, his intelligence, his integrity (which in business is as often as not considered to be an impediment), his gift of language which allowed the whole mix that was him to come alive."

You think of the river of effort McGuire and his advertising sales guys made in those early years. All the days, weeks, months, years of plane flights (late, cancelled, baggage lost), taxis that wouldn't stop for you in the rain, appointments broken at the last instant, every known pronounceable reason for a rejection (gone all-broadcast; regional magazine? . . . no way; lost you on the last cut; aren't doing women's books; readers: too old, too poor; too damn many "C" and "D" counties; no product in the South; who needs the bloody South, you're last in everything).

If McGuire or any of our salesmen, and later saleswomen, could have seen all at once, as through a telescope, every rejection, every awkward effort, heard every lying dog and every unsympathetic phone call from Birmingham—"What happened to AT&T? Thought we had them in the bag?"—then they would have thrown themselves under a train in Chicago, or under a bus in Atlanta or Dallas or under a streetcar in San Francisco, or jumped out of the window of the old Marine Midland Building at 250 Park in New York.

Of course they didn't do any of those things. "No" to them was simply the "new yes" that hadn't been spoken.

This narrative is not finished with McGuire. His old colleagues will be telling stories about him so long as there are any of them left who knew him.

Now to introduce this man Jim DeVira, whom you've only known so far by his name. Well, DeVira was a city boy. He was born in Jersey City, New Jersey, across the river from Manhattan. He went to the same high school as—and played basketball with—Tommy Heinsohn, later famous as the shooting forward and then the coach of the great Boston Celtic teams in the NBA. Also in the same high school class was the pitcher Johnny Kucks. "I remember watching Johnny win two games for the Yankees in the World Series," said DeVira. He'd won twenty games in the regular season.

Kucks hurt his arm a couple of years later. He made a comeback with

the Atlanta Crackers of the International League. Ironically, Logue was
the baseball writer for the *Atlanta Journal* that year. Kucks won fourteen
games and pitched the Crackers to the Little World Series championship.
"He was a hell of a competitor," said Logue. "Just like DeVira and Heinsohn, he took no prisoners. They must've put something in the beer in
Jersey City."

The full-grown DeVira, about six feet three inches high, was not hard
to look at. Tall and dark, he would remind you in those days of the singer
Robert Goulet. And you know what the late Judy Garland said about
him: "He's an eight-by-ten glossy." That was DeVira. There were, admit-
tedly, two or three women on Manhattan Island who did not watch him
go by on the street.

We cornered DeVira in the still-new Southern Progress headquarters
building in Birmingham. He was visiting from Hilton Head Island, where
he lives in retirement. He looked fit and ready to charge hell with a
bucket of water. The advertising world would have presented a more
fiendish challenge. But nothing DeVira hadn't handled in the past.

He told of his first job, which was selling Spalding Bros. sporting
goods in New York State. "I replaced a guy named Bert Purvis. He'd been
the Spalding salesman there for twenty-five years. He had a lot of friends.
But he also had a drinking problem. They'd warned him and finally let
him go.

"I started my rounds making sales calls," said DeVira. "I went by Oak
Hill Country Club in Rochester, a beautiful club, big stone building, fabulous course. The pro there was Charlie McKenna, a cranky old guy. We
chatted awhile. He put his arm around my shoulder and said, 'Come on
back to the stockroom.'

"In those days, if you belonged to a country club, you were rich and
supported your pro by buying all your equipment at the club. Charlie
said, 'See all this Spalding stuff,' shelves and shelves of irons and woods.
'Jim, I want you to take it all out and send it back.' I said, 'Charlie, I'm
here to sell you some equipment, not to take it out.' He said, 'Well, Bert
Purvis was a good friend of mine for twenty-five years, and if that's the
best they can treat him, I don't want to do business with Spalding.' "

DeVira squinted as if he could still feel the pain. "It took me two years
before I was selling more stuff than I was taking back. I realized I wasn't
going to make my fortune in the sporting goods business." One thing the
Spalding experience taught Jim, the strength of good friends in powerful
places.

It was a friend, Jeff Spier, who pointed DeVira toward an advertising career. Spier had a friend, Frank Hill, who ran a small group of guys selling national advertising for all the Hearst newspapers. "This Frank Hill was the slickest-looking guy I ever met in my life," said DeVira. "He'd grown up poor in the Bronx and lived in Brooklyn. He always said that one of these days he was going to marry a rich woman. He did, an heiress to one of the tobacco fortunes. He wound up living on Park Avenue, with a big country house in Jersey with horses and the whole nine yards. He used to walk in at 10 A.M. in a camel's hair coat. Three of us worked for him. One guy would make a few calls and stay drunk the rest of the day. The other guy couldn't get out of his own way selling ads. I wound up with most of the accounts and was doing very well. Until they had a cutback. I figured, *I'm king of the hill around here. No one is going to fool with me.*

"Frank called me in. He said, 'Jim, we have to let someone go.' I said, 'Frank, I'm sorry to hear that.' He said, 'You know Bill has a drinking problem, and he's getting old, and he'd never be able to get another job. And Paul is a good guy, but fumbles around and can't get out of his own way. He'd never be able to get another job either. Jim, I'm going to let you go because you are not going to have any problem getting another job.' "

DeVira shook his head and rapped on the desk, still unable to believe it. "So, I was unemployed for doing the best job."

But not for long. He went directly to Hearst's *New York Journal-American.* He had all the big department store accounts, Gimbel's, Macy's. He was content. Until he met a fellow named Jim Cusack, who sold advertising for *Progressive Farmer* magazine. Cusack said they had an opening on their staff, and why didn't he apply?

"So, I went up and met Bill Bentley," said DeVira. "Don Cunningham had been the New York manager and had just left to open the Atlanta office. Bill and I hit it off immediately. He was a great guy. He had this Southern accent and was just a ball of fire. He was kinda tall, balding, smoked these small cigars. He'd only been in New York a short time. They'd moved him up from Alabama. In fact, Logue's father once hired him as an assistant county agricultural agent."

"Until the day he died, my father said that Bentley was the brightest young man he ever hired," said Logue.

"Bentley was a good salesman," said DeVira. "He knew all the agricultural accounts. Everybody loved him."

Before he could be hired, DeVira had to fly down to the Progressive Farmer home office in Birmingham. "I remember Smith Moseley met me at the airport. And drove me to the old building on 19th Street. What did I think of the old building? I couldn't believe it. They put me up in the old Redmont Hotel. I remember walking into this creaky old elevator, and this old black man took me up to my floor, and I said to myself, 'My God, this is Birmingham?' "

DeVira remembered he met the general manager, Fowler Dugger, who of course had had his voice box removed, and it was not easy trying to have a conversation with him. He met Fowler's brother Oscar, who was the advertising director. And he met Advertising Manager Emory Cunningham, who reported to Oscar.

"*Progressive Farmer* was one of the great magazines in America," said DeVira. "It was fourteenth or fifteenth among all magazines in advertising pages. It carried lots of agricultural ads but also consumer ads. I sold mostly consumer ads: food companies, appliance companies, cigarette companies, also insurance companies. It was a great opportunity."

What did he know about agriculture, coming from Jersey City?

"I knew zero," said DeVira, laughing. "One of the accounts Bentley gave me was a big one, Merck, the drug company. I don't know if they are still in the agricultural business. They were in it big-time then. One of Bentley's old friends, who was advertising director of Merck, said to me, 'Why in the hell did they send you over here? You don't know a goddamn pig from a horse.' But this guy kind of took me under his wing and told me what I needed to know. But I spent most of my time on consumer accounts. That first year with *Progressive Farmer* I came in second in the company sales contest. I got $250. That was 1964. At the time I thought it was a lot of money."

When did he first hear about the possibility of starting *Southern Living?*

"Emory came up to New York," said Jim, "and had a meeting with Bentley. They later called in the whole staff: myself and Jim Cusack and Paul Hickman and Jim Martise, and told us the company was going to start this new magazine to reach the urban market. Oh, we thought it was a great idea to start *Southern Living.* I was selling mostly consumer advertising in *Progressive Farmer.* And it was getting more difficult. The farm market was shrinking."

DeVira interrupted himself—he always had a weakness for eccentrics—"This Martise was a funny guy, came up from Louisiana. Didn't know a knife from a spoon when he got to New York. Carried about eighteen pens and pencils in his shirt pocket. Wore white socks, had these taps all around the outer soles of his shoes to keep 'em from wearing out—you could hear him coming like a poor man's tap dancer. He was a good salesman. Later went to *Redbook*."

What kind of impression did Emory Cunningham make on him?

"He was impressive," said DeVira. "A big, tall, good-looking guy. I always thought he was slick and smooth, always said the right thing to the public. I understood he had been a great salesman in Chicago. I'd met him in Birmingham. He and Roger McGuire, who was eventually going to be the advertising director of *Southern Living*, were both big, good-looking guys. And smart. Roger had just rejoined the company when I was hired. He'd left briefly for *This Week*, which appeared in millions of Sunday newspapers.

"McGuire had a good reputation in Chicago and Detroit, where he'd gotten the ball rolling for *Progressive Farmer*," said DeVira. "He was a friendly guy. He didn't have an enemy in the world. In future years, the big joke was McGuire wanted to hire everybody. He'd say, 'I met this great guy on a plane.' Or, 'I met this great guy in a bar. He'd make a good salesman. I think we should hire him.' Half the time he would be wrong. You see, Roger liked *everybody*. In those days, he loved Emory. He once told me he loved him like a father."

DeVira thought a minute. "I'll tell you the kind of guy McGuire was. When we published our first two-hundred-page issue of *Southern Living*, he came up to New York. The guys who were on the staff still talk about it until this day. You know Roger never had a whole lot of discretionary money to spend. We ran a tight ship. But he bought tickets for everybody and their families to the Broadway play *The Championship Season*. He wanted us to know we'd also had a championship season."

Southern Living held the advertising sales meeting in 1965 that we mentioned earlier, at the Heart of Atlanta Motel. DeVira and McCalla could not remember if they met one another at that meeting. DeVira did remember Herb Manloveg of BBD&O saying, " 'You better take another look at this thing. You might be making the biggest mistake you ever made.' Manloveg was considered one of the top media guys in America," said Jim. "But it didn't cast a pall over the sales meeting. We were too excited about the possibilities of the new magazine. You have to give Emory and Mr. Butler a lot of credit for not backing down. You know

Manloveg put the Pepsi Cola ad in the first issue of *Southern Living*. And he became a great supporter of the magazine."

DeVira said, "We were almost too early with *Southern Living*. We were close on the heels of the Civil Rights Movement in the South and a lot of awful publicity. But in 1965 the South had just begun to grow, and that was our story. We talked about the market almost as much as we talked about the magazine. Of course, the *differences* in the South, the many ways *Southern Living* serves those differences, was our main story. It had better still be our main story. The South became the biggest, fastest-growing market in America. Advertisers couldn't ignore it. And *no other* magazine was addressing it. They were selling more Cadillacs in Texas and Florida than anywhere in the country. If you wanted to sell Cadillacs or BMWs, you had better be selling them in those states.

"We had some strong early believers," said DeVira. "Arthur Pardhel gave us the Clairol business. He was with Foote, Cone, and Belding." (Pardhel gave his old tennis buddy Devira the Clairol business, which was critical to the magazine's survival the first year. How that came about is pretty funny. Nobody tells it better than DeVira's once protégé Mike Fitzgerald. We will wind up Fitzgerald and set him loose later in this narrative. Fitzgerald imitating DeVira is one of the joys of this book, if it can be said to have any joys.)

DeVira said, "As an agency, Young & Rubicam really understood what we were trying to do. They gave us a good hearing and put a lot of advertising into *Southern Living*. Dick Anderson, Roger McGuire's great friend, was at Y&R, with his assistant, the former Greek Orthodox priest Constantine Kazanas. Steve Frankfort was the youngest president in Y&R history. He later formed Frankfort Communications, and Anderson joined him. McGuire hired them to produce Tony Silva's two films on *Southern Living*. The damn films were terrific. Remember the one, *Coming Home*, that started in Savannah with the kids riding bicycles around the city squares? And the one, *The Now South*, that began with big diesel trucks rolling down from Jersey?"

"Yes," said Logue, "the narrator quoted from the introduction Willie Morris wrote for our first art book, *A Southern Album*: 'Driving out of Manhattan at nightfall, following the big diesels on the great eastern turnpikes. Down the wastes of New Jersey into Delaware and Maryland, past the monuments of Washington which beckoned like trusted companions in the surrounding darkness, on through the Dismal Swamp, the Carolinas, then skirting the mighty skyline of Atlanta, the red hills of Ala-

bama, and across the line into Mr. Bill Faulkner's country.' And Willie
Morris was home, where he was at last happy to be living." (And God
bless him, he was to die before his time.)

"Those first films really got everybody's juices flowing," said DeVira.
"Dick Anderson moved to Needham, Harper, and Steers in Chicago, and
then went in business with a former Y&R copywriter, Gary Comer.
Comer started the mail-order catalog *Land's End.* He's now one of the
richest men in America. Dick ran it as president, and he's now retired,
with a condo on the river in Boston. JoAnn and I go up to see him on his
farm in Vermont. Dick loves horse racing and is part owner in a couple
of thoroughbreds. He was one of the greatest friends *Southern Living*
ever had."

"I thought Dick had lost his mind when he got out of advertising,"
said Logue. "He had such a gift for it. But I guess he did the right thing.
Fifteen or twenty million dollars never stymied a man's retirement. I believed *Southern Living* would survive after McCalla became editor, but I
did not understand that if we got it right, it would be a driving force in
American publishing—not until I heard Anderson's speech in 1968 at
Lakeway Inn in Texas."

"Let me tell you my Dick Anderson story," said DeVira. "McGuire
knew Anderson. He had called on him in Chicago. Anderson moved to
New York as director of media relations at Y&R. But he didn't get involved in too many accounts directly. So I hadn't met him. McGuire tells
me, 'I invited this friend of mine, Dick Anderson, to come talk to us at
the sales meeting at Lakeway. I'd like for you to go over and fill Dick in
on the magazine.'

"So," said DeVira, "I went over with my damn briefcase full of stuff.
I walked in, and here was this skinny little guy sitting behind a desk. I
proceeded to give him the whole deal . . . I mean pounding on his desk,
'National magazines don't reach the South!' and I'm going on and on,
giving this great presentation. He says nothing, sitting there looking at
me. I say to myself, 'Crap, I'm not making much headway with this guy.'
So I finish. I asked him, 'Dick, do you have any questions?' He asked me
one question. I forget what. I answered it. He said, 'I don't have any more
questions. I think I've got it.' So, I walked out, and I said to myself, 'Mc-
Guire is making the biggest goddamn mistake. This guy can't even talk.'

"About a week later, I got a call from Anderson's office. He wanted
me to come back and bring some more information on such and such. I
don't remember what. I get back over there with stacks and stacks of pa-

pers. Do my usual thing. Pound on the desk, give him the whole presentation. He said, 'Hmmmmmm. Good.' I mean he didn't say ten words. I walked out, and I said to myself, 'This is going to be a disaster.'

"Well, you guys remember, Anderson came down, with Constantine Kazanas. And gave a fabulous presentation. Mike Fitzgerald still says it was the best presentation he ever heard."

"It was the first time," said Logue, "I ever heard anybody in the big time say that *Southern Living* was going to be a success and it was going to be a huge success. Anderson's words filled up that room until I thought the roof was gonna fly off."

"It wouldn't remind you of the first time we gave an editorial presentation in New York," said McCalla.

"Oh, God," said Logue.

The two of us and Foods Editor Lena Sturges took a pitiful half-tray of thirty-five-millimeter slides to Manhattan to take on the advertising world. This would have been about 1968. We started out at nine o'clock in the morning at the largest advertising agency in America, J. Walter Thompson. They put us downstairs in a room with no windows. It looked like a storm cellar. The room was full of kids. Because they couldn't coerce anybody over twenty-three down there to hear us.

"We were supposed to have twenty minutes among us," Logue said. "Lena led off. She got up and talked *forty-five* minutes and wasn't finished. One boy on the front row got up to leave. Sturges said, 'Sit down, young man! You might learn something. When I got started in this business, we shot our food out of the trees.' You never saw a hotshot New York ad guy sit down so fast. McCalla and I collapsed our talks into less than one minute each, and staggered out of there. I said, 'DeVira, if they are all going to be this tough, I'd rather do a little head-on tackling with the New York Giants.'

"After that, we put Lena last," Logue said, "threatened to turn out the lights if she talked over seven minutes. She was tough. She was great. McCalla made them understand that we were a 'down-home' magazine, a word that drove DeVira crazy. He thought it sounded low-rent. It didn't. McCalla said we were like a hometown newspaper. I told them that college football in the South wasn't life and death; it was more serious than that. What other family magazine would give you 'Seven Ways with Cornbread' and 'Auburn Versus Georgia Football'?

"We weren't up for a Tony Award. But we didn't flop either," said Logue.

New York was a hard town and a fearful place for on-the-job-training in the art of giving an editorial pitch. But McCalla and Logue grew to love it.

Actually, McCalla nearly landed in New York. His uncle Robert Klaeger was one of the early pioneers in the television commercial business. He handled some of Eisenhower's TV campaign for president. And his Klaeger Film Productions won the Academy Award in 1961 for the documentary film *Project Hope*.

"Bob Klaeger was my number one hero," McCalla said. "I don't think he ever finished high school. He worked as a theater projectionist back home and wound up in the Army Signal Corps. By the time World War II was over, he was one of the top film editors in the Army. A lot of New York and Hollywood film people served with him at Fort Monmouth, New Jersey. That's how he got his start."

McCalla himself came out of the Army with a wife and a child on the way. His uncle convinced him he would be happier working back home in Oklahoma or Texas, rather than in the fatally stressful streets of New York. It was good advice. His uncle fell dead of a cerebral hemorrhage at age forty-nine in April, 1965, the year his nephew joined *Southern Living*.

But McCalla and Logue have lots of memories of New York: Catching a matinee in the opening week of *Grease*, before that musical caught fire; seeing the play *Lenny Bruce*, about a raging comic who would drown to-day's timid lightweights on HBO, who only know to fall back for laughs on the twelve-letter noun that used to get you a five-hundred-dollar fine in the National League when Logue was writing baseball; listening to the very New York musical *Company*; sitting with McGuire and his great friend Philip Morris, our brilliant design editor whom you will meet shortly, through the musical *The Man of La Mancha*, before driving the next day to Lancaster, Pennsylvania, to give their pitch to Armstrong Cork, and McGuire having a cake brought out for Philip's birthday; seeing Jack Lemmon in an underpraised performance of *Long Day's Journey into Night*, still America's greatest dramatic play; getting off the subway, running into a guy outside Yankee Stadium who was selling two tickets behind third base, for regular price, and stepping inside with Tom Angelillo, the future president of Southern Progress, just as the Old-Timers' Game began, seeing the Giants' once-great Willie Mays dive and make a rolling catch, and seeing Joe DiMaggio accept a convertible auto-mobile and ride around the Stadium in it, tipping his hat to the fans; Oxmoor throwing a party at the swank Pierre Hotel for the artist Richard Stone Reeves and his book *Classic Lines*, and Zero Mostel showing up with his huge eyes and bawdy wisecracks, and Salvador Dali, who had a suite at the Pierre, crashing the party in his long, black cape, like Count Dracula, and Logue standing with the billionaire banker Paul Mellon and the great Argentine horse trainer Horatio Luro, as the two men compared riding to the hounds in their own countries, and Luro asking Logue if they rode to the hounds in Alabama, and Logue, answering without a missing a beat, "No, we ride to the coon, a nocturnal beast"; they were impressed.

Oh, the joints hit were too many to separate in the mind. Time passes, and time takes a heavy toll. On their last trip to New York, to interview Don Logan for this book, McCalla and Logue walked all over Manhattan Island, and even saw *Sunset Boulevard*, but were in bed by midnight. That's their story and they're sticking to it.

"One of the differences in our company in those days," said DeVira, "was the relationship between advertising and editorial."

"We all had a passion to make it work," said McCalla.

"That's exactly right," said DeVira. "We invented ourselves as we went along. I remember Emory Cunningham came up to New York, and we were talking about should we take tobacco advertising. Emory said he liked some tobacco advertising, but most of it he didn't like. He said, 'I like those Marlboro ads with the cowboy on the horse. We can take those. We can't take the others.' I said, 'Emory, I don't believe we can get away with that.' "

DeVira said, "Later, Emory sent a note out that we're not going to take any tobacco advertising. I guess Eugene Butler saw the note and called Emory and said, 'Listen, *Progressive Farmer* is telling these farmers how to grow tobacco—I don't believe we are going to cut tobacco advertising out of *Southern Living*.' I'm just guessing here. But a week or so after the tobacco memo, and the only time I remember this happening, Emory sent out a note saying, 'Well, we've reconsidered, we're going to take tobacco.' "

Years later DeVira became publisher of *Southern Living*, whose advertising star never dimmed, not to this day. But Cunningham never let up on the troops. "We would have a good year," said DeVira. "In fact, after all those good years, Emory would get us in the conference room, and say, 'Next year we've got to do this or we've got to do that. The economy is going to be tough next year.' He never just said, 'Guys, that was a great year.' He could never enjoy it."

DeVira said, "One night at The Club, Emory said we were not doing this right, we were not doing that right. I felt it was a slap at the sales force, and I challenged him. I said, 'Wait a second, baloney, that's just not right.' He hated that. Emory could make you feel good. And he could make you feel miserable. I don't think he gave people the credit they deserved for whatever success the magazine had. He sort of wanted to take all of that himself. At one time Roger McGuire told me Emory was like a father to him, but as time went on I think he really pushed Roger out of the company."

McCalla and Logue did not disagree with Jim. And the three of them also agreed there was no question Emory got *Southern Living* started, and that he was a formidable president, that he represented the company, within the industry and outside of it, as well as it could possibly have been done. And there was never a guy more fun to go on a trip with, especially hunting or fishing. Emory fought his way up, and he was not a man to let go of any rung on the ladder.

What kind of year did DeVira have selling *Southern Living* that first year?

"Well, I sold 35 percent of the ads that were in the first issue," said Jim. "I sold 38 percent of all the ads we carried that first year." Only Ted Williams hit for that average when he was playing in the American League.

"I grew up in the business with guys who were going to run the companies and the ad agencies," said Jim. "I could get an appointment to see them. And give my pitch. Not so easy today. Now maybe they send you a letter: 'We're doing a campaign for Pepsi Cola. Give us your best rates and whatever merchandising you can afford.' They have all the research on you. They don't necessarily want to hear your story. You can still tell it, but it's tougher to get an audience. Of course, *Southern Living* is well established. It would be harder now to sell our story—the differences in the South—if you were just starting out. You call a client and you get voice mail."

That most depraved act of American communication, *voice mail*, did not exist in 1965. Bill Bentley could get on the telephone to any advertising executive with a body temperature. Unhappily, too many of them wanted a three-martini lunch. Bentley, great guy that he was, fell an early casualty to Demon Alcohol. McCalla and Logue both remember an advertising sales meeting in Callaway Gardens, Georgia, when Bentley was unable to get up to give his presentation and had to be helped onto the plane back to New York.

"The company did everything it could," said DeVira.

Emory Cunningham flew Bentley down to Birmingham to spend the day. But Bentley would not recognize that he had a serious alcohol problem. The company was prepared to send him to the treatment center of his choice. Bentley went back to New York and stayed sober for a short while. But then he fell hopelessly off the wagon and was reluctantly terminated. He moved back to North Alabama and in all too short a while was killed in an automobile accident.

"He was one of the best guys and one of the best salesmen I ever knew," said DeVira, whose job it was then to replace him as New York advertising manager.

What kind of staff did DeVira assemble? "They just had to hit me. I had to have a gut feeling about them—that they sincerely wanted to work for the magazine—and they would get out there and work their butts off. I mean in those early days that's what you had to do," said DeVira.

"They had to believe in the magazine," said Jim. "It didn't work for them to try and sell *Southern Living* by saying, *they* do this. It had to be *we* do this, *we* are different. They had to get themselves into the *Southern Living* story. A lot of people could never do that. You had to put yourself right in the middle of our magazine and our market. We wound up with a lot of diverse personalities. All of them strong."

Some of them were stronger than Octagon soap. Mike Fitzgerald could talk more Irish blarney than the population of Dublin. He would not sell you an ad if you were lying in the Bellevue Hospital morgue with a tag on your toe.

Which brings us to Milt Lieberman, a very serious young man whose talent actually equaled his ambition. He was famous among the staff for selling a series of ads in the early issues to After Six, the formal wear people. Now you must realize that one-half of the first subscribers to *Southern Living* had been arbitrarily moved over from the rolls of *Progressive Farmer*, and these good folk were inclined to barbecue ribs over open coals wearing Liberty overalls. The closest they'd ever been to a tuxedo was the previews of a Cary Grant movie while they were waiting for Gene Autry to come on.

Lieberman once gave a presentation to a dog food company of *Southern Living*'s cost per thousand *dogs* (among readers). Of course they bought it. Every other presentation in the history of American advertising had been of a magazine's cost per thousand *people*. Lieberman left the company early in his career and ultimately became a publisher with *Mc-Call's* and later retired from *Parade*.

"Milton was so serious," said DeVira, whose own formula for success was about as happy-go-lucky as a heart attack. "I called him in one day, and I said, 'Look, Milt, we've got a problem. Somebody in the office is gay.' 'Who? Who? Who?' said Milt. I said, 'We've got to keep this quiet.' And I leaned over and kissed him on the cheek. Oh, Lieberman fell for it. 'What are you doin', what are you doin'?' He jumped up out of his chair terrified. Roger McGuire used to love that story," said DeVira.

Then there was Steve Berezney. Strong, compact, looked like he could still play defensive halfback for West Virginia University. You could tell him no, but pronounce it politely. Berezney never should have left the company. He himself always regretted it, though he has done very well with *Family Circle*.

Which brings us to Jerry Latzky. Latzky looked like Woody Allen on a bad hair day. Off duty he would cram his big bare feet into open sandals and walk around midtown Manhattan in a ghastly flowery shirt he might have found in a rummage sale in Hawaii. And probably did. Latsky would argue with a lamp post, lit or unlit (him and/or the lamp).

The magazine, the company were fighting for their existence in June, 1967. Latsky told DeVira he was taking a week's vacation in Israel. DeVira said, no way. We got to have you here. Latzky said, I'm gone. DeVira said, no way. Latzky landed in Israel the morning the Six-Day War broke out. Of course, he couldn't get home for two weeks.

DeVira was biting ten-penny nails into tacks. He swore that the war wasn't about the Golan Heights, the West Bank, or Palestine. But that Egypt, Jordan, and Syria thought Israel was trying to unload Latzky on them.

Of course it couldn't happen again. Of course it did. Our man Latzky went back to Israel and got caught up in the rematch. DeVira still swears the Israelis and Arabs should forget about territory and concentrate on keeping Jerry Latzky out of the Middle East.

The old offices at the Marine Midland Building at 250 Park were a zoo. Fitzgerald will tell us about the time the boys decided to form a union to fend off the iron boot of DeVira. The Czar of Russia never put down an insurrection more emphatically.

DeVira denies nothing. "I wanted the person who wouldn't take no for an answer. Tomorrow, or next week, or eventually, you were going to tell him, *yes*.

"Of course, it wasn't always a him," said DeVira, "I hired the first woman advertising salesperson, Jan Bingham. She was working for Orville Demaree in research, a bright person and a beautiful redhead. We moved her to Atlanta. She was outstanding. Later, she left the company and died tragically young.

"Joan Walton joined our staff in Chicago and was really inventive," said DeVira. She once gave a presentation at an advertising sales meeting in the breathless tones of a 1940s bobby-soxer, wearing bobby-sox and sweater; you could've cast her in a movie with the young Judy Garland.

"Jo Craiglow became our first woman advertising manager, of the Dallas office," said DeVira. "Now we have many terrific women in advertising sales. In fact, it's becoming a woman's world. If you have ten good applicants for an advertising sales job, eight of the best are going to be women. They have a gift for it. And they are hungry." It pleased DeVira to no end that one of those young women in advertising sales was his daughter Susan, who was made manager of *Southern Living*'s New York office a few years ago. (She recently resigned to take a year off and see the world. Logue and McCalla were glad they weren't there when she broke the news to the Old Man.)

"You've got to be hungry and tenacious," said DeVira. "I think of the special section we sold Seagram, 'The Sounds of the South.' All original American music came from the South. It took us nearly ten years to sell it. We had to rebuild the dummy because it fell apart with age and handling. When we finally sold it, I went out and got a big gold record that said: 'Sounds of the South.' And the caption said, 'We finally sold it.' That was the kind of tenacity it took."

"Our young writer Mark Childress wrote it," said Logue. "He knew music. It made a terrific special section. Readers loved it. And we went on to do three special football sections with Seagram. They ran inside our own All-South Football section. Kevin Lynch sold them, and he's now publisher of *Southern Living*. See what the football section could do for your career?"

The old sales offices at 250 Park were a three-ring circus, with DeVira cracking the whip.

6

Tribulations

Meanwhile, the domestic wars continued to rage among the nouns and verbs of the editorial offices, with new editor Dr. O. B. Copeland the reluctant captive of Dr. Alexander Nunn.

A likely subject would appear, only to be subverted by its written treatment, or its photography, or its page design, or by all three hands-on afflictions.

Some rather promising early moments, too often subverted by this or that:

John McKinney made an excellent cover photograph of the *Delta Queen* riverboat for the second issue, but went a bridge too far by composing the story himself. Big John quoted a passenger, "If you don't bring me anything else, bring me some of that fried cornmeal mush—I haven't had any of that since my mother cooked it in a cast-iron kettle." That was Big John: cast-iron corn.

A profile in the March issue of the great San Antonio architect O'Neil Ford cried for the ear and the design understanding of Philip Morris, who, unfortunately, was still some years away from joining the magazine staff.

Never before had an innocent, and delicious, Lane Cake been committed to so garish a red-curtained photograph as in the story by Lena Sturges in the same issue. It looked like dessert in a Hong Kong pleasure palace. Good advice was offered in "Sure Cures for Weedy Lawns" by a pair of free-lance writers, in company with a design layout as ugly as nut sedge.

There was a nifty black-and-white piece in April: "Study and Storage for Children." It anticipated the savvy homes shorts of the future. Oh, yeah, McCalla shot it and wrote it. Sturges compiled a solid set of lamb recipes, and they came with a photograph that was a cut above the other food shots. Only, from readers' letters word arrived that lamb was not high on their food chain.

The May issue featured on the cover a rather warm photograph of a home in the North Carolina pines, but the other photography of the house was colder than the inside of a hailstone. Also in May, the company's own Nathan Glick painted truly beautiful portraits of the state birds of the South. A friendlier text, however, could be found in a cheap encyclopedia. Rather fine photography appeared in a survey of beaches on the Outer Banks, North Carolina; Padre Island, Texas; and the Panhandle of Florida; and with a second-person narrative that stands up okay.

McKinney outdid himself with a cover shot for June of walking horses in Tennessee. But that was it: the cover shot. John gave the art director *ninety* versions of the man and woman on horseback at exactly the same spot, and not one other photograph of them riding or saddling or watering or doing any other thing with the horses at any other location. June did offer a well-photographed, well-thought-out, well-designed look at urban landscaping in Fort Lauderdale, Florida. It actually stands up to the genuinely professional interpretations of urban design for which *Southern Living* would eventually be famous.

Maybe the best thing—certainly the best visual thing—that appeared in *Southern Living* that first year were the drawings by one Don Davey in July to go with Paul Plawin's famous New Orleans story. Two of the full-page illustrations of the French Quarter—they resemble copper plate engravings—will knock your hat off. In a rare offering of reader recipes, Sturges published four versions of jams and jellies. The short narratives were interesting of the women—one of them age ninety-four—who created the recipes. Such reader recipes would one day become the heartbeat of the food section.

Fashion never made it as an advertising/editorial category in *Southern*

Living. But if you will look at the layout in the September, 1966, issue, you will swear you are looking in the 1966 *Vogue.* Bonnie Carr set up the models in the open atrium of the Hyatt Regency Hotel in Atlanta, while it was still under construction. A guy named Raf Tanksley knocked out the photography, which is superb. The models—one of whom looks like a young Audrey Hepburn—are smashing against the strange, raw, unfinished concrete space. And the language of the text is appropriately sexy. And all of it belonged in the magazine like cholera.

McCalla's cover photograph of October foliage in the Great Smokies holds its own. Sturges comes through again with apple recipes from readers, and the people seem real. A color illustration of apples looks rather contemporary, though it is rather odd to see a mouse and an earthworm, napkins about their necks, sitting at the table to eat a newly halved apple.

In November, free-lancer Gordon Schenck took the best photograph of the ill-fated City Salutes. He sat the director of Richmond's Confederate Museum in Jefferson Davis's leather chair in front of a statue of a mounted Robert E. Lee. The museum director, Peter Rippe, was holding Lee's uniform in his lap, and the boots Lee wore when he surrendered his army at Appomattox were standing empty beside him. Rippe was looking dead ahead, as if back into a tragic past. It was a great photograph, however deliberately composed. Schenck also photographed a Knoxville, Tennessee, home in the mountains that might hold its own in today's magazine.

Perhaps the most successful all-around cover story—photograph and text—published in the first fourteen months of *Southern Living* was in the April issue of 1967. The magazine had found the brilliant people photographer Bruce Roberts, who later became its chief of photography. Bruce assembled all of the citizens of Abingdon, Virginia, who had performed in its famous Barter Theatre and posed them in costume. No more challenging or successful photograph has appeared on the cover of *Southern Living.* Paul Plawin's last story in the magazine about the town and the theatre was brief but excellent.

So much for a sampling of early stories of some promise. There were others. Also, there was a long line of "subject failure," a wonderful expression coined years later by Homes Editor Louis Joyner while looking at a particularly unhappy architectural result. We are concerned here with stories that confused the mission of *Southern Living*:

The March issue included a long, convoluted story on the state of Florida's "experiments in education." It was a piece that would have been more appropriate in *The Chronicle of Higher Education*, though it didn't cut deeply enough to meet their standards. God knows what *Southern Living*'s early subscribers made of it.

The same issue had the most amazingly ghastly photograph of a left foot and a right foot bearing the most tacky jewelry around toes and insteps that a depraved imagination could conceive. The feet themselves seemed abnormal; then you realized they belonged to separate women, whose faces were mercifully not shown. And there was this delicate sentence: "If you can count ragged cuticles, shaggy heels, or callused soles among present possessions, it's time to take stock." Problem was, readers were taking stock who counted this magazine among their possessions.

The March issue wouldn't let go. Next came a story entitled "Teenage Drivers a Problem?" Why the hell did they need a question mark? Of course teenage drivers were a problem. That's why their insurance rates were higher than Mount McKinley. But what the heck was *Southern Living* going to do about it?

Again the question arose: were we going to be *Field & Stream*? The longtime outdoor free-lancer Russell Tinsley kicked in with a story: "For Lunker Bass, Try Bottom-Bumping," with one of his patented phony photographs of a bass with a worm in his mouth leaping in the air behind a boat. The hard-core outdoor layout had no place in *Southern Living*, which years later evolved its own more civilized way of translating the out-of-doors.

"Stay South, Young Man," wrote Romaine Smith, young-folks editor. The story had this sentence: "Union Bag–Camp Paper Corp., Savannah, Ga., is the largest pulp and paper plant in the South, employing 280 college graduates, 1,260 skilled workers, 2,050 semiskilled, and 1,500 clerical workers." Question: Could you build a consumer magazine on that sentence? Answer: Not hardly.

You could not believe "The World of Wigs" in the May issue. This young woman was gazing out from under some kind of wild animal pelt. One thing she was not seeing was any kind of advertising support for our fashion and cosmetic efforts.

"Lifesaving Information Is Yours in This Tiny Book" appeared in the June issue. Here we had a method of keeping your child's medical records, a worthy idea, but it belonged in somebody else's magazine.

The story on the next page was McCalla's all-time favorite from early *Southern Living*: "Selecting the First Bra." He has chortled over this story for decades. It came wrapped around one of the Modess ads sold by Jim DeVira. The story opened: "Carol Ann, stand up straight. Carol Ann, don't slump." The narrative heightened: "Her mother was delighted when the trip was made and Carol Ann had her first brassiere, because she didn't slump."

If a camera had been set up at ground level the instant the bomb exploded over Hiroshima, it would have recorded the August, 1966, cover of the magazine. It was a night shot of a house, apparently on fire, if fire could be said to burn green, red, and black. It was described on the contents page as "cheerful night lighting."

In September, the magazine ventured to celebrate the director of the Texas prison system. The story carried the humane title: "Desperate Men Call Him 'The Man': When Dr. George Beto was named director of the Texas prison system, inmates discovered quickly that 'the preacher-man don't push.' "

The story didn't point out that Texas executed more prisoners than any other state. Or that Texas was being accused of having one of the most brutal prison systems in America.

"I had a guy who worked for me in Huntsville, who did time in the Texas prison system," said McCalla. "His nose lay over on one side of his face. He said if you did something they didn't like, they made you stand on a milk stool all night and beat you if you fell off." Just the kind of prison system *Southern Living* needed to be celebrating.

The Old Guard at *Southern Living* didn't have the true grit to get into the prison system and tear it apart to identify any inhumane weaknesses or true strengths (if they existed). The Old-Timers wanted to *play* at reform without getting their hands bloody. This subject was a perfect example of why McCalla felt the magazine "should publish on subjects it understood, and on subjects that were positive, and let everybody else take care of the negative, which plenty of people were doing."

Now reader, you must go over to your public library and look up page 45 of the November, 1966, issue of *Southern Living*. You will find the magazine's version of Thanksgiving dinner in *outer space*. It is the damndest thing you will have ever seen: plates and saucers and knives and forks and turkey and dressing and sour cream pecan pie and string beans and sweet potatoes and pumpkin pie floating in space, with a family clad in the full masks and helmets of astronauts giving prayerful thanks. McCalla swears he had nothing to do it, though Lena Sturges always blamed it on him, since he had done work for NASA.

"There was one great thing about this caper," said McCalla. "When the bill came from photographer Bill Langley in Dallas, it was for *eigh-teen hundred dollars*. O. B. Copeland almost fainted. You see, *Progressive Farmer* was used to paying maybe *ten dollars* for a black-and-white photograph. After that, it was much easier to pay Bruce Roberts a couple of hundred dollars a day to work for us."

All the fun went out of everything on page 70 of the same November, 1966, issue. Here was printed the first opinion editorial in the brief history of *Southern Living*. The essay had a deceptively innocent headline: "A Bright, Modern South That Writers Are Missing." What followed was all malicious and reactionary and Old South and wrongheaded. It began: "Ever since Georgian Erskine Caldwell's typewriter got involved with *Tobacco Road*, the South has been the country's Literary Problem No. 1, no fault of its own.

"Us Southern cats on a hot tin roof have had many a long hot summer of our discontent based in the kind of literary treatment this region has been given."

The writer goes on to say, "With the advent of TV, we have become accustomed to additional attention, in drama form as well as in dinner-hour newscasts much too often. Not happily, but interestingly, of late the newscasts have dealt increasingly with other portions of the country. Maybe there are no strictly 'regional problems.' "

What the writer is saying here, and he is saying it as the puppet of Dr. Alexander Nunn, is that racial strife in other regions of America in 1966 is interestingly dominating the news, rather than the old-hat racial strife in the South. The sentence denied that the national news was now *happy*, but the writer's gleefulness rang through the denial.

Consider this paragraph: "In continuing basic sets of images handed down to them, in refusing to consider the South's mid-20th century awakening into as much steel, chrome, and plate glass as any other geographic section, the fictional progenitors have continued to conform as if they would be lynched for *not* doing so." The verb *lynched* is deliberately and ruthlessly employed, careless of the hundreds of black victims of that terminal abuse over the years in the American South.

Dr. Nunn had raided the local *Birmingham News* for its editorial page editor, E. L. ("Red") Holland. He was given the title of associate editor of The Progressive Farmer Company.

McCalla believes absolutely that Dr. Nunn brought Holland into the company to be the next editor of *Southern Living*. Emory Cunningham agrees. "Alec was fond of him. He was Alec's man. He would have been the editor if he had lived." And *Southern Living* would have died within the year.

Holland was a bright guy, a graduate of Birmingham Southern and a Nieman Fellow at Harvard. His brightness made him all the more dangerous. Nunn hired him to drag the magazine into the political wars, and the political battle that mattered most to Nunn was an undeclared defense of segregation, using all the code words acceptable to polite society.

Holland's editorial railed madly against the literature of the South, one of its true glories even in its darkest moments of civil unrest. It also insulted the literature of the nation at large. In truth, *Tobacco Road* was fully as real as The Progressive Farmer Company, and so were the best plays of Tennessee Williams, which Holland also debased. That's why these works endure. A magazine tilted to deny its region's and its nation's true literary voices would not only die, but would deserve to die.

Fate can be cruel. For it was E. L. Holland who was dying when he wrote the one editorial that ever appeared in *Southern Living*. In fact, the physical examination he took after he was hired discovered the cancer that would kill him.

Still, the magazine would benefit for years from the good intelligence and the gentle presence of his widow, Jomarion, who lent her considerable skills to the copy desk until her retirement.

In the spring of 1966 the *Southern Living* editorial staff retreated to Dauphin Island on the Alabama coast, just south of Mobile. The consultants, Herb Mayes of *McCall's* and Wilson Hicks, formerly of *LIFE*, came to give their opinions of what the magazine had published in its first four issues. *Progressive Farmer*'s editors were also meeting on the island at the same time.

"The company was having a fish fry over on the Eastern Shore of Mobile Bay," said McCalla. "Mayes said he didn't want to go. Oh, he was a dapper guy. He'd never been outside of New York City except for the time he lived in London. Bradley Byers and Paul Plawin and I stayed and ate dinner with Herb and talked about our organization.

"Mayes said, 'O. B. Copeland is a fine man. But if he continues to edit this thing, it will never work.'"

And what did Hicks think? "Wilson said that John McKinney's photography was all right, but it was 'dated.' That he was shooting 'back in the thirties or forties.' He said the magazine 'looked badly out of date.' And of course he was right.

"Hicks, coming from *LIFE*, wanted 'more people on the covers. I miss people,' he said. 'I want more exciting Southerners.' Wilson had some good ideas," said McCalla, "but he wanted to make us into a people magazine, just as Mayes wanted to make us into a women's magazine. We didn't do a good job of sorting out their good advice from their advice that would ruin us.

"Mayes, for instance, suggested these story ideas that would have more happily fit into *McCall's*: 'What Women Need to Know About Stocks' [which Byers actually researched and wrote and we published]; 'Short, Soft 'n' Sweet Hair Styles'; 'Scholarships You Can Apply For.' Mayes suggested 'An Apartment for Two in Gulfport,' thinking that our readers in Gulfport, Mississippi, lived in small apartments as people did in Manhattan," said McCalla. "He offered other good ideas: 'Big Soups for Winter Days'; 'Cover Your Walls with Cloth.' We published one of his worst ideas: '*Southern Living* Jr.' It was a monthly feature of kids' artwork."

"By the time I got to the magazine the next spring, it's amazing how much the readers hated it," said Logue. "They put their own kids' artwork on their refrigerator doors, but they complained on the telephone that they had no interest in incomprehensible stuff by other people's kids. And it took up two precious color pages."

Numerous other voices in the magazine business registered complaints about the early issues of *Southern Living*. Warren Osterwald, media director for Alfred Auerbach Associates, wrote to ad salesman Milt Lieberman: "The general format of the magazine is dull and insipid. Perhaps the close association with your sister publication, *Progressive Farmer*, has been reflected in the makeup of *Southern Living*." No truer observation was ever made. Osterwald was also critical of the editorial material reproduction and pointed out that the advertisements "had been reproduced satisfactorily." The problem had to be in the editorial material and not in the printing.

A friend of Roger McGuire's at *Better Homes & Gardens*, Dan Matthews, advised in a memo: "Don't say 'Southern' [in headlines] just to prove to yourselves it's a Southern magazine." Too true; years later McCalla put a virtual ban on "Southern" in headlines. Matthews said, "Take [Gene] Butler's picture and throw it out the window." He liked the typeface of the magazine, if not the face of the company president. He hated the homes photography. He didn't like the travel writing. He didn't like much. He finished, "It's a good magazine *idea* that needs a lot of polishing."

McGuire's good friend at Leo Burnett, Bob Ross, wrote comparing the sexy titles of the ads in the magazine with the clumsy titles of the editorial material: " 'Coats & Clark—You've Got the Best Set of Teeth a Zipper Can Have.' President Butler's [opening column]: 'City and Rural People Brothers.' "

Ross said, "The tone of the editorial voice is a generation or two behind the tone of the advertising voice in my opinion." He said he "could not believe Herb Mayes consulted on this magazine. Mayes's secret was [to hire] a great designer given maximum amount of design freedom." Ross said, further, "The writing is terrible, low grade *National Geographic* style." The rest of his critique was no kinder.

McCalla remembered with much laughter that Herb Mayes asked if he could drive McCalla's car to the Mobile airport after the editorial conference was finished. "Sure," said McCalla.

Mayes started up the rental car and backed it directly into the side of the motel. "He hadn't learned to drive until he was fifty or sixty years old," said McCalla, "and he'd never before driven a stick shift. That rental car took just about as big a hit as our magazine had taken."

Byers wrote "confidential" letters (of which McCalla still has copies) to Herb Mayes and Wilson Hicks after the Dauphin Island meeting. Byers recommended that six major features be added to each issue of the magazine, one of travel, one of food, one of homes, and one titled "What I Like About the South," and one feature "of substance . . . art, politics, music, education, problems, personalities." He proposed eliminating twelve items. And he suggested forty-seven story ideas. Byers wrote, "These are *my* ideas, in outline form."

McCalla, who has kept every note he made during those months and years, counted thirteen of the story ideas as advanced by himself in writing, and two of them actually advanced by Mayes. And McCalla had long argued to dump the state and city articles, dress patterns (which were horribly dated), beauty stories, the Chromaster house plans (for small and dreadful houses, which he later killed), and fashions. Byers also wanted to cut the number of recipes published, and McCalla thought, and still thinks, he was nuts.

Byers wrote Mayes, "Please treat these suggestions as confidential. If you should have occasion to refer to them, it could be as if they were made to you verbally at Dauphin Island."

Politics were bursting out all over, and Byers obviously wanted to get his sword out of the scabbard in the event there was a palace insurrection.

Fall came, and winter, and the natives were restless. Bradley Byers was the first to hand in his resignation. "I was convinced the magazine could not succeed on the homespun path it was following," said Byers, looking back on that time. "Herb Mayes felt it could not succeed and advised me to leave before it failed. When I decided to leave, I put my recommendations for the success of the magazine in a letter to Eugene Butler, and removing Cope's decision-making authority was one of my ten or eleven recommendations. If I recall correctly, within six months, all of the recommendations were put into effect."

In fact, Cope continued as editor of *Southern Living* for more than two years, and it was that long before Emory Cunningham was put in overall charge of the magazine.

Byers left something else: a prediction. Carey Hinds, who nowadays is back in the work force in Birmingham, having raised with her lawyer-husband a family of bright students, remembers the gist of Byers's note, but not the exact wording. It went something like this: *The Progressive Farmer Company Board of Directors met in Birmingham in January, 196?, and quietly voted to fold* Southern Living *magazine.*

"That's exactly true," said Hinds, "But I can't remember the precise date of his prediction."

Happily, at the time, Carey didn't also leave, though she had some cause. She started out as a part-time editorial assistant in 1965. It was pretty funny how she came to apply for a job, and we'll have her tell about it in a minute. But by the winter of 1966 she was researching and writing her own stories, and rewriting awkward stories by other editors, while holding on to her many other odd-lot jobs. The magazine had hired a young woman just out of college as an editor and was paying her considerably more money that it was paying Hinds.

"I went to see Dr. Copeland," said Carey. "I told him I felt that the work I was doing was on a par with that of the editor he had hired. And that I should be paid accordingly. He said, 'Carey, the difference is that you are married, and your income is not as essential to you. On the other hand, the other editor has to make it on her own.' "

Hinds was not persuaded. "That's not fair," she said. And of course it was not. Today, Time, Inc., would have to add to its fifty-nine lawyers to defend a similar salary policy.

Byers went on to a career in Washington, D.C., with one of the government agencies.

Paul Plawin stayed only long enough to finish his cover story for the April issue on the Barter Theatre in Abington, Virginia. He left on friendly terms with no dire predictions.

McCalla tracked Plawin down in Falls Church, Virginia. Plawin wrote him an account of his days with the early *Southern Living*. He said Eugene Methvin of *Reader's Digest* recommended him to O. B. Copeland, who had been Methvin's college classmate. Being a city boy, Plawin himself thought *Progressive Farmer* "was an oxymoron," but it turned out his mother- and father-in-law knew about farming and the magazine and vouched for the company.

Plawin wrote, "My job interview was conducted by Dr. Alexander Nunn. I recall his office was large, but somewhat outdated. There was a large brass spittoon on the floor to the side of his desk. I was amazed. He asked me during the interview if I drank alcohol. I figured there was something going on here, and I better answer judiciously. So I said, 'Yes, I drink beer.' 'How much?' he said. 'Maybe a six pack a week,' I said. I've gotten many laughs over this story through the years."

Nunn told Plawin that the magazine wanted to appeal to younger, city people in the South. The idea appealed to him. But now he remembers visiting Nunn's own peach farm near Loachapoka, Alabama. "All those black people serving us nice eats and drinks on silver trays," he wrote. "And, then, before the soiree ended, he had them line up and introduced them to us, in quite a polite manner, and with a sense of pride, but also ownership: 'Now this is Maysie; she's been with my family since I was a boy. Good woman; cooks good cornbread. And this is Willie; works in the groves and also helps in the house . . .' and so on. I thought Virginia was South. But *this was South*."

Plawin said his recollections of Red Youngsteadt were "not nearly as vivid," that he didn't see him "as the editor type." He remembered that Red's wife "was really happy to be back in Alabama, but Red longed for the overseas life." Youngsteadt, of course, did return to Africa after being replaced very early on as *Southern Living* editor.

He remembered O. B. Copeland: "He was a bit too buttoned up, but he was a nice person, and got things done. I recall once thinking he wasn't tough enough, even though his lack of toughness was surely to my benefit. I was in a doldrums period, when the Birmingham son, Butler, and perhaps Dr. Nunn, were wanting this 'new magazine of the urban South' to carry the *Hambone Sez* comic strip, an Amos and Andy type spoof . . . and a *Prayer of the Month* up front in the magazine."

This "Birmingham son, Butler," was the same Britt who insisted that employee pregnancy be identified as a disease. And his father was the company president and principal owner, Eugene Butler.

Plawin said about that time he volunteered to go to New York and do "a dog and pony show" for some of the advertising agencies, describing the intent of the new magazine. "I heard these ad agency guys smirking about our dummy magazine and its 'prayer of the month,' and so forth. I recall one of those guys pointing to a Spring Maid Sheet ad and saying: 'For your magazine, you ought to have Spring Maid show their sheets as pointed hats with eye slits in them.' "

Plawin wrote, "Another guy pointed to a very avant garde Oldsmobile ad and said, 'Do you expect an advertiser like this to want to be next to the *prayer of the month* and *Hambone?*' " Plawin said he then "mouthed off to our advertising sales guys in the New York office. . . . I probably said the old boys in Birmingham weren't letting the new young boys do the right things. . . . When I got back to Birmingham . . . at the very next staff meeting, O. B. passed around a memo to all hands in which he said, without naming any names, that someone on the staff had been spreading dissension in the New York office and that . . . it should stop. If O. B. had had any guts he would have fired me. But, of course, I was grateful he did not. And somehow, we got on with the job, and we didn't have to run Hambone or the prayer.

"My fondest memories of those great early days, when we all felt we were inventing a great new thing," said Plawin, "were the sessions when we'd review cover and inside photographs by photo chief John McKinney. . . . We'd go over every slide, with all of us picking his shots apart. . . . But he'd plow on. Then one time he flashed on the screen pictures he'd taken of a remodeled kitchen. And every drawer was open, every cabinet door was open. It looked exactly like a bomb had gone off in the kitchen and blown open all these drawers and doors. It was hilarious. I think we all just broke up. And he was very defensive. He said, 'Well, you told me to show how much storage space she had.' "

Plawin remembered "getting so frustrated with the ancient phone system, where we had to yell over the partitions to one another to 'pick up on line two,' since all calls came through on a single line. I suggested to

Dixie Snell . . . that we should throw our phones out the window to call attention to the dilapidated system."

Plawin went on to be travel editor for *Better Homes & Gardens*, until Iowa winters sent him packing for a twenty-year career with Kiplinger's *Changing Times*. He then became Assistant Executive Director for Communications for the American Vocational Association, and is looking forward to a second retirement.

So how did Carey Hinds come to work as an editorial assistant for *Southern Living* in December, 1965?

"I was just recently married," said Carey, "and I would drive my husband to work every morning and then take 8th Avenue to Birmingham Southern. I noticed this big old building with a water tower on top. It said THE PROGRESSIVE FARMER. It looked more like a cotton mill than a publishing company. I thought maybe the farm magazine leased its name to some factory. I wondered what they did there. I had worked for *Family Circle* magazine in New York during the summer. So I was interested in journalism."

Carey remembered, "One December morning my husband said to me, 'How are you, an English major, going to be gainfully employed when you graduate?' I said, 'I don't know.' I passed the water tower again. So I went that very day to the Birmingham Southern development office and asked if they knew what The Progressive Farmer Company did in Birmingham. The man said, 'This is their main office. As a matter of fact, they are starting a new magazine. My friend O. B. Copeland is going to be the editor.' He said another Birmingham Southern student had worked there part-time but was moving away. And that they might need someone. So, I set up an appointment to see Dr. Copeland and got the job."

Hinds went to work full-time after she graduated, with the understanding, she said, that she would go to the Massey School of Business and learn to take shorthand dictation. Did she?

"*No!*" said Carey.

Hinds was an excellent editor and very good writer. McCalla and Logue used to kid her about being a terrible typist. "I would have been the valedictorian of my class at Central High School in Shelbyville, Tennessee," said Carey, "except I made a 'B' in typing. Sondra Locke, the actress and movie producer, won it. You know her—she lived for years with Clint Eastwood. Except in high school she was 'Sandra.' "

Carey remembered how everybody at *S.L.* smoked cigarettes. "I smoked like a fiend and drank coffee," she said, "Beth Carlson smoked. Lena Sturges smoked. Gary smoked. We all smoked all the time."

"I didn't have to smoke," said Logue. "All I had to do was breathe."

Carey had to laugh, thinking of Lena. "Remember we pinned up the galley proofs on the long board toward the back of our offices," she said. "Lena used the word 'pimento,' in a story.

"It looked weird to me. I put a question mark by it so we would check the spelling, and I initialed the page. So Lena came by my office and plopped this jar of pimentos on my desk and said, '*This* is how you spell *pimento*.' "

"You are lucky she didn't hit you with it," said Logue.

"That was the first time I understood that Lena thought she could get away with anything because she was from Texas," said Hinds.

"Not only thought she could, she did," said Logue.

In those days, Hinds did one of everything, from clipping Southern newspapers, to working on the Travel Calendar before Dixie Snell took it over, to typing, to editing, and finally to writing and rewriting other editors' material.

"After 5 P.M.," said Carey, "they used to give me a list of subscribers to call to find out if they liked *Southern Living*. I'm afraid I didn't do a very good job, because having grown up in Tennessee and gone to college in Virginia and Alabama, I would start chatting with people to see who they knew that I knew."

"That's as Southern as it gets," said Logue.

"I know I made people feel really good talking to the magazine. Whether they liked what they read or not, I couldn't say."

Carey took an important role in the infamous July 4 issue of 1967, and a critical role in 1968 in helping shape a White Paper that dramatically influenced the direction of the magazine. We'll get to those moments shortly. She set up, and directed the photography, and wrote one of the best fashion stories the magazine ever carried before it happily dropped fashion from it pages. But it was an offstage player in the drama who in time proved most interesting.

After the frightful July issue of 1967, when the magazine had been downsized and readers were in rebellion, a strong emphasis was put on added four-color pages for September. Carey was asked to produce a college fashion layout, never having turned a hand at fashion.

"I was given the assignment—no ifs, ands, or buts," said Carey. "I had to come up with an idea, and I knew that Tanner clothes in North Carolina were clothes that I enjoyed wearing, being five ten, because they were long-waisted. They sent me this huge box of clothes."

"Did you send them back?" asked Logue.

"Yes."

"You should never have sent them back."

"I know. It was terrible. Anyway, I called Sweet Briar, and I asked, 'Could you tell me the name of an attractive young woman who may be dating a boy at Chapel Hill? Because we want to do a fashion shoot in North Carolina?' And I always wanted to go to Chapel Hill. And so they gave me the name of this girl, Kathy Porter. She was from Atlanta. And she was dating a boy at Chapel Hill.

"I got in touch with her," said Hinds, "and she said, fine, she'd do it. Bruce Roberts took the photographs. We had a wonderful time."

The layout, the story, the clothes, the kids, the college football weekend, were a smash. It made you almost believe in fashions in *Southern Living*."

"Almost," said McCalla.

But, you see, the real story, ultimately, was not the clothes. It was the *boy* she was dating, who was caught by the camera swinging romantically on a rope pulled by Ms. Porter. His name was Taylor Branch. And he would go on to write *Parting the Waters: America in the King Years, 1954–63*, which won the Pulitzer Prize and the nation's applause as the definitive record of the Civil Rights Movement under Martin Luther King.

Lots of wonderful things have happened to people whose photographs were published in *Southern Living*. Not to mention some rather awkward things. There was the bartender who appeared on the cover and his ex-wife's lawyers found him and hit him up for back alimony. Served him right. There was the wife who wound up in a sizable statehouse scandal. At first, it was a political scandal if your name came up in connection with hers. And then it got to be something of a scandal if it didn't. Maybe you were out of the loop.

And there was the guy whose helicopter landed on Cumberland Island off the coast of Georgia. He carefully helped a young lady step to the ground, only to have a photographer from *Southern Living* take their picture. Here they were landing on a wilderness island, the same island John Kennedy, Jr., chose to be married on in a secret ceremony, an island you could only get to by boat or plane, and here, by God, was a magazine with *twelve million* readers about to publish the photograph of the guy and the babe stepping down from the helicopter. The man called the magazine the next week in a panic, and McCalla killed the photograph.

Some guys weren't so lucky. The magazine held a focus group interview of subscribers and nonsubscribers in Atlanta. One group was made up entirely of men. They were shown various photographs and story ideas and asked what they did and did not like. When it was over, one guy, who hadn't said a word, sheepishly identified himself to Gary McCalla. He said, "Hey, you fellows once got me in deep trouble with my wife. You ran a photograph of me and my girlfriend holding hands in a mall. My wife and I are still together. But it got pretty rocky."

The moral of all this is: if you are slipping around and see a *Southern Living* photographer coming, smile; you want your wife and/or your husband to see you looking your best.

"Carey," said Logue, "do you remember how the *Progressive Farmer* staff used to have a Monday morning coffee break, a kind of show-and-tell, of where editors had been, what they had done?"

She remembered.

"They used to make us *Southern Living* editors pay ten cents for our coffee and cookies," said Logue. "They got theirs free. And do you remember the time—I can't believe we did it—because neither you nor I could hum, much less carry a tune, but you wrote a sort of bawdy ditty— bawdy is too strong a word—but a sort of suggestive ditty—about what all the *Southern Living* editors and photographers had been doing that past week? And you got a damn pitch pipe from somewhere, and piped the proper key, and you and I sang this ditty, I can't remember to what tune." Logue could not continue for laughing. "We never got asked back to Monday morning show-and-tell. McCalla, are you keeping up with all the things we never got asked back to?"

"I like to remember that I had a hand in recruiting several of the company's most talented editors," said Carey. And, indeed, she did.

"Candace Franklin, now Candace Conard, was a dear friend of mine, and she had never had a permanent job," said Carey. Candace became a star executive editor with Oxmoor House and now enjoys a successful book-packaging career in New York City.

"Candace started out as a proofreader or something," said Logue. "She still teases me about passing her a notice of her first fifty-cent raise, facedown on a piece of paper. We never had a more talented editor."

"Then there was Karen Phillips, now Karen Irons," said Carey. "She was another close friend I recommended." Karen was rescued out of the bank and became a major force in both Oxmoor House and *Southern Accents* magazine. No editor in the company had a greater eye for excellence in design.

"And there was Vicky Ingham," said Carey, still boasting of her recruiting skills. "I was on the vestry at St. Luke's Church, and we had a terrible downturn in contributions. We had to let several employees go, the last hired the first fired. Vicky was so talented. I felt terrible. She needed a job, and I recommended her to Southern Progress." Vicky proved to be an outstanding editor at Oxmoor House and later moved to an even more responsible job with *Better Homes & Gardens*.

"You batted a perfect one thousand," said McCalla, "they were all smart. And beautiful, too."

"You noticed that," said Logue. "Carey, if you hadn't been looking at that water tank on the old building, we would have missed you and your talented buddies. And what might have become of McCalla's and my White Paper to Emory, and the whole *Southern Living* operation?"

Carey Hinds could only smile the same impish smile of her extreme youth, looking hardly older than herself as an undergraduate.

To quote Dreamer Tatum, in Dan Jenkins's rowdy American football classic *Semi-Tough*: "Everything that could 'a' happen, did happen."

Progressive Farmer's entire staff, looking as rough and ready as the James Gang, gathers outside its headquarters in Winston-Salem, North Carolina, on June 11, 1892. Seated are Business Manager J. W. Denmark (*left*) and Editor J. L. Ramsey. Standing (*left to right*) are printers Jim Medlin, W. A. Fulcher, Walter Womble, and Wiley Jones, and an unidentified assistant.

P.F.'s staff, looking by 1903 as prosperous as Republicans, pose in front of their first Birmingham offices. The principal owners (*beginning fourth from the left and continuing right*) are Editor Clarence Poe, John S. Pearson, Dr. Tait Butler, and Dr. B.W. Kilgore. The men flanking them are unidentified.

Friends and rivals Clarence Poe (*left*) and Eugene Butler. Poe edited *Progressive Farmer* for sixty-seven years, but Butler easily outlasted him as Southwest Edition Editor and company president.

Three generations of Butlers have held down the fort at *Progressive Farmer*. *Left to right*, Tait Butler, Eugene Butler, and Britt Butler.

Progressive Farmer's editors and advertising salesmen tour a cattle farm in Mississippi in 1964. Gene Butler (*second from the left*), Roger McGuire (*in checked shirt*), Emory Cunningham (*fourth from right*), and Jim DiVira (*second from right*) all look solemn. This was two years before the launching of *Southern Living*.

Roger McGuire (*left*) with his arm around Emory Cunningham during their Chicago days, sometime in the late 1940s or early 1950s, when they wore gangster hats and were as close as brothers.

A view from across Birmingham's 19th Street at the old Progressive Farmer building that Philip Morris later described as "vintage cotton gin."

Consultants Herb Mayes of *McCall's* (*left*) and Wilson Hicks of *LIFE* (*center*) suspend their disbelief while looking over a ghastly preview dummy of the early *Southern Living* with Editor Norman ("Red") Youngsteadt.

Left to right, Editor O. B. Copeland, Birmingham Mayor Albert Boutwell, and *Progressive Farmer* Editorial Director Dr. Alexander Nunn open the first issue of *Southern Living* in February, 1966.

S.L. Managing Editor Gary McCalla sports the thick beard he grew after his surprise heart attack in 1968. John Logue passed him the word that if he'd shave it off, he could change his title to Editor of *S.L.*, and McCalla complied.

Carey Hinds helped convince Emory Cunningham that McCalla was the right choice as *S.L.* Editor.

Cunningham and Butler officially name McCalla Editor of the listing ship *Southern Living* in 1968. All three look as if their best dog has just died.

John Logue (*left*), Paul Cook, and McCalla land in Mobile for a Southern Travel Directors Conference. A few years earlier, it was Cook, McCalla's longtime friend, who tipped him off that *S.L.* was about to be started up.

McCalla, Travel Editor Caleb Pirtle, Logue, Travel Assistant Karen Lingo, photographer Gerald Crawford, and Editorial Assistant Judy Richardson helped the improving *Southern Living* win its first national magazine travel award in 1969.

This is it—the 1970 senior *S.L.* editorial staff. *Left to right*: Travel's Caleb Pirtle, Gardens' Hurley Thompson, Managing Editor Logue, Editor McCalla, Copy Desk's Felicia Butsch, Foods' Lena Sturges, Homes' Philip Morris, and the Art Department's Art Curl.

McCalla interviewed Atlanta architect/developer John Portman for his first issue as *S.L.* Editor.

Happy days come to *Southern Living*. *Left to right*, Roger McGuire, Emory Cunningham, and Gary McCalla smile at the magazine's new prosperity during an advertising conference in Houston in the early 1970s.

McGuire and Logue look through some of the 70,000 entries in *S.L.*'s first photo contest. Actor and Air Force Brigadier General Jimmy Stewart notified the winner, who was on active duty in the military.

The cover of the company's in-house magazine, *Ink Pot Farmer*, never sizzled so fiercely as in December, 1971, when it featured Judy Richardson (*left*) and Barbara Pettway (later McCalla).

Left to right, Karen Baucum, Peggy Smith, the formidable Lena Sturges, and Jean Liles lift a glass to the Foods Department's good health in Lena's backyard, in December, 1971. Peggy is still with the magazine, and Karen has risen to supervise employee benefits.

Philip Morris in September, 1974. He'd been the object of a vast search for a design editor. "He and Jean Liles are the most important hires we ever made," says McCalla.

The Old South lives again in this *S.L.* send-up, featuring *(left to right)* Morris, Bill McDougald, Liles, McCalla, Tom Ford, and Karen Lingo.

Jean Liles unloads a day's groceries for the test kitchens from her beloved Karmann Ghia.

McCalla presides over the test-kitchen staff, as he did for twenty-two years. It's easier for a camel to pass through the eye of a needle than for a recipe to make its way into *Southern Living*.

Foods editors (*left to right*) Phyllis Cordell, Susan Payne, Susan Dosier, Deborah Hastings, and Jean Liles load up for an editorial conference in 1988. "We built our empire in the Foods Department," says McCalla.

Lois Chaplin bringing instant life to the garden staff. She now works as a free-lancer.

Kaye Adams (*left*) and Susan Payne help make *Annual Recipes*, year after year, the most profitable single book title in America. Kaye rose to become an executive editor of *S.L.* and Susan moved to a senior position at Oxmoor House.

7

"It'll Survive"

So, this story passes into The Winter of Our Discontent, 1967. Bradley Byers and Paul Plawin had gone to their future careers, with Byers leaving his signed prophecy of disastrous times ahead for *Southern Living*. All that was needed to complete his dirge of ruin were three witches chanting around a boiling pot. It couldn't happen in the old building on 19th Street; there was only one eye working on the test-kitchen stove, and it would barely boil water and couldn't be expected to raise the temperature on a newt or a toad.

The telephone rang at 1776 Remington Road, Atlanta, Georgia. The call was from O. B. Copeland. John Logue sat on the edge of the bed, holding the receiver. He covered the mouthpiece with one hand and asked his wife, Helen: "Have you ever heard of a magazine, *Southern Living*?" She said, "Yes, but you can hang up. We are not moving to Birmingham."

John was in absolute agreement. Atlanta was a city on the go, a city in those heady days claiming itself to be "too busy to hate." Writing sports for the *Atlanta Journal* had been a ten-year pleasure ride, if you didn't mind the seven-day weeks and the low pay. But what do the very young know about long hours and low pay? And the major leagues had come to town. You couldn't say the Atlanta Braves were setting the National League of baseball on its ear. You could say the National Football League was knocking the Atlanta Falcons on their anatomy. University of Georgia and Georgia Tech football were still the Big Noise in sports in the state, and Logue was the *Journal*'s college editor. But he was pushing thirty-five, with three growing sons, and it wouldn't cost anything to listen.

He hung up the phone with zero interest in *Southern Living*. Then Dr. O. B. Copeland came to Atlanta for a round of interviews. He took a room on the second floor of the already weary Travel Lodge off Highway 85.

Logue started up the outside stairs and met the *Journal*'s former Washington correspondent on the way down. He shook his head and said one word: "Hopeless."

Okay. Logue shook hands with Cope, and the first words out of his own mouth were not designed to impress a future employer: "You are not holing up in the high rent district."

Cope smiled his agreement. You had to like his sort of lop-sided smile. He had sent a few recent issues of the magazine to Logue, who had been underwhelmed with the writing. He didn't know enough about magazines to understand exactly what *Southern Living* was trying to do. After he learned a little more about magazines, he had no idea what *Southern Living* was up to.

Cope talked about The Progressive Farmer Company. Logue was very much aware of it, as his father had once been a county agent, and for years had been the State 4-H Club Leader of Alabama. Cope said Logue's Auburn journalism professor Paul Burnett had recommended him for the job, as had Logue's brother Mickey, who was an assistant professor on Burnett's staff. Logue appreciated the votes of confidence but came to realize that top Southern journalists were not throwing their careers out the window to apply for the job.

Southern Living was to be a magazine for the "modern South," said Copeland. He didn't go into great editorial detail. The magazine was lying open to speak for itself. Logue deflected questions as to his own opinion of *Southern Living*. He still had no interest whatever in moving to Birmingham.

Then O. B. Copeland said, "This job as features editor will play *thirteen thousand five hundred dollars*." Logue looked at Dr. Copeland as if they had just been introduced. He had recently been raised, after ten years, to $170 a week. He knew that *Journal* Sports Editor Furman Bisher made only about thirteen thousand dollars a year, and Bisher was a young man and not about to leave Atlanta.

"Jim Minter and myself and Gregory Favre used to laugh about how one day we would succeed Bisher as sports editor," said Logue. "Jim would get it for two years, and then I would have it for two, and Greg would have a long five-year career. Of course, it's 1996, and Jim is retired as editor of the *Atlanta Journal-Constitution*, and I am retired from Southern Progress, and Greg is a big shot on the *Sacramento* [California] *Bee*, and Bisher is still writing the most literate sports column in the South in the *Journal*. I hope he goes on forever."

This much Minter, Logue, and Favre could tell you: if you could work for Furman Bisher for ten years, and hold your own on the *Atlanta Journal* sports staff of the 1950s and '60s, you could make it any place they paid you to write the news in the English language. "You got a minute," was Bisher's favorite expression when he was displeased. No one ever confused it with a question . . . but once. And a small note folded into your mailbox was not to tell you what a swell fellow you were. "We loved him, and we hated him. We loved him a lot more the further in time we traveled from the experience of working for him," said Logue.

If you loved sports you would have loved those years in Atlanta, the fifties and sixties. They were the glory years of Southern college football. Even the stadiums are now named after the coaches: Robert Lee ("Bobby") Dodd of Georgia Tech, Ralph ("Shug") Jordan of Auburn, and, of course, Paul ("Bear") Bryant of Alabama, not to forget Wally Butts and then Vince Dooley of Georgia, and Johnny Vaught of Ole Miss, and Paul Dietzel and Charlie McClendon of LSU, and Ray Graves of Florida, and Bowden Wyatt of Tennessee, who might have been the best of them all if Demon Alcohol had not cut short his career and his life, and Frank Howard of Clemson, and Jim Tatum of Maryland, and Frank Broyles of Arkansas, and his good buddy Darrell Royal of Texas. And all the assistant coaches, seething with ambition, who worked under them, desperate for a chance at a team of their own.

"We knew those guys," Logue said, "in their glory and generosity and in their despair and drunkenness and in our own. We wrote about the games when they beat the mortal hell out of somebody else's team. We wrote most compellingly when they went to war against one another and dog-cussed one another across fifty-five yards and accused one another and murdered one another's teams and laughed together like hell about it when they teed the golf ball up, lying about their handicaps, at some conference outing in the spring. And when they died, they went to one another's funerals." Logue still has the image in his memory of Bryant, with his black hat off, at the grave of General Robert R. Neyland of Tennessee, whom Bryant never beat once in eight bloody games when he coached at Kentucky.

Logue said, "We laughed with those guys who were growing older in front of our eyes while mortality hadn't yet occurred to ourselves; we fussed with them; their football wives were wont to chew us out from time to time; we drank with them, oh, yes, we drank with them, almost always *their* whiskey. [We sportswriters of that era had the shortest arms in America; we couldn't afford to pick up a check at a Krystal Café.] We wrote nasty things when the coaches cheated and went on probation. We were welcome in their offices and in their stadiums and in their dens where the old stories climbed up to the ceiling with the cigar smoke. Funny thing, they trusted us, and did not edit their recollections in front of us. You could argue we should have been writing who was gambling in Las Vegas, who was at the track in New Orleans, who was over his head in debt, who was drunker than he ought to be, who was sleeping with some young thing. But we left that world to the next generation of sportswriters, and they are welcome to it.

"Oh, I didn't mention the players of those times," said Logue, "but we dare not call up their separate names or this book would never get back to Birmingham."

These were also glamorous years for golf in Georgia: Bobby Jones himself still lived and ruled Augusta National in a time, first, of Hogan and Snead, and then of Palmer and Player and the man-god Nicklaus. The Atlanta Crackers won seventeen pennants until giving way to the mediocrity of the early Braves. Jim Minter, some years later, wrote on the editorial page of the *Atlanta Constitution* of those sports-writing days of the fifties and sixties: "It was a good time to do what we did."

But another circumstance compounded Logue's interest in this new magazine *Southern Living*. In the not too distant past, he had been dropped as *Sports Illustrated*'s correspondent in Atlanta. He'd refused to report any "inside" material on the infamous Bear Bryant/Wally Butts football "scandal" that was raging in *The Saturday Evening Post*. The two coaches were accused of "fixing" the 1962 Alabama-Georgia football game, which Logue had covered at Birmingham's Legion Field. Alabama's Joe Namath had truly fixed Georgia's wagon, 35–0, with his touchdown passes.

Sports Illustrated's chief of correspondents accused Logue "of sitting on the biggest sports story of the last fifty years." Logue said, "I think it's a three-million-dollar libel suit." He was naive; it was a ten-million-dollar libel suit. The first judgment in favor of Wally Butts was for three million dollars, an American libel record. It was later reduced to several hundred thousand dollars. And *The Saturday Evening Post* settled out of court with Bear Bryant for several hundred thousand more. The entire episode destroyed the once great American magazine's last vestige of credibility.

By the end of the Butts trial, *Sports Illustrated* was glad to have kept its mouth shut. But before that trial, *S.I.* sent Logue a "There's a time for good men to go their separate ways" wire. Gone was a nice piece of regular pocket change. Some nineteen years later, when Time, Inc., bought *Southern Living* for nearly a half-billion dollars, Logue would tell Time, Inc., President Dick Monroe, "We're even." Logue and McCalla only wished they'd had more than a tiny piece of the action when the sale came about.

Suddenly Logue was ready to fly over to Birmingham and explore the idea of working for this new magazine. Helen Logue was not thrilled with the possibility.

Birmingham was only about two decades behind 1967. There hadn't been a new high-rise building built in the city since before World War II. The old open-hearth Sloss Furnace was still raging fire and smoke off First Avenue North, in the middle of town. The air had plenty of body to it. You could breathe it or stir it. The taxi ride in from the small, posthumous airport passed through old, dying neighborhoods. Of course, there was no freeway through the city.

Logue remembered many generous things he had written about Birmingham, covering the Atlanta Cracker baseball team when it played the Birmingham Barons in wonderful, decrepit Rickwood Field. Such friendly observations as: "DATELINE—Slagtown, USA." And: "Here we are in Birmingham, which calls itself the 'Magic City,' which is an accurate alias as it disappears once a day in the smog." Other generous, charitable thoughts came to mind on the grim taxi ride into the city.

"Take me to The Progressive Farmer building . . . at 821 North 19th Street," he told the driver, an old hand driving a beat-up Chevrolet.

"Can't. They tore 'at buildin' down years ago," he said.

Logue looked again at the address in his hand. He had the feeling he was trapped in a time warp. "Well, take it up 19th Street anyway."

The driver turned by the low, seedy Boutwell Auditorium, which sported large color posters for professional wrestling. Kelley Ingram Park, where many of the most violent civil rights battles had been fought only a few years before, was a couple of blocks south and west.

"Eye God," said the driver, "it's still here." As if some miracle had saved the building, the very company, from oblivion. And maybe it would take a miracle.

Logue climbed out of the cab. He stared at the metal awnings over the unwashed windows. The building looked exactly like the warehouse it was constructed to be in the first quarter of the century. It reminded him of the old *Montgomery Advertiser* building where he'd first gone to work in 1955, where the ink would settle on your face if you walked through the newsroom without touching any solid surface, and where the hand-operated copy basket rumbled down like a bowel movement into the composing room and the old, iron-legged Linotype machines creaked and racked and dipped black arms like lost souls. Logue looked at the God-abandoned Progressive Farmer building, and he liked it.

Dr. Copeland was all cordiality. Introduced him to Beth Carlson and Dixie Snell, obviously two live wires. Logue wondered what they did. He'd never been in a newspaper office with a secretary or editorial assistant. Turns out they did *everything*. He met the thin, jumpy Art Director Bob Simmons, and Carey Hinds, the all-purpose editor who would become a good friend. He met the fearsome Foods Editor Lena Sturges. He'd seen her kind around the newspaper; God help any elected official one of them lit out after. And he met the older, suspicious horticulture editor, whose office looked like it had imploded with loose papers.

Logue didn't meet Gary McCalla that morning. He did go to lunch with Cope and Dr. Alexander Nunn and President Eugene Butler, who had flown in from Dallas for the interview. Two of *Southern Living*'s three writers had called it quits in a matter of two months. The magazine was struggling to find itself. All three executives were obviously suspicious of some hotshot sportswriter from pagan Atlanta. As well they might have been. Logue couldn't figure out how the magazine, as chaotic as it appeared to him, was coming together at all.

The three company officers walked Logue across the park to the Downtown Club. A waitress stopped by their table and Gene Butler said, "I think I'll have a glass of skim milk." Dr. Nunn said, "That sounds good, I'll also have a glass of skim milk." Dr. Copeland said, "Alec, I believe I will also have a glass of skim milk."

Logue said, "Gentlemen, I don't normally drink at lunch. Not a big drinker anytime. But I drink an occasional vodka-tonic. If that's a problem, we better talk about it."

From the expression on his face, it was a problem for Dr. Nunn. But Gene Butler, who Logue later learned would lift a glass of bourbon from time to time, said, no, if it wasn't a problem for Logue, moderate drinking wouldn't be a problem for the company. Dr. Nunn bit his tongue. Dr. Copeland drank his skim milk. They all knew or had met Logue's father, Hanchey Logue, the State 4-H Club Leader. Dr. Nunn knew him very well and respected him. That's almost certainly why his son was sitting across from them at the table.

Logue spoke of his brief tenure at the *Montgomery Advertiser* as police reporter/sportswriter before entering the Air Force, and his brief tour of duty on the United Press radio wire before his ten years of writing sports for the *Atlanta Journal*. He mentioned that he wrote fiction on his own time, but that no publisher had shown the least interest in any of it. Butler said that what a man wrote on his own time was his own business. Logue spoke of his wife, Helen, and three sons, Johnny, Mac, Joey. Not much was said of the direction of *Southern Living* itself.

Logue was not impressed. There was such vagueness, the very air might have been bottled in the nineteenth century. His interest in the magazine dipped below zero. He stole a look at his watch. He was glad he was not spending the night.

Back in the old building, Logue came face-to-face with Gary McCalla. He was short, thick in the chest, had a pelt of black hair combed straight back and black eyes to match. And he was smoking a pipe. It didn't take long to learn he was a Choctaw Indian from Oklahoma. McCalla stood just outside his cubicle, having no problem with where to put his hands and was in no way trying to impress anybody.

"Tell me something, who the hell is putting this magazine out?" asked Logue. "You?"

"Mostly," McCalla admitted. "In fact, I'm responsible for the July issue. Cope turned it over to me. It may be a disaster. We are reducing the page size. And the whole issue will be built around the Fourth of July. Anyway, it ought to shake things up. Somebody will have to make a decision about something."

McCalla was not censoring anything that he said, as if he'd known Logue ten years instead of ten minutes. "You know two writers left?"

"Why'd they leave?" asked Logue.

"Rats off a sinking ship," said McCalla, laughing this deep, harsh laugh that he still laughs.

"Is this thing going down?" asked Logue.

"Maybe."

"Why are you hanging around?"

"Maybe it's not," said McCalla, puffing on his pipe, the only person at ease and confident in his own judgment Logue had met in the old warehouse of a building. "It beats bidding for contracts with NASA." He told Logue something of his dangerous years in Huntsville, the two of them still standing there at the entrance to his cubicle, careless of who might overhear their conversation.

Up walked a tall, good-looking guy with a great smile and a suit he didn't buy in Birmingham.

"Roger McGuire, meet John Logue," said McCalla.

McGuire was a big guy, a half-a-head taller than both of them. He looked you straight in the eye when he shook hands. There was more than a little mischief in his eyes.

"Logue's a sportswriter from the *Atlanta Journal*," said McCalla.

"Must be a brave one," said McGuire, now laughing. He had a great laugh, like he was laughing at the world, or at least at himself.

"McGuire's the advertising director of the magazine," said McCalla, back puffing on his pipe.

"Are you selling any ads?" were the first words Logue ever spoke to McGuire. He can still see him formulating his answer, which took a few seconds.

"We could sell more," he said, all the emphasis on the word *more*. He had a way of standing back, his shoulders very much back, as if about to meet the firing squad, except you soon learned that he was holding all the spoken ammunition. He offered no apology. No gushy promise. Like McCalla, he had no problem with what to do with his hands and arms.

Logue asked, "Do you think this magazine will survive?"

McGuire's exact answer was, "It'll survive." Just that direct sentence. No more, no less.

In those fifteen minutes, talking with McCalla and then McGuire, Logue went from having less than zero interest in *Southern Living* to wanting the damn job, the challenge. Even if it was in Birmingham. He had worked for ten years with an assortment of extremely gifted writers; he could tell when he'd met a talented, significant person, though they come in many shapes and sexes.

Logue later said, "I knew I was in the presence of two substantial, though very different, people. There was no question in my mind that either one of them could make a living anywhere. If McGuire was working here, he believed it made sense. And McCalla, too."

John Logue went back to Atlanta and Helen Logue didn't flinch from the possibility of the challenge, even if it meant leaving her beloved Atlanta. The deal was, Logue would write a couple of stories, for a modest fee. And O. B. Copeland, on the strength of them, would or would not offer him the job as Features Editor. The job was offered, and accepted.

It was not as hard to leave the *Journal* as Logue had imagined. The great old sports gang was already breaking up. Greg Favre had gone to Washington on the staff of an idealistic young congressman, and would hold many newspaper jobs until he wound up a vice-president in Sacramento. Lee Walburn would soon leave the baseball beat to flack for the Atlanta Braves themselves and later edit *Atlanta Magazine*. Terry Kay would give up sports to write drama criticism and then wonderful novels. Jerry Chatham would run his own public relations agency. Gene Asher would leave prep sports, which he and the *Constitution*'s Charlie Roberts had invented, to make millions in insurance. Bill Robinson would disappear for years, only to return to the sports staff like a ghost from Christmas past. Only Tom McCollister stayed on, taking over Ed Miles's old golf beat (only to be killed too young in a car accident in the summer of 1999). Jim Minter would become editor of the *Constitution*. And Miles, the last gentleman and president of America's golf writers, had put on his hat and gone to the gin rummy tables at the Atlanta Athletic Club, never to return.

8

A White Paper

Remember, there was no freeway in Birmingham in 1967. The shortest route over the mountain from the suburbs to the south was straight up Highway 31. "Over the mountain" was a real estate euphemism for any community far enough south to escape the dreadful smoke and grit from the Sloss and other furnaces still making steel in the city limits. The town of Homewood chose the role of bottleneck, with never a traffic officer in sight during rush hour. It took Helen an hour to drive Logue eight miles from their home in the suburbs to 821 North 19th Street, with three small sons perched on the back seat like displaced persons.

Logue stepped out of the aging Pontiac and looked at the metal awnings over the soot-stained windows and asked himself: "What the hell have I done with my life?"

There was a great deal more chaos inside the building than outside, although Gary McCalla had the July issue by the throat. He knew where *it* was going. The direction and fate of *Southern Living* magazine was what hung in the balance.

Dr. O. B. Copeland had called Dixie Snell into his office and asked her to "look out" for the new editor coming in from Atlanta. It was Dixie's lot to babysit all the new editors.

"Oh, I remember John didn't want any files," said Dixie, recently, passing on the dessert at O'Charley's. "He said, 'I'll research a story, and I'll write it the day I get back. I don't need a filing system.' And he threw all the press releases in the trash basket. The first thing in the morning he read the newspaper. He wouldn't speak. He might grumble behind the paper. He said they had a rule on the newspaper, they didn't speak before 10 A.M., unless they had to.

"This went on for about a month," said Dixie. "I came in and took the newspaper out of his hand. I said, 'This is *Southern Living*. We speak at eight in the morning.' "

"That's the trouble with Dixie, she never forgets a damn thing," said Logue. "And God, did I need a filing system. I didn't realize I would be working on thirty stories at the same time."

"You got so attached to those files that nobody, *nobody* went in them but you and me," said Dixie. "Cope looked in them once to check on some statistic in the story you wrote on the Coca-Cola company, and you pitched a fit."

"I hope I did," said Logue.

That first day Copeland had given Logue a list of maybe a hundred story ideas that had been kicked around from time to time in planning sessions.

"I wish I had that list," said Logue. "It was the strangest mix of story ideas you could imagine. Luckily, I wasn't ordered to write any of them. McCalla gave me my first assignment. And it was a startling one: interview two veterans of the Vietnam War, which was raging as we spoke. It was for the 'Fourth of July' issue coming up. This issue opened with 1767 and ran for two hundred years right up to 1967. It was a bizarre magazine. But it had some gutsy stuff in it."

"It nearly put us out of business," said McCalla. "We'd gone to the smaller page size. And nobody could figure out from the July cover design what was going on inside. It was a fiasco which I orchestrated. Nobody would make a decision about July, so I said, 'Hell, I will.' Cope turned over to me the responsibility for getting out the entire issue. And I never really turned that responsibility back."

The first confusion, as McCalla said, was in the July cover design. Three photographs were cropped to make a big 4. One was of cowboys about to barbecue three hundred pounds of beef, one was a very cool fashion photograph, and one was of a small boy in a high hat in a parade. The montage was not outlined, and nobody could see that it made a 4 against a solid white background. It just looked like three wildly different subjects stacked improbably together. McCalla shot the first two photographs, the cowboys in West Texas and the fashion models in Savannah.

Advertising and circulation response was catastrophic. The advertising staff never showed the issue to one media buyer. Subscription renewals dropped through the floor. McCalla learned a gigantic lesson he never forgot: single-subject issues will get you killed. From that July forward, he insisted on total balance of subject matter in *Southern Living*. And he never allowed anything but a full-bleed image to appear on the cover of the magazine.

Not that there weren't some lively stories inside that July issue. Carey Hinds wrote two of them. She made a pilgrimage to the James River Road in Virginia, where her family's ancestral home, Ampthill, built in 1732, had been relocated. Her first-person account had a bit of the power of a novel by Jane Austen.

Carey got permission from the *Virginia Gazette*, published since 1736, to create "a reasonable facsimile of news and events, reported as they might have been in 1767" in that newspaper. Hinds rendered a terrific account of what was happening in the Southern colonies with everybody from Thomas Jefferson to Daniel Boone. She signed her maiden name, "C. Gates Thomas."

In between her two classic stories was a garish handout preview of the Daytona Firecracker 400 stock car race. A ghastly blue tint was printed over the photographs of good ol' boy drivers Curtis Turner, David Pearson, Richard Petty, Bobby Allison, and Sam McQuagg, giving them a posthumous look in a dangerous profession, all of it a long way from the James River Road.

Bruce Roberts shot a marvelous photographic essay of "The Fourth at Faith," North Carolina, surviving even the eccentric page design by Simmons.

McCalla pulled together, with much satisfaction, the fashion layout of handsome young women wearing red, white, and, of course, blue. He called it "The Siege of Savannah, 1967."

"Gerald Crawford and I did the shoot," said McCalla, nearly spilling his iced tea at the memory. "We were working out of this hotel in Savannah. And we were running in and out of the room these attractive young women, dressed in different outfits. This activity concerned the assistant manager, a woman, who came up to see if we'd turned her hotel into a bordello."

"That would have been a lively addition to the July issue," said Logue.

He could never have imagined his own assignment to interview two Vietnam vets, each headed back to the horror of that ongoing war. Logue spoke with enlisted man John Martin, the son of his old friend Harold Martin, longtime Foreign Editor of *The Saturday Evening Post* and Atlanta columnist. John described how his outfit had been ambushed and twenty-three of the thirty-seven guys wounded, including himself, and two killed. His leave was up, and he was heading back into action.

Logue spoke with Lieutenant Dennis Graham, a fighter pilot who had won the Distinguished Flying Cross for destroying a SAM missile site. He said, full of mischief, "I'm not married. I can't find anybody to ask me. But I know now about the Fourth of July. If I have any boys, I am going to see that they do."

Lieutenant Graham never had any boys. A family member called Logue a short while after the July issue appeared. The lieutenant was killed in a plane crash. Logue can still hear the lively energy and the fun in the lieutenant's voice. Years later, he looked up Graham's name on the Vietnam Memorial in Washington, D.C. The war never seemed a more tragic human waste.

The same issue of the magazine—if you can imagine it—had a story by Lena Sturges on "Fourth of July Barbecue." Excellent photographs by "The Mad Mexican," as McCalla named Gil Barrera, a free-lancer from San Antonio. Barrera would be shooting a naked young woman for *Playboy* one day and barbecue beef for *Southern Living* the next; you can imagine who got first call on his services. Barrera also took the most compelling photograph McCalla and Logue had ever seen of President Jack Kennedy, the day before he was killed in Dallas. They urged him to give a print to the Kennedy Library. They still wonder if he ever did.

The ex-governor of North Carolina, Luther Hodges, and the sitting Governor of Arkansas, Winthrop Rockefeller, wrote for July first-person, self-serving accounts of industrial growth in those states. And there was a gardening piece on espaliering plants.

How could the readers and advertisers have imagined what was going on in *Southern Living*? Of course, they couldn't. But it wasn't boring; it was only insane.

Certainly the July issue didn't bore Emory Cunningham. It terrified him. President Eugene Butler had named Emory publisher of both *Progressive Farmer* and *Southern Living* magazines in March of 1967. Advertising and circulation staffs of both magazines would report to Emory, representing a new direction in the eighty-one-year history of the company. But *Ink Pot Farmer*, the company's in-house publication, emphasized, "Editors will continue to be responsible to the Executive Editor, Alexander Nunn."

Even so, Dr. Nunn's days were numbered. The appointment of Cunningham as publisher of both magazines, and the decision by *Southern Living* to accept whiskey advertising, hurt the old man deeply and left him without a power base. Dr. Nunn consulted with his family and resigned from the company. His resignation occurred that spring of 1967 and was announced in July, but was not effective until November. He had been with The Progressive Farmer Company forty-three years.

After it was announced that Emory would be in complete charge of *Southern Living*, he ran into Harold Dobson of the Circulation Department. "He met me at the elevator," remembered Emory. "He said, 'Do you realize what's happening?' I said, 'What do you mean?' He said, 'They are putting you in charge of a sinking ship.' Charlie Scruggs of *Progressive Farmer* said something similar to me. And others. We'd gone backwards [editorially]. It was a whole lot tougher to restart the magazine than it would have been [to launch it right] in the beginning."

Everybody had an opinion to offer Cunningham. "I don't think I ever told this to anybody," said Emory, "but Herb Mayes and Wilson Hicks had told me, 'If you start this magazine here [in Birmingham], you are going to ruin this fine old company. You've got a better chance to make it work if you move your headquarters to Atlanta. Birmingham is just not a place to have a magazine like this.' Mayes was the most outspoken about that. And then the two of them said, 'You've got to find an editor with big league experience who knows about magazines of this kind.' They said that so much to me that I went to New York [looking for an editor] soon after Gene put me in charge of *Southern Living*." More about that later.

The July issue of *Southern Living* stunned Cunningham. He was now in a position not only to persuade but to direct the editorial staff. He offered no ultimatums or new editorial directions. But he persuaded Copeland and McCalla that something had to be done with *Southern Living* to counter the negative response to the reduced page size and the puzzling July magazine.

"The August issue had already gone to press," remembered McCalla.

"September was our first chance to improve things. We decided to pour the color to it. Luckily, we had good color photography for September."

Logue had knocked out his first major story for the magazine in August: "The Carbonated Kingdom," a look at the history of that Southern phenomenon Coca-Cola, as well as at Pepsi Cola and the tagalong Royal Crown Cola. He wrote of Coca-Cola: "Brewed in a three-legged iron pot in the backyard of 'Dr.' John S. Pemberton in Atlanta, Georgia in 1886, and stirred—if you will—with an oar, it now is a $979 million-a-year business." (These days that would be petty cash for Coke.)

"One thing you can say about that story—it wasn't too short," said McCalla.

"Yes, it jumped twice," said Logue with some glee. The truth was that being the lone writer in the *Southern Living* stable, he had to pick big subjects and write long to fill up the magazine. McCalla now functioned as Senior Editor and Travel Editor, but with the undeclared responsibility of putting out the magazine. He didn't have time to write.

Logue hadn't been there a month. He was walking up the stairs to the third floor of the old building. Coming down the stairs, walking on the insteps of his feet, was a middle-aged man, rather thin, slightly slumped, wearing glasses. He wore his hair combed straight back and had a twitchy mustache, giving him more than a casual resemblance to Groucho Marx.

"Boy," he said, "are you Logue?"

"That's right."

"You know you are putting out the sorriest magazine in the United States." That was Orville Demaree, market research expert, always a man to let you down easy.

Orville was not the least eccentric man in the building. He loved to cuss. It was sort of comforting to Logue, who was reminded of the baseball language in the dugouts of the old Southern League. Demaree paid an astrologist three hundred dollars a year to help him coordinate the colors he wore. His bow tie, his pants, his shirt were coordinated in rather spectacular colors, every day. He'd pull the tops of his undershorts out of his pants to show you they were also coordinated to his "colors" for the day.

Demaree was something of a genius at analyzing the complex figures of market research. He did it in his head, with the help of a pencil or a calculator. Until the day he retired, he never lowered himself to work on a computer. He was one guy who, after some controversial company decision, would walk into Cunningham's office and say, "Emory, you're crazy." It wasn't that Demaree was right or that Emory would ever take his advice that amazed us, but that Orville got away with how he gave it. Maybe we should have all hired the same astrologist.

The September issue did brighten a lot of faces around the old building, maybe even Demaree's. Cope and McCalla poured seventeen pages of color to it, rather than the usual five or six.

"The cover wasn't bad," said Gary. It was a fall shot of a Chattanooga family riding by boat up the Tennessee River to a football game at the University of Tennessee in Knoxville. Logue produced the first of his twenty-seven All-South Football sections, which were to prove popular with men and women and advertisers over the years.

McCalla was careful to lace the issue with recipes and entertaining, with a house sporting assorted decks, and with garden pools in the landscape. No more single subject issues. But it was a matter of one step forward and two steps backward. A catastrophic step backward was the October cover. Bruce Roberts took the cover photograph, an excellent image of a woman taking a horse over a jump against the Virginia landscape in glorious fall color. Only the color separator in Nashville missed the fall foliage and a good deal of the horse.

"They just went in with a router and routed out the mane of the horse. It was the damndest thing you ever saw," said McCalla, still hot about it thirty years later.

Mike Fitzgerald, of the New York ad staff, remembers going by a newsstand with Emory Cunningham the week that October issue came out in 1967. "We looked at it," said Mike, "and the cover photograph was out of register about a quarter of an inch. I said to Emory, 'That's not a horse. That's a bad outline of a horse.' He said, 'It happens all the time to all kinds of magazines.' We're looking at eighty magazines on that newsstand, and none of the others is out of register."

McCalla took it on himself to move half of the next batch of color transparencies to Dallas, Texas, to be separated. He kept firing separators until he found another outfit in Nashville that could do the job. They are still doing it.

October was the last issue designed by Art Director Bob Simmons. He took his Afghan hounds and swipe file and hit the road, leaving behind more dire predictions for the fate of the magazine. McCalla and Logue remembered going over to Oxmoor Printing Company—owned by The Progressive Farmer—to interview Art Curl for the art director's job. Curl was the living opposite of Simmons, quiet, reserved, gentlemanly. Copeland hired him, and he ultimately brought to the magazine a classic, full-page bleed look—one photograph occupying the entire page. Curl would not dazzle you with his design invention, but he lent an organized, rather formal look that the magazine needed at the time, for the editorial content still flew off in sometimes manic directions.

It was in the November issue that the first classic, two-page color spread of food appeared, a pecan pie shot by free-lancer Taylor Lewis, himself as great a character as ever stepped in the door at *Southern Living*. He photographed a pecan pie, sitting among whole and shelled pecans, uncracked eggs, an iron nutcracker in the shape of a dog with a pecan in its mouth, and a kerosene lamp illuminating the entire tableau. It looked like a painting by one of the early Dutch Masters and set the standard for thirty years of food photography in *Southern Living*. And that photograph was to influence Emory Cunningham's choice for the future editor of the magazine.

Taylor Lewis was a trip in himself. Jean Liles can bring him to life better than anybody and will in this book.

McCalla felt that Art Curl designed the magazine's first feature layout with a "truly professional look" in the December issue of 1967: "Missions Imperishable." It was a feature on the Spanish missions of San Antonio, with exquisite photography by "The Mad Mexican," Barrera.

"The story wasn't shabby," said Logue, fishing for a compliment.

"Yeah, and it was longer than the two hundred years the missions had been around," said McCalla, "but it was a great piece," he said with fake reluctance.

"I always went for distance and not accuracy," said Logue.

Karen Lingo's name came up a few chapters back. Like Carey Hinds, she first heard of *Southern Living* as an art student at Birmingham Southern College, but a bit later, in the spring of 1967. "I needed money to pay for art supplies," said Lingo. "*Southern Living* had a listing for 'an assistant to a secretary.' I walked into that old building. And was interviewed by Sara Bagwell. Remember her?"

"I remember she was run over by a car in front of the building," said McCalla. "A very nice person. She never came back to work."

"I said to myself, 'Uh-uh, no way,' " said Lingo, " 'I'll see what other jobs the college has listed.' But Sara called me and asked me to come to work the next Monday. I said, 'Well, okay.' I worked three hours a day, three days a week. It paid around twenty-five dollars. But enough for my paints and canvas."

Lingo collated and took over clipping newspapers. "But the thing that almost did me in," she said, "was taking reader complaints. We were just converting subscriptions over to the computer, and some people were getting six or seven copies of the magazine every month. Then I got the people who were upset because we changed the size of the magazine, from large to small. They hated the new size. It was so depressing to walk out of there every day after hearing so many complaints."

Sara Bagwell, Lingo remembered, had it worse. "Charles, the Horticulture Editor, made her cry every day. I don't know what the man said to her, but she was always coming into my office crying."

"That sounds like one of Sturges's assistants," said Logue.

"Then the other Horticulture Editor, Hank, almost did me in, too," said Karen. "His office was a mess, stuff everywhere. His filing system was simply stacking papers along the bookshelves, just a mess of papers. Talk about depressing. He went out of town, and I came in on a Saturday and worked all weekend. It was a long weekend. I categorized everything. I filed begonias under 'B.' I had everything in a filing cabinet. Organized. You could find anything. The shelves were neat.

"I came in from classes the day after he got back from his trip," said Lingo. "He had taken everything out of the filing cabinet and just spread it again over those shelves. I could not believe it." Lingo could laugh thirty years later. "He never said a word. I never said a word. And I never touched his stuff again."

"He cleaned out those files one more time, when he was leaving," said McCalla. "I found a box in his office—all the gardening photography we had at the time—*all of it*. I got the box and locked it in my office. He never said a word. I never said a word."

"Communication, that's what saved us," said Logue, laughing.

"I got switched over to Homes and worked with Nez Calhoun," said Lingo. "I worked everywhere except Photography and Food."

Nez was an alert and extremely likable editor, on her first job from the University of Georgia. It was not her fault that she had never had training in architecture or any form of design. Copeland hired her out of the blue as Homes Editor. She went on to make an outstanding career for herself in the Birmingham city school system.

Lingo remembers the time Lena Sturges baked a cake for the editorial assistants. "There was this little bitty kitchen with a door that folded back," Karen said.

"And one eye and the oven barely worked," Logue said.

"I never knew Lena cooked," Lingo said of the longtime Foods Editor.

"It wasn't her main thing," Logue said.

"But she went in there and baked us a cake," said Karen. "We dug into it, and there were *eggshells* throughout the cake. She had put the eggs, shells and all, in the cake."

"I believe it." Logue and McCalla could not swallow their lunch for laughing.

"I was not impressed," said Lingo.

"Do you remember after you finished college, you walked into Mc-Calla's office and said, 'Well, I'm ready to go to work.' Do you remember that?" asked Logue.

"Yeah, I remember saying it, and he said, 'Oh, okay.' "

"McCalla, you weren't the editor. You didn't have authorization to hire anybody," Logue said.

"You're right."

"I was so naive," said Karen, "I didn't realize I couldn't just waltz in, and say, 'I'm coming back.' It never occurred to me."

"You just hid her on the payroll, which was one of the luckiest things ever to happen to the magazine," said Logue.

Lingo went on to become one of the outstanding Travel Editors in the history of *Southern Living*, and today edits special publications for the company.

"All I knew was that it was absolutely fascinating," said Lingo, "and I felt I was part of something important. I really enjoyed the atmosphere, what was going on. It was exciting."

"I remember *you*, you had this frizzy hair, wore these long print dresses, like somebody out of 1938," said Logue. "It didn't take you long to become a fashion plate. Of course, today all the women in New York spend three hundred dollars trying to frizz up their hair."

"I know I was the first woman to wear a pants suit to work," said Lingo. "Remember that rule against pants suits? Nobody said anything to me. I just wore them."

"Oh, yes," said Logue, "and do you remember the memo that Britt Butler sent around, that mini-skirts could only be a certain height from the floor?" Logue pounded the table until water was spilling out of all their glasses. "And, of course, I was right at the door the first day after the memo, measuring skirts with a ruler. Remember McCalla's assistant Joan Bates? Wore the wonderful short skirts. I said, 'Bates, this skirt is one inch *too long*. You have got to go home and put on a shorter skirt.' "

"Oh, God, the jail wouldn't hold us today," said McCalla. "Not that a single one of our *Southern Living* editors paid a damn bit of attention to Britt's amazing rules."

"And don't forget the famous *toilet paper incident*," said Logue. Other customers in the Hollywood Restaurant were staring, as if this one table of two aging men and one still-youthful woman had gone slightly berserk. "Britt, always acute to save his daddy's money, told the department heads they had a 'serious situation' in the women's bathroom. The women, he said, were using *twice as much toilet paper as the men*. Something had to be done." Logue struggled to breathe. "I don't know if anyone ever gave him an anatomy lesson. Luckily, *Southern Living* began to make money and for all these years it has been able to bear the burden of the women's profligate use of toilet paper."

"Did you ever work for Al Livingston?" asked McCalla, changing the subject.

"I worked for Al," said Lingo. "The whole time I did he took one week-long trip—drove all the way out to West Texas—and did one story on the little oak trees at Monahan State Park. That was it."

McCalla winced. "Al was a terrific writer. He worked for me in Huntsville. But a travel writer has to travel."

Livingston, a quiet, introspective young man, was something of a Goren on poker. He wrote an excellent, best-selling novel about a poker player. He'd written stories for *LIFE* on the game big-time poker players preferred (Tennessee Hold Me Darling) and stories on how to hold up a high-stakes poker game (with a sawed-off shotgun). Just the writer *Southern Living* needed at the time, being the biggest magazine gamble going.

"I know he was just sitting there with his feet up on the desk, reading books, 'doing research,' " said Karen.

"I remember he said he would never marry a woman who read Shelley," said Logue. "I met his wife recently, a very bright woman; I bet she doesn't read Shelley. Al lives somewhere down in Florida. But he did one good thing for the cause. He really improved our poker games. *In seven-card, high-low poker, if you don't improve your hand with the fourth card, fold it. In high-low poker, always go low. You might draw out and win either way.* Ah, the game according to Livingston."

"Yeah, after Al left, Logue and I had our own poker tables at the advertising sales meetings," said McCalla. "I'd close down Chicago. And he'd close down New York. But I had to let Al go."

And at Logue's suggestion, he hired a lively Texan with the improbable name Caleb Pirtle. Caleb deserves his own moment on the stage, and in due course, he'll have it.

"I lucked out and got assigned to Caleb," said Lingo. "Bill Hardman promoted 'Springtime in Tallahassee' [Florida] to a group of travel writers. Caleb asked me if I wanted to go. 'Yeah, I'd love to go.' It was my first trip, myself and five men. They wouldn't let me pay for anything. I hadn't been given a travel advance anyway. When I got back Gary called me in his office and said, 'Karen, you are going to ruin it for the rest of us. You can't go traveling for a week on *nine dollars*.' He sat me down and 'adjusted' my expense account. I mean I got back twenty-five dollars. Ever since that time, I've been very careful to pay my share when I am on trips."

Lingo finally was freed from her filing and typing duties and became a full-time travel writer when Pirtle hired as his editorial assistant Judy Richardson, known as "J.J." Judy and Barbara Pettway (now McCalla) became inseparable buddies, even appearing together on the cover of *Ink Pot Farmer*, which had never before sported such a combination of brains and sex appeal.

"I'd been so busy, I hadn't had a chance to file anything," remembered Lingo. "We had a stack of folders higher than my head. They *fell* on J.J., her first day, covered her up. She was not hurt, but was very upset." Ah, those were the days.

During 1968, the magazine would lurch forward and fall back a notch, but was gaining ground, certainly in design. Travel and Homes, with McCalla lending a direct hand in Homes, made progress, but Gardening was essentially a disaster, compounded by astonishingly inelegant flower arrangements. Taylor Lewis continued to set a new standard in food photography. He even took an acceptable golf photograph on Hilton Head Island that made the January cover for Logue's story "The Golf Coast." Leave it to Logue to assign himself the arduous job of playing the best golf courses on the South's Atlantic coast.

The South was truly beginning to boom, and nowhere more obviously than on Hilton Head, with Charlie Fraser's Sea Pines Plantation about to assert itself as one of the great family and resort communities in America. When McCalla first stepped on the island, it had the Plantation and less than one hundred homes and condominiums. When Logue did the January golf story, Harbortown was a round hole in the earth, a long way from the trendy shops and restaurants and world class golf course and yachts that routinely anchor in the harbor today. Hilton Head now has a population of over forty thousand and a multitude of golf course communities. Its growth and affluence have almost directly paralleled *Southern Living*'s.

Back to that golf story. Logue was playing the great Seaside nine of the Sea Island Course (which is actually on St. Simons), when he caught up with a gentleman from Connecticut, a very nice man, very trim, about fifty, we'll call Mr. Samford. They enjoyed each other's company and agreed to meet for breakfast. When Samford was late for breakfast, Logue inquired at The Cloisters' front desk. The clerk, in a very quiet voice, said, "I'm sorry to tell you, Mr. Samford died in the night." Logue said, "It confirmed my lifelong belief that whatever it is you are going to do in this world, you better get on with it—if it's publish a magazine or go to Scotland or write a novel."

For February of 1968, Taylor Lewis applied his considerable skills to an oyster roast on Longboat Key near Sarasota to good effect, but the cover ran dark. There were also appealing black-and-white photographs of Williamsburg craftsmen, and a "decent home," and a knowledgeable look at the Everglades by talented free-lancer Mike Frome, an early environmental activist. But then followed a godawful flower arrangement. And the food section fell apart with no photography.

So went the year, up and down. A pretty good azalea cover for March, though the hems of the skirts on the young women were too long, about a year out of date. Lewis took a great restaurant shot of Perdita's of Charleston that also set a standard for shooting restaurants for years to come. Taylor Lewis made his mark on *Southern Living* with his powerful photography, and he loved to devil Lena Sturges, both remarkable achievements.

McCalla and Logue waded through flooded downtown San Antonio to help Barrera shoot maybe the best cover yet for the young magazine. The subject was a 1,440-square-foot mosaic by celebrated artist Carlos Merida of Guatemala. It occupied the main entrance to the exhibit hall of San Antonio's HemisFair of 1968. At the time the photograph was taken, in 1967, everything else in the future World's Fair grounds was underwater.

Lewis struck with a lovely shot, "Au Fromage," that lifted cheese to an art form. And then there was a "Create Your Own Easter Corsage" that would have made the pope blush.

In May even McCalla enjoyed the story on "Jazz, New Orleans Style," being a great friend of jazz pianist Ronnie Kole. "All it needed was more color," McCalla said. No mention of how long Logue's story ran. Lena Sturges did herself proud with a barbecue story.

So it went. "We would catch the arts and crafts of the Southern Highlands fine," said McCalla, "but we had nothing but trouble with the black-and-white food shots. More progress in Travel, but the garden section was awful. We were struggling to find our direction with the homes section."

To distort a line from a broadway musical: Some things were about right, but the damn thing didn't come out right. McCalla and Logue finally agreed: the magazine had gone about as far as it could go without a firm editorial direction and a more disciplined system. Not to mention without an infusion of talent.

Bill Capps, who will bounce into this narrative shortly, took over from J. L. Rogers in 1968 as circulation director for *Southern Living* and ran it for the next twenty years. Capps made available to this book circulation figures for the magazine in its early years. Only in 1968 did the circulation effort suffer a promotion deficit in selling *Southern Living*. The loss that year was $121,620. It represented the difference in the amount of money spent in recruiting subscribers as opposed to how much the subscribers paid. It did not include the high cost of creating and printing and distributing the magazine.

Capps always said he could sell *Southern Living* the first year, but once the subscriber had read it the magazine had to sell itself. Readers were unimpressed by what they read in 1968. And the trend was *downward*. In 1966, circulation's promotion profit was $71,995. In 1967, it was $18,000. And by 1968 came the big loss.

All during the first two weeks of July, McCalla and Logue talked about what had to be done editorially if the magazine was to survive, oftentimes taking the discussion into the night over a favored bar. Even good bourbon couldn't drown the magazine's obvious editorial problems.

Remember the scene in the great movie about the life of Pancho Villa,

Viva Zapata—when the bandit is poised with his wire cutters over the telegraph line, and to cut it means revolution, and Marlon Brando says: "Cut it!" In the last week of July, 1968, McCalla and Logue decided to cut the telegraph line. They determined to write a "White Paper" to Publisher Emory Cunningham, telling him precisely what had to be done if *Southern Living* was to survive, not to mention realize its potential.

The decision was not made out of any disloyalty to Dr. O. B. Copeland. He had held things together through chaotic times. He was a man of great character. But although he was no longer under the thumb of Dr. Alexander Nunn, who had resigned over a year before and had been gone since the previous November, Cope had offered no explicit new direction for *Southern Living*. Nor had Cunningham implemented one, though he had considered and was pursuing the idea of bringing in an editor from New York. Hang on, this story will get to that.

Southern Living was going into its fourth year of publication. The company did not have an inexhaustible supply of money to fuel it. Circulation's promotion income was in the middle of a three-year downtrend and was currently suffering its only loss and that a significant one. The advertising world was not famous for its patience; only a brilliant ad staff had been able to counter the magazine's homely and confusing start.

The *idea* of creating the South's own magazine had been so powerful that it had sustained the enterprise. But the public's patience was running thin. It was now necessary for the magazine to stand on its own merit—if it could.

After McCalla and Logue had discussed their thoughts in the sober light of day and into the less sober night, Logue knocked out a rough, rough draft of ten major recommendations for the direction of the magazine. The old, thin original sheet of memo paper still exists, with all the hand edits. It needed much work to become an official recommendation to Publisher Emory Cunningham, who was about to be named president of the company.

McCalla and Logue agreed to stay in the office that night, late in July, 1968, until the White Paper was done. And they would leave it for Cunningham, consequences be damned. Carey Hinds was a willing accomplice.

"Oh, I knew it was insurrection," said Hinds, "but I didn't feel scared. I thought, 'Here is something to be involved in. Something that can make a real difference.' There was no reticence on my part. I was really happy to be included. My conversation with Dr. Copeland about my salary situation probably heightened my enthusiasm."

The three of them worked through several drafts of their recommendations, two of which have survived. McCalla and Logue are not dead sure which was the final draft. Hinds sat at the typewriter, McCalla stood on her left, and Logue on her right. McCalla, working off Logue's original draft, formulated each recommendation aloud. Logue translated it into spoken sentences. And Hinds typed it onto the page, often recommending changes which were adopted.

They didn't finish until 11 P.M. The document was four pages long with a cover letter, of which none of them kept a copy. The letter strongly recommended that an editor be placed in charge of *Southern Living* who could make quick, hard decisions, and who was capable of executing their enclosed recommendations. They expressed no preference as to whether the editor came from inside or outside of the company; either choice was acceptable.

Here is an abbreviated summary of their recommendations:

AUDIENCE: *Southern Living* will be aimed at the young, affluent, urban families of the South.

PURPOSE: The magazine will illustrate those aspects of living which are uniquely Southern.

CONTENT: Four basic categories will constitute *Southern Living*'s editorial content: food, travel, gardening and landscaping, and homes.

QUALIFICATION: as defined, *Southern Living* will be "the *Sunset* magazine of the South," with these modifications.

a. Extensive use of color photography to capitalize on the South's scenic beauty, and to brighten the magazine.

b. A general story, not confined to the four basic categories, will be carried from time to time. Such a story would have to be so uniquely Southern that the most obvious magazine to publish it would be *Southern Living*.

CONTEXT: Major emphasis will be placed upon travel and its related activities . . . capitalizing on the South's great variety of scenic attractions, historical landmarks, mountains, lakes, rivers, thousands of miles of ocean beaches . . . and its temperate climate . . . to make it the playground of eastern America. Travel . . . will also encompass related articles . . . emphasizing the where, when, how and who of . . . hiking, camping, fishing, boating, skiing, etc.

FOODS: Each issue will carry a featured article on foods, added emphasis will be placed on entertaining and complete menus for specific occasions will be introduced. We will continue to print the well-received Southern reader recipes which have formed the core of the foods section. When warranted, unique restaurants will be included, in conjunction with major travel articles.

HOMES: There will be one major homes article each month. In at least six issues each year complete coverage will be given to a unique Southern home . . . traditional or modern. In the other months, the major homes article will be devoted to a specific element of a home . . . decks, kitchens, fireplaces, etc. Short items of a practical nature will show how Southerners have creatively solved problems and increased the convenience and comfort of their homes. Remodeling will also be treated.

GARDENING AND LANDSCAPING: The Garden Calendar and Letters to Garden Editors will be continued. Whenever possible, we will coordinate landscaping with homes and entertaining for a major, featured article. Occasionally, original floral designs will be created . . . to show our readers how to use native Southern plant materials decoratively. All articles will continue to stress the practical, how-to-do-it aspect of gardening and landscaping.

GENERAL CATEGORY: These stories must be unique to the South. They must involve the reader to the extent she is able to actively participate in what is discussed, or be a spectator to it, such as "How to Watch the Masters," facts and figures for suburbanites who would like to be horseowners; or a personality story about the man who is carving Stone Mountain.

These stories will not deal with civic problems, socio-economic issues, or politics. Further, there will be no salutes to cities or states, or similar survey-type articles which interest only a limited number of people. Individual aspects of cities which fall naturally into the four basic categories of the magazine will be treated in those categories. Truly unique communities, such as Key West, Fairhope, Alabama, Gatlinburg, Tennessee, Jefferson and Presidio, Texas may be dealt with in travel articles.

It will be *imperative* that each article considered under this category be weighed carefully and judged particularly for its adherence to the basic philosophy of *Southern Living* as expressed in the editorial concept.

COVERS: The cover, in its visual impact, will say *Southern Living*. Whenever possible, the cover photograph will be drawn from the main, featured article for the month. All covers will be a single picture, full bleed. Cover subjects . . . should be weighted in this manner in a 12-month schedule: Travel 4, Foods 3, Homes 3, Gardening and Landscaping 1.

PHOTOGRAPHY: There is no better way to portray the essence of *Southern Living* to readers and advertisers than through imaginative photography. Good, functional photographs will illustrate practical, how-to articles. A more selective use of color photography can give *Southern Living* a great dimension of vitality.

That was it. No more problem teenage drivers, no more beehive hairdos, no more foot jewelry, no more fashions, no more education solutions, no more sermons. The magazine would publish what it understood: travel, food, homes, and gardens, and interesting Southern people doing creative things.

In future years, when editors with specific talents joined the magazine staff, certain editorial categories were broadened. Philip Morris would create powerful and influential stories on how certain small towns and historic neighborhoods in cities saved or restored their essential character. The magazine would grow to include travel sections to Mexico and to the Caribbean and even to Europe. But McCalla's greatest contribution as the editor would be to see that the magazine stayed true to its mission, to interpret the good life in the American South.

But first Emory Cunningham had to buy into the premise.

Immediately upon leaving the White Paper for Emory, McCalla left for Biloxi, Mississippi, to be a judge in a beauty contest. "Somebody had to sacrifice," said Logue.

On August 3, the phone rang in the old building at 821 North 19th Street. McCalla had suffered a heart attack in the shower. And was in the hospital in Biloxi. He was still a very young man at thirty-seven. There was an odd tradition of the men in his family of having a heart attack early and then living up into their eighties.

Logue drove down to Biloxi to pick up McCalla's wife and kids and an antique chair she had bought. McCalla was lying up in the hospital bed growing a beard. "My God, he grew a beard like a black bear," said

Logue. "I thought Indians didn't have to shave." (The aspect of the bearded McCalla can be seen in a photograph in the first illustrations section). Logue told McCalla, "If I had known the women in this contest were so beautiful they would give a man a heart attack, I would have rolled you for the job."

In those days, heart attacks put you out for three months. McCalla wouldn't return to work until November. "You had it easy," said Logue to McCalla, "all you had was a heart attack. I was down there at the office dying. If you think things were already slow to happen at the magazine, with you out we couldn't make a decision if our pants were on fire."

McCalla had been named managing editor by the beginning of 1968, when Logue was named Travel and Features Editor. Gary had actually been responsible for getting out the magazine since the infamous July issue of 1967. He didn't have the authority to hire and fire a staff, or to decide what subjects went into the magazine—but he pulled the damn thing together and got it into print, everything from selecting the well lead to the cover photograph. His sudden absence left a frightful power vacuum. Decisions were harder to come by than a pay raise.

But The Progressive Farmer Company that August made one huge decision. It named Emory Cunningham president, succeeding Eugene Butler, who was to remain chairman and keep his editorial office in Dallas until his death. The destiny of the company was now in Emory's hands. Cunningham, forty-seven years old, became only the third president in the company's history.

"I had this advantage, that they let me run it almost as if it were my own company," said Emory. He had one large opportunity/problem on his mind: *Southern Living*. He would rise or fall on the success or failure of that magazine. And he was obviously unsure of what steps to take to reinvent the editorial package.

But with McCalla out recovering from his heart attack, Emory had time to think before responding to his and Logue's long memorandum. Even to hire an established, outside editor to run the show.

In the past year, *Southern Living* had gotten out from under the thumb of the retired Dr. Nunn. It had been a long time since he approved the color that went into the magazine. But suddenly with McCalla out, and with a new company president who felt himself under the gun to improve the magazine, every editorial move at *Southern Living* was a decision by committee.

The All-South Football section came off without a hitch (with Logue's old school, Auburn, "miraculously" appearing on the September cover). There was a reasonably beautiful photographic interpretation of "Five Faces of October," with Logue slipping in a favored, haunting quotation from Thomas Wolfe's *Of Time and the River*: "Now October has come again which in our land is different from October in other lands. The ripe, the golden month has come again, and in Virginia the chinkapins are falling. Frost sharps the middle music of the seasons, and all things living on the earth turn home again."

"McCalla, you get your anatomy back to work," advised Logue, who was scrambling in all directions like a one-armed short order cook. He remembered one day when he and photographer Gerald Crawford flew to Dallas, Texas. They started with a daylight interview with Dallas Cowboy quarterback Don Meredith. Question was, why had the nine leading quarterbacks in the National Football League grown up and played their college ball in the South, while fourteen in all came from the South? Meredith cited the good weather to pass in and the fact he, like many Southern boys, had been playing quarterback "since the second grade."

Logue and Crawford skipped lunch and toured the Amon Carter Museum of Western Art in Fort Worth. They crammed a subject that deserved a couple of days into a couple of hours. Some years later Logue, as editor-in-chief of Oxmoor House, was to publish a stunning book, *Masterworks of American Photography*, on the museum's photographic collection, one of the finest in existence.

Crawford and Logue beat it out of Fort Worth to the tiny Rockwall Municipal Airport. They hooked up with the North Dallas Glider Club, and despite twenty-five-mile-an-hour winds went up with Dr. John Smale, an Englishman, who said, comfortingly: "Soaring is jolly good sport. . . . If you don't have an engine, there's no chance of losing it."

Crawford had himself tied into the tow plane and the door taken off that side so he could lean out and shoot Logue's glider unimpeded. Crawford was an otherwise sane young man. His long, fine hair was blown into such knots that he finally had to give up on combing it and cut it.

Logue and he burned rubber on the rental car to meet their flight from old Love Field in Dallas. "Stop!" shouted Logue, before they cleared the Rockwall residential area. Crawford jumped out, picked up a camera, and shot an espalier magnolia growing against the side of a house that later ran in the garden section. They made their plane back to Birmingham with a good three minutes to spare. All three stories from that day's trip ran in the fall and winter as major features. It was a fun, hectic time—so long as you didn't think about what was and was not happening back on North 19th Street.

Logue's one favorite memory of those desperate months was of a cover pick for the November issue. He had written a story on the golf courses along the Gulf Coast. "McCalla was not the only one making sacrifices," said Logue. Gerald Crawford had gone along and shot some excellent stuff, particularly on the two courses of the Grand Hotel on Mobile Bay. Nobody could make a decision of what photograph to put on the November cover.

For the one time in the history of *Southern Living*, the president, Emory Cunningham himself, sat in on the cover selection, as did Big John McKinney in his last days as *Progressive Farmer*'s chief photographer. Emory asked McKinney his opinion of a particular image that was projected on the screen. Big John stood and talked five minutes—while the film sizzled in the carousel; he talked up one side of that photograph and down the other, and God himself couldn't have puzzled out if he was for it or against it. Logue, smothering his laughter, had more tears in his eyes than anytime since he'd watched the last scene of *Doctor Zhivago*.

But Logue was in no way a hero of that cover selection. He hunkered down in the dark and kept his mouth shut, which few who know him would readily believe. "I was more interested in the question of who would ultimately run the magazine," said Logue. "Better silence than to muddy that consideration over a single cover." Arguments of hilarious lunacy flew around the viewing room. Crawford's fine shot through a flowering fruit tree to a green on the Grand Hotel course bit the dust. And Copeland and Cunningham and McKinney and Curl and Crawford and Lancaster and the strangely silent Logue went back into the files and chose a cover photograph taken by Taylor Lewis on, for God's sake, *Hilton Head Island*, which is one hell of a long way from the Gulf Coast of the South. This shot chosen for the November cover came from the discard pile from which a very similar cover had been chosen only ten months before for the January issue.

"Get well, McCalla, we are losing ground," telephoned Logue. The two of them still make merry over the idea of a Gulf Coast cover from the Atlantic Ocean. The cover choice was a prime example of why presidents should preside and editors should edit. It never happened again.

Before McCalla came back to work full-time, he stopped by the office one day in October to pick up his mail. He walked into the building like Admiral Richard Byrd returning from the North Pole, only he smiled behind a beard that might have grown on a Bolshevik general. All the women who were brave enough to stand that close to the beard hugged him, including Dixie Snell, who let out a scream of disapproval at the sight of him.

McCalla met Emory in the hall. Cunningham did not comment on his beard. It was like not commenting on an electrical fire which had suddenly broken out in the building. "Did you get our memo?" asked McCalla. Emory indicated that he had, that he was "thinking about it." No more, no less.

Come November, Logue picked up McCalla at his house and drove him back to work, as he was to do for the next couple of years. "I wanted to make damn sure he was there to take the heat," said Logue. Color picks went back to their old, rowdy familiarity, chaired by McCalla: "Well, damn, what else you got?"

9

Time for a Change

Logue said to Cunningham, "The magazine was still struggling in 1968. After you became president, why didn't you let us all go? Copeland, McCalla, Logue, all of us. And bring in a proven magazine editor and staff?"

Emory thought about that for a minute. "There was a lot of pressure on me at the time [to improve the magazine]. Well, I went to New York. I had a lot of appointments lined up with editors, and they almost sneered at me—the idea of getting off the beaten path and coming to Birmingham, Alabama, for a new magazine. When magazines were having so much trouble."

Cunningham continued, "The people I talked to were all Ivy League types. And I didn't like any of them. I didn't meet one that I wanted to hire. I'd heard so much about this—that I should get somebody in the business who knows how to do it. And I didn't know how to start out [finding somebody]. I didn't find one that I would even think about hiring. And they wouldn't think about coming to work for me. So it was a mutual thing, and I came back here. I knew I had to make a change."

In the winter of 1969, Cunningham had still not responded to the White Paper suggesting that *Southern Living* take on a new editor and become the *Sunset* magazine of the South, with certain modifications of color photography and more general features absolutely married to Southern people and to the Southern experience. In point of fact, he never did respond to it, except by the ultimate action of hiring Gary McCalla as editor. And that did not come about readily.

First, there was the matter of Dr. O. B. Copeland. "I was worried about Cope, because I thought the world of him," said Emory. "I also knew all the circumstances he had worked under. There was Alec Nunn and John McKinney after him, and he's the editor, and I was after him, and he didn't know what to do."

But Dr. Nunn had been gone over a year, and Emory was now in complete charge of the company and the magazine.

"I'll never forget," said Emory, "O. B. called me one day about this time [winter of 1968–69]. And he wanted to go to lunch. And we went down to La Paree, and he was sort of nervous, and he had this little card, a three-by-five card. He said, 'Emory, I may not—I haven't done a very good job as the editor of *Southern Living*. But one thing I have left is a lot of pride.' He said, 'I've always had a lot of pride. I guess coming from a poor family over in Georgia and we had pride and I still do.'

"He went over the points on this three-by-five card," said Emory, "and it was very unusual to go to lunch with someone who had what he wanted to say outlined that way. He said some other things, and he said, 'I want to offer my resignation from the company.' "

Cunningham said, "I had already thought Cope was the ideal person to play the role as an assistant to me. I said, 'You disappoint me, because I wanted to tell you that I want you to be my assistant.' And I had a pretty hard time during this lunch getting him to come back, but at the end of the lunch, he said, 'All right, I'll do it, and I'll never mention this again.' And he's never mentioned it again."

Dr. O. B. Copeland was, and is, a very classy man, with the sort of integrity that has allowed Southern Progress to endure as a company since 1886.

"So, how did you have the insight, the nerve to name Gary McCalla editor?" asked Logue. "I mean, I was with him every day. I understood his knowledge of photography, of graphics, his ability to get things done. You weren't there. How did you know that? I mean, you couldn't look at McCalla and know how bright he was," said Logue, laughing.

"I wasn't as distant [from the editorial staff] as you might think," said Cunningham. "Later on, I kept my distance, but at that time I was pretty close. I knew what was going on. I never told about this: I liked Carey

Hinds. I knew her well and her husband was a good friend. I wanted to talk to somebody back there who knew what was going on, who would keep it confidential, so I wouldn't get myself in a lot of trouble.

"I showed her a number of things in the magazine that I felt were good, on the right track," said Emory. "For instance, the pecan pie photograph by Taylor Lewis, and I asked Carey, 'Who was responsible for that?' And each time, she said, 'McCalla.' And it helped me make up my mind. I thought you'd like to know that."

McCalla nodded.

"And then Alec Nunn," said Emory, "he was heart-broken, and mad at me, when I took over the magazine, and I asked him about Gary. He said, 'Emory, I can tell you one thing, he has more stamina, more mental and physical stamina, than anybody else back there, and that includes you at your age. He's got more than any of us, and that's an important part of the job, just being able to take it.' I don't remember Alec's final judgment, but he must have thought it would work, I don't know. But I remember that conversation with him, and I decided to go ahead and do it."

McCalla and Logue, at that moment, across from Emory, both felt a certain empathy, not to go so far as say guilt, as regards the old man, Alexander Nunn. He was the captive of another century. But he was a stand-up guy. Logue remembered that some years after *Southern Living* had hit its stride as a popular, highly profitable magazine, Dr. Nunn came by the building, stuck his head in Logue's office, and said hello. They talked a minute, and Logue asked, impishly, "Dr. Nunn, did you hold on to your Progressive Farmer stock?" And he laughed and said, "Yes, I did." "Good thinking," said Logue, and years later, at the moment of this conversation with Emory Cunningham, he was particularly glad the old man, long dead, had died rich.

Emory hadn't mentioned the White Paper to Carey Hinds when he quizzed her in 1969 about the magazine. Nor did he ever mention it to McCalla or Logue during their quarter century on the magazine. Hinds said that she remembered the conversation with Emory those many years ago.

"All the stockholders who cashed in their rich chips when Southern Progress sold to Time, Inc., might tip their hats to Hinds, not to mention to you, McCalla, you old goat," said Logue.

McCalla denied nothing. "I believe this," he said. "After the memo we sent him, Emory knew I understood what *Sunset* magazine was doing, and how we could adapt it to the South. I think that's why he finally gave me the job. And Carey's endorsement didn't hurt." Logue agreed.

But Emory did not immediately give McCalla the job, even after he had made up his mind. He called Logue into his office and said, "Tell your buddy if he will shave off that beard, I'll let him run the magazine."

Logue stopped by McCalla's office. He said, "If you will stand nearer your razor tonight, I believe your career will be looking up."

McCalla shaved off everything except this gigantic mustache, which made him look for the world like the old radio comic Jerry Colonna. The laughter was so great that the mustache only lasted one day.

Cunningham called McCalla into his office. He offered him the job of editing the magazine, but he did not offer him the title of *editor*. "I'm going to leave you as managing editor," said Emory. The *Southern Living* mastheads in May and June actually listed no editor.

"I said, 'Wait a minute,' " remembered McCalla. " 'I'm going to replace Cope, and he's editor? And I'm going to be managing editor? You won't have done anything for me.' I debated with him. I said, 'I'm not going to do it without the title of editor.' Because if we'd faltered just a bit, he could have brought in somebody over me very quickly."

Emory finally conceded the argument. And in the July issue of the house magazine, *Ink Pot Farmer*, Gary McCalla, age thirty-eight, was announced as the new *Southern Living* editor. He and Emory and Eugene Butler appeared in one of the most solemn photographs ever struck, all looking as if their favorite dog had died. Emory was quoted as saying, "Gary McCalla and a talented team of editors working with him will continue to strengthen and expand the editorial format of the publication."

This "talented team" had just been reduced by one editor. That left five editors who actually wrote copy, covering sixteen states. And the Travel Editor and the Horticulture Editor and the Homes Editor would be gone within the year. These were volatile times.

Gary was first listed as editor of *Southern Living* in the July, 1969, issue. Typical of McCalla, his "Life at *Southern Living*" column, which was to carry his name for twenty-two years, did not mention his promotion, but only his conversation with Atlanta architect John Portman. He did submit to a photograph of himself and Portman, shot through a Gutmann sculpture. Good Lord, could he have been that young?

McCalla knew improvement had to come quickly. The magazine, with its thin and not very gifted staff, lived on the ragged edge of running out of even mediocre copy. McCalla came up with an ingenious idea for increasing the staff's capability by one-fifth without hiring another soul. Everybody could work every Saturday. Which they did for about eighteen Saturdays. Logue, who'd never had a Saturday off in ten years in the newspaper business, said McCalla's attitude reminded him of the motto in the Japanese prison camp in the movie *The Bridge on the River Kwai*: "Be happy in our work."

The idea was to move toward a seriously departmentalized magazine: Travel, Homes, Food, and Gardening, with features and people mixed in when worthy. Easier hoped for than achieved, with the magazine's weakness in Homes, Food, and Gardening and overall thinness of talent. To try and sharpen things a bit, McCalla ran the copy from Homes and Gardening through his typewriter, while Logue worked with Travel and features and tried to make nouns and verbs out of food, which his wife, Helen, still finds hilarious. Here's a man who once opened a can of Vienna sausage by himself.

To fill up the magazine, it was still necessary to use stories from freelance writers, which varied from the awkward to the awful to the occasionally very good. Atlantan Harold Martin's story on architect Portman proved absolutely excellent. Hub Mason of San Antonio wrote an insightful piece on Padre Island, but his photographs and the magazine's reproduction of them were ghastly. Walter Osborne, the rare combination of excellent writer and brilliant photographer, brought both skills to the page in translating the vanishing lives of skipjack fishermen on Chesapeake Bay. Osborne was a terrific guy, who lived in St. Michaels, Maryland. He'd been one of the original editors of *Newsweek*. You could see his photographs, mostly of horse racing, in the Philadelphia Fine Arts Museum. But he was a lousy tout for the Kentucky Derby.

In 1970, McCalla had been following the hoof prints of a thoroughbred, Dust Commander, who won the Bluegrass Stakes at Keeneland. Osborne, the great-grandson of Herman Melville, said, "Forget this Dust Commander." He was at the Derby and put McCalla's and Logue's bucks on another horse. Dust Commander with Mike Manganello aboard powered through the mud to win the race, paying about thirty-two dollars. McCalla showed great restraint. He did not contract for the assassination of a horse photographer. But he thought about it.

McCalla and Logue once joined Osborne on a visit to Mrs. Richard C. Dupont's horse farm on the Eastern Shore of Maryland to see the great thoroughbred Kelso. Osborne had published a book on Kelso. Mrs. Dupont showed them about the farm in an old station wagon running over with about twelve dogs. Her vet was examining the retired Kelso, first racehorse to win two million dollars. Kelso, unhappily, was a gelding. "They paid me three hundred dollars to take 'em out. They'd pay me three million if I could put 'em back," said the vet.

McCalla and Logue promoted a contract with Walter to produce for Oxmoor House a photographic book on the great Southeastern seaboard. And it would have been a beauty if Walter hadn't died, a victim of the small black cigars he loved to smoke.

Well, there was only one Walter Osborne. So McCalla determined early on that he would build *Southern Living* into a staff-produced magazine, the better to control its written and visual quality. He also determined that he would hire specialists—architects, landscape architects, food experts, horticulture experts—and blame any written inadequacy on Logue, who had replaced him as managing editor in September. Now all they had to do was find the experts.

They did make a bit of headway on headlines: "Broyles and Royal, Friends to the Death," a profile of the two great coaching rivals and best buddies from the Southwest Conference; "Confectionately Yours, for Christmas," Lena's big cake extravaganza; "Nancy Lee, Meet the Mountain," a photographic essay by Bruce Roberts of a young girl in the Blue Ridge Mountains. And with "Sister" Sharon Watkins ultimately taking over the copy desk, you couldn't find a typographical mistake with a microscope. Some literary type once said, "A poet can survive anything but a typographical error." Try a recipe. The slightest typo can create a catastrophe in one million kitchens. Much of the readers' great trust in *Southern Living* can be traced to its accuracy, its authenticity—in short, to its ever-vigilant copy desk.

McCalla and Logue flew to Menlo Park, California, to look over *Sunset* magazine to see what ideas they could lift. *Sunset* owner and President Bill Lane had approved the visit. If he could have imagined *Southern Living*'s success-to-come he might have said not only "No," but "Hell, no." McCalla had met *Sunset*'s editor, Proctor Mellquist, in Mexico, and he proved friendly enough.

After a couple of days, Logue and McCalla figured they had learned all they could effectively steal from the *Sunset* formula. They also had a great time crawling over the hills of San Francisco. "Damn, I'd hate to be driving on this double-decker freeway if they had an earthquake," said Logue, steering the rental car across the bay. He remembered some years later that queasy feeling when the freeway collapsed on itself in a major quake.

When they got back to Birmingham, after filling out his expense account (which ran higher than nine dollars), Logue knocked out a four-page, single-spaced account of their observations, including these:

1. *Sunset* was planning, editing, and producing the next four magazines at one time.

2. The *Editorial* Department placed the ads in the magazine (a luxury—and a responsibility—McCalla was never to have).

3. The *Sunset* advertising staff could contact only Mellquist on the editorial staff. (McCalla never imposed such a ban at *Southern Living*, and a tight but independent relationship between Editorial and Advertising has been one of *S.L.*'s greatest strengths over the years.)

4. The copy desk ruled inviolately over every story in *Sunset*, with total power to rewrite a story entirely or kill it, with no input from the editor who wrote it. "The copy desk creates a good bit of tension on the magazine," said Mellquist. (It also created a disembodied text without tone or voice. The text might have been a "one note" tape recording. McCalla and Logue agreed to encourage separate voices among editors who sang in the same key. And to capture in words the voices of Southerners in nearly every story they published. The copy desk would be critical in insuring accuracy and consistency.)

5. Mellquist himself wrote every *Sunset* headline. (And impotent headlines were one of the weaknesses of the magazine.)

6. *Sunset* maintained a complete workshop, and how-to-do-it projects were the strengths of the magazine.

7. Their test kitchens were to be envied; all of their recipes were actually kitchen-tested. (It would be years before this was true at *Southern Living*.)

8. *Sunset* fought to save the redwood forests and had much influence environmentally. But the magazine did it in a non-confrontational style. ("We should go and do likewise," thought McCalla and Logue.)

9. *Sunset* had no central filing system for photographs. (Neither did *S.L.* for a decade, a terrible oversight.)

10. *Sunset* had *one* staff photographer. (McCalla determined to eventually build the best photographic staff in consumer magazine publishing. And he did.)

11. *Sunset* books operated entirely independently of the magazine, with no collaboration between them. (A terrible mistake, which Oxmoor House was to duplicate for some years.)

The trip confirmed for McCalla and Logue their belief that the *Sunset* formula of travel, food, homes, and gardens was appropriate for *Southern Living*, but they were also convinced the South loved its quirky personalities and memorable voices, and that people going about productive lives must be central to the South's new magazine.

Early in 1968, Gerald Crawford had taken timeless photographs of the rugged Guadalupe Mountains in West Texas. But the photographs needed a text to make it into the February issue of 1969. Texas Travel Director Frank Hildebrand, whose friendship with *Southern Living* was critical to its success, put Logue on to his assistant with the peculiar name of Caleb Pirtle. Pirtle agreed to write the text for a modest fee. It couldn't carry his by-line, because he still worked for the state of Texas.

Pirtle described the Guadalupe guide Noel Kincaid: "He is a slender man, almost lanky. His voice is low, sanded perhaps by years of shouting against the winds whipping up the canyons. He seldom speaks, striding across the flatlands of Frijole Valley, watching the clouds over the mountains." Noel's son Jack Kincaid was also a guide in the Guadalupes.

But it was what Logue had to cut out of his story that made him tell McCalla, "If we ever have the chance to hire another travel writer around here, let's hire this Pirtle."

Here's the gist of what Pirtle wrote that didn't run in *Southern Living*, his unedited text being lost to time: Jack Kincaid guided into the Guadalupe Mountains Supreme Court Justice William O. Douglas, a man into his seventies, but as rough and ready as the mountains. The occasion was Douglas's honeymoon with his bride, a young thing, still in her twenties. The first few nights, the three of them would eat by the campfire, and Justice Douglas and his bride would repair to their tent, leaving Kincaid alone with the wind and the hobbled horses. About the fourth night out, the justice stayed behind to pour himself and Kincaid a stout drink, and gaze into the campfire and up into the star-flung heavens. Neither man spoke for a long time. And now Logue can remember Pirtle's written words:

"Mr. Kincaid," said the justice, "you haven't commented on my young bride. What do you make of her?" There was a long silence.

"Judge," said Kincaid, "I think you've done overstocked your pasture."

"How could you not hire a man who wrote that?" said Logue. McCalla agreed, and when he became editor the deed was done. Pirtle joined the staff in September and showed up on the magazine masthead in November, 1969.

Caleb Pirtle was a trip. He wore cowboy boots and a big cowboy hat, and when he put it in the overhead rack on an airplane he turned to everybody in the aisle and said, "Don't nobody put nothin' on the hat." They didn't. He also affected flowery, long-sleeved, open-collar shirts, sometimes with lace around the cuffs, like the great Texas sportswriter Blackie Sherrod. Pirtle played a little guitar, and if you didn't watch him, he'd sing, badly—maybe the song he wrote about the cowboy's senorita: "My girl lives south of the border / But last night she came across." Vintage Pirtle.

It wasn't long before he knew everybody, not just in his native Texas, but everybody that had a body temperature in the travel business.

There is such a thing as being too popular within the travel industry. The good folks at Six Flags Over Texas so admired the work of Pirtle and Crawford that they hired them "on the side" to write and photograph a promotion brochure for the theme park. McCalla preferred to have an unwritten understanding that staff members would not participate in free-lance work, knowing full well over the years that many of them did it through the back door. Out of sight, out of mind. Wouldn't you know the Six Flags people sent the considerable check, not to Pirtle and Crawford, but to The Progressive Farmer's *chief financial officer, Vernon Owens,* who, like Queen Victoria, was not amused? It would have been less embarrassing if they had sent it to the Internal Revenue Service. McCalla had to drop the hammer on the boys and have them send back the check.

If you didn't watch him, Pirtle would not only sing but also speak. Or he'd give "The Speech," as Jerry Flemmons called it. Flemmons, who died in late 1999 of lung cancer, had long been the Travel Editor for the *Fort Worth Star-Telegram*, and long been the best in the business. "We've been listening to Caleb give that speech for twenty-five years," Flemmons said to McCalla as they sat in a big meeting of travel folks, listening to it again. Pirtle's best move was to reach in his pocket and grab a fistful of dimes and fling them into the crowd. That got their attention, if it didn't knock out an eye. And he always ended "The Speech" by turning and walking off the stage and out of the building.

"My God, following Pirtle on *Southern Living* was like following Will Rogers," said Les Thomas, another Texan you will meet. "The man knew everybody."

"We did have some characters," said Dixie Snell, of the early magazine staff. "I got along with Caleb. He and I were pals. My daughters made me pierce my ears. Caleb said if I would do it, he would get me a pair of gold earrings, and he did. Caleb was a good fellow."

When he'd come back from Mardi Gras in New Orleans, or from the State Fair of Texas, or from Old Mexico or Haiti, Pirtle would bring all manner of trinkets to the editorial assistants trapped in the office: beads, chili powders, voodoo dolls, glass bracelets. It was like Marco Polo unpacking his pack.

Not that he couldn't get a bit testy. When the company first moved into its new building on Shades Creek Parkway, the administration went a tad overboard in policing the tidiness of each office. Photographs of your family were not considered acceptable on your desk. And you were supposed to keep in your desk only items related to your work, or you might be left a note by a midnight spy: "These items are not appropriate."

After such a note, Pirtle bought a foot-long rattrap, strong enough to catch a boa constrictor, and baited it with his own note: "Keep your ———— hands out of my desk." Don't know if the trap did the job, but gradually the company fell back into its employee-friendly ways, and Caleb's desk once again looked like the wreck of the *Hesperus*.

Pirtle was also a popular writer, though he was something of a Johnny-one-note, with a folksy, spoken, troubadour sort of style. Here's Caleb's introduction to "The Rich, Sad Song of Nashville":

> Porter, sing a sad song. That's what you do best.
> Sing about a lonely and frightened man who awaits a guard and

sad old padre . . . a man who waits to walk at daybreak and dreams, once again, about the green, green grass of home.

Sing of the girl who was crying when you met her, but cries harder today. And tell us not to blame her because life turned her that way.

Sing of the day Walter Browning died in the Carroll County accident. And don't forget the matchbox circled by a rubber band that held the golden wedding ring from Walter's hand.

Remember the cold hard facts of life and the forgotten dreams of Skid Row Joe.

Porter, sing a sad song. That's what you do best.

That's Pirtle. Of course the singer was Porter Wagoner in 1971, the year he and Dolly Parton were named country music's singing duo of the year. Caleb talked his way onto Dolly's bus and interviewed her while she was sitting on her bed.

Southern Living's lively travel pages, even before Pirtle, did not go unnoticed in the industry. The magazine won the DATO Award in 1969 for its travel editorial, competing against all consumer magazines in America. And then with Pirtle as Travel Editor and Karen Lingo as his assistant won it again in 1971. DATO discontinued the award in future years, or *Southern Living* might have kept right on winning it.

In addition to its "Travel South" package in 1971, the magazine was cited by DATO for its editorial support of the Bankhead National Forest wilderness proposal in Alabama, for its support of the preservation of the Big Thicket in East Texas, for helping save seven endangered historic homes in Lexington, Kentucky, for speaking out against the pollution of Sanibel-Captiva Islands in Florida, for the magazine's salute to San Antonio for the protection of its scenic downtown river, and for its salute to Kentucky for the protection of its Land Between the Lakes.

Southern Living, from the beginning, has been a strong but reasonable "voice in the wilderness," not to stop thoughtful development but to help protect what is best about the South's unique landscape, both in the wild and in urban and neighborhood settings. The magazine has always approached controversial subjects from the aspect of a solution; therefore its voice has been listened to by those with the power to make a difference.

If Caleb Pirtle was not so versatile as a writer, he was surely indefatigable. When he joined the magazine, he hit the typewriter with all eight fingers and both thumbs and was soon filling up two hundred columns a year in *Southern Living*. Pirtle also found time to collaborate with Crawford on a visual book for Oxmoor House on Callaway Gardens, Georgia, and he wrote the text for Oxmoor's art book with ten living cowboy artists, titled *XIT: The American Cowboy*.

Gerald Crawford's images appeared so often in the magazine that in April, 1975, a package addressed simply: *Crawford, USA* was delivered to him personally by one Newt Goodwin of the Birmingham Post Office.

Another truism was that two hundred columns a year was too much of the same note in the same but maturing magazine. *Southern Living* by 1977 had a variety of talented voices, all competing for space in the magazine.

For whatever reason, Pirtle and Crawford grew restless in their work at *Southern Living*. Without discussing their discontent with the magazine formula with McCalla, they set about researching and photographing a story on the Smoky Mountains—in a "new" interpretation. McCalla, a cold cup of coffee in hand, as was his habit, got with Pirtle and Crawford to review their photographs of the mountains in all their fall glory. Up on the wall went the one photograph of a blind mountain beekeeper, at least eighty years old. That was it.

"Where's the damn mountains?" McCalla thundered.

"The old man is it. He's the lead to our story. Not the mountains," said Pirtle, with a shy assist from Crawford.

"The hell he is," said McCalla.

Speaking today, McCalla says, "It was an okay picture of the old man. We could have used him in a tight shot. But we needed fall color in the mountains for the October issue. They were looking for an 'artsy' interpretation. I said it was baloney. I sent 'em back to the mountains."

McCalla agrees the failed stand by Pirtle and Crawford was symptomatic of their—especially's Pirtle's—burnout in the job. They used McCalla's volatile response to their old blind man as evidence that he was turning his back on the rustic folksy ways of the South.

Pirtle and Crawford that year quit the magazine with a rather astonishing letter of resignation:

Dear Mr. McCalla:

Gerald Crawford, for more than 11 years, and Caleb Pirtle, for more than 7 years, have been basically responsible for the travel coverage in *Southern Living* magazine. During that time, they—

with the talented assistance of their co-workers—have produced a product that is one of the nation's most respected domestic travel magazines. In addition, it now ranks second in the nation in resort and travel advertising, a tribute to both the salesmen and the product they have to sell. Moreover, *Southern Living* has won awards from Discover America three times, as well as awards from the Southern Travel Directors Council, Arkansas, Texas, South Carolina, and Virginia.

Now, however, it has been decided outside the travel department that the magazine's travel concept and philosophy be changed. In the past we tried to provide entertainment, as well as service. Now, we are told, the section is to be nothing more than a hard-core service section, providing that information which is available on most of your brochures.

That is a philosophy we cannot accept. The South is a land that is proud of her people, her legends, her rural festivals, her story telling ability. That is the Southern mystique. To turn our back on that is to turn our back on the South.

As a result, Crawford and Pirtle submit their resignation.

They added that because of their love of the magazine they would work through March to meet the deadlines for the large spring issues.

Emory Cunningham took it on himself to reply to the letter, obviously constructed by Pirtle:

Dear Gerald and Caleb:

In a faculty convocation address Chancellor McGehee quoted Mark Twain,

In the space of one hundred and seventy-six years the Lower Mississippi has shortened itself two hundred and forty-two miles. That is an average of a trifle over one mile and a third per year. Therefore, any calm person, who is not blind or idiotic, can see that in the old Oolitic Silurian Period, just a million years ago next November, the Lower Mississippi River was upward of one million three hundred thousand miles long, and stuck out over the Gulf of Mexico like a fishing rod. And by the same token any person can see that seven hundred and forty-two years from now, the Lower Mississippi will be only a mile and three-quarters long, and Cairo and New Orleans will have joined their streets together. . . . There

*is something fascinating about science. One gets such wholesale re-
turns of conjecture out of such a trifling investment of fact.*

The . . . statements from your letter to Gary are *even* greater returns of conjecture from *no* investment of fact.

. . . Of course, no such change of policy has been or will be
made, and I sincerely request that you refrain from making such
derogatory statements about *Southern Living* and its leadership. To
state or imply that *Southern Living* will no longer publish articles
about Southern people, rural festivals, and the Southern mystique
is an absurdity and needs to be called just that.

If you say we aren't perfect, make mistakes—some very bad
ones—I readily agree. But you surely know the magazine has not
changed policy in such a way that its writers will have to "turn
their backs on the South."

Both of you should be ashamed for saying it. If you can't stand
the heat, say so and leave with your heads up and your self respect
intact.

Sincerely Yours,

Emory Cunningham

McCalla offered no written response to the prodigal sons, true to his
philosophy: "They can't hang you for what you don't write down."

"So they quit over a blind beekeeper?" said Logue, "I don't think so.
I believe Pirtle had had it, and was just looking for an exit line to get back
to Texas. And took Crawford with him as his alter ego. I didn't want Pirtle to quit like that. But I *hated* to see Crawford leave. I knew he was
making a mistake. And I tried to talk him out of it." As did McCalla and
even Cunningham.

"Yeah," said McCalla. "Pirtle had connections. He could make it
back in Texas. Crawford made a big mistake. He tried to come back two
or three times in later years, but I'd seen his stuff. I didn't think he'd
grown as a photographer, and we'd grown as a magazine. But he's a good
photographer and a good guy."

Crawford came a long way, from putting the flag up on top of the old
building to chief photographer of the most successful monthly magazine
in America. And he took down his own flag over a blind beekeeper. Still,
he left his mark on the magazine, and so did Pirtle, to be fair. Both of
them missed the true glory years of *Southern Living* in the eighties and
nineties. Pirtle wrote a conciliatory note to McCalla before he left, but
he's never stepped back inside the *Southern Living* building.

10

Recipes for Success

One of the forces which drove *Southern Living* to its astonishing success slipped into the old building on North 19th Street in 1970, unrecruited and unknown. Her name at the time was Jean Wickstrom. She's long been married, and her name is now Jean Liles. To avoid confusion, that's the name this book will use.

Liles is tiny, about a perfect size four. She seems not to have changed at all in thirty years, not in her size, not in her vital appearance, certainly not in her unsinkable enthusiasm for even the most abhorrent assignment.

In 1970, Jean had left an unhappy marriage and moved to Birmingham to teach school. But teaching jobs were scarce, and she signed up with the Kelly Girl service for part-time work. "I was home vacuuming in the middle of the day, and the woman from Kelly Girl called," said Liles. "She said, 'I hate to call you on such short notice, but the folks at *Progressive Farmer* have a project that's got to get in the mail by tonight.' I said, 'I can unplug this vacuum cleaner in no time. Give me a few minutes to spiff up, and I'll be out the door.' I got in my little green 1966 Karmann Ghia, which I still have, and went looking for the address on North 19th Street.

"It was pretty depressing, that old building," said the ever-cheerful Liles, who could find favor with a volcanic eruption, "and it was a mess. It was half up and half torn down."

It hasn't been mentioned here, but in 1970 the city was taking down the north half of the old Progressive Farmer building to build a freeway, making the most godawful noise and horrendous mess imaginable. The city was also trying to steal the other half of the building at an absurd price to put up a parking deck. Emory Cunningham was fighting to get a fair price. His close friendship with two United States senators finally put the squeeze on Birmingham, and he did get fair market value for the building, which led to the company's first new building, which is another story.

Liles went to work for *Progressive Farmer* collating "a mountain of material" to put in the mail for the Advertising Department. It was a part-time job that went on for several months. "The funniest thing, in all my photocopying and my collating, I had to work with Mr. Demaree," said Liles, laughing over her lunch with McCalla and Logue at their now familiar table in the quirky little Holly Wood Grill.

"He was a great character, Mr. Demaree," said Jean, "and every other word was a cuss word."

"That got you prepared for McCalla," said Logue.

"He just sort of grew on you," Jean said of the ornery Orville Demaree. "He either liked you, or he didn't like you. Well, I was lucky. I guess he liked me okay. He found out I had a home economics degree from the University of Alabama. He asked me if I'd ever met Lena Sturges. I hadn't. He said, 'I'm taking you down to meet Lena.' So, away we went. We visited. Lena asked me if I'd ever considered doing any freelance editorial work. She needed help. She'd been ill; she'd had her mastectomy about that time. I said, 'I'm interested, just give me a call.' "

And what was her first impression of the formidable Lena Sturges? "Tell the truth, Liles," said Logue.

"The first impression of Lena could fool you a bit," she hedged; "you could see the Texas farm girl in her. Lena was a bit stern, so I'm sure her sternness was present."

"Lena was a bit stern," said Logue, "and Stalin enjoyed a bit of power."

As time passed, the *P.F.* Advertising Department offered Jean a job. "But the pay was so low I decided I could make more money teaching school," she said. *P.F.* made her the "heavyweight" offer of six thousand dollars a year.

The months and years passed. "I went to work part-time for Simon and Moginer," said Liles. "They made children's clothes. They were in financial trouble, and had a time-and-motion person from Atlanta studying their operation, and I worked with this fellow. They offered me a full-time job. I was to price out buttons or trim, that sort of thing, to see if they could afford to make that particular item. I liked the work. I'm a believer in organization." Which is to say, Sir Isaac Newton was a believer in gravity.

"Simon and Moginer offered me a full-time job," said Jean. "I knew they were in a financial bind. I said, 'Let me think about it a week. I'll let you know Friday morning.' Guess who called me at a quarter to four on Thursday?"

"Lena Sturges," said Logue.

"Asking me if I would be interested in a job," said Liles. "I had done two free-lance stories for her, one a pasta story and the other, I believe, a spinach story. I told her I had to let these other people who'd offered me a job know something by nine o'clock tomorrow morning. I said, 'How about I meet with you at 8 A.M.?' " This was the summer of 1972.

Sturges brought Jean Liles by to see McCalla and Logue. "The impression I still have of you both, when Lena introduced me," she said, "was of you reared back in your chairs with your feet propped up on the desk."

"That was us, going down the drain, all confidence," said Logue.

"Gary knew that I had written the pasta story," said Liles, "and he said, 'Tell me how you cook pasta,' and he wanted to know, 'How do you drain it?' "

"Great God, how do you remember that, after twenty-four years?" asked Logue, in no way surprised, as Jean Liles has never forgotten one tiny thing in her entire life.

"This was in August," said Jean, "and Lena told me I could work three days a week, until the magazine moved into the new building in January and would have test kitchens. Then I could work full-time. And so I said, 'Yes.' I figured I could work two days a week as a Kelly Girl or I could substitute teach.

"The very next week Taylor Lewis was coming to town to shoot food photography, and I was a little, I guess, *scared*, would be the word," said Liles.

"If you had known Taylor, *amused* would have been a better word," said Logue.

"No, I was scared I wouldn't be able to test recipes to suit Lena," said Liles. "We couldn't test recipes in the old building. The refrigerator was the only thing that worked—and one eye on the stove. All we could test there was a congealed salad recipe. So all the testing we did wound up at Lena's house. Of course, not every recipe we published was tested," said Liles, in a massive understatement. Many, if not most of them, in those days came from industry: Kellogg's, Pillsbury, General Mills, etc. The days of "reader recipes" in *Southern Living* were in the future, though the myth was already alive.

So the recipe testing and photography would be done the next week at Lena's house on Lakeshore Drive in Homewood, just south of Birmingham. Lena's Editorial Assistant Cathy Criss, who would not last long, was there, as well as Taylor Lewis, in his scraggly Vandyke beard, with wickedness in both eyes.

Taylor had grown up in San Francisco. His father had been a rather famous magazine illustrator, in the glory days of illustrators John Whitcomb and Coby Whitmore. Taylor was, you might say, unconventional. He lived on the beach in Norfolk, Virginia, in a house with a stairway to nowhere. His studio was an arrested hurricane of clutter. But the man didn't shoot with a camera, he painted with it.

Liles said, "Taylor would come into the building at Shades Creek Parkway wearing tennis shorts and shoes and a plaid sports coat. Remember that? Lena said, 'Well, did you decide to show up in your underwear?' "

"I'm the guilty party," said Logue. "Taylor was a good tennis player, and after he shot awhile, we would sneak off and play a couple of sets."

"And Lena would be waiting there, furious," said Jean. "Taylor was comic relief. And no doubt he loved to get Lena's goat. Oh, he had an eye for props. Once he told Lena over the phone he wanted to use some old lumber in the shots we were going to do the next week. Lena called me that Sunday, and we took that little mountain road, where the Wildwood Mall is now, and found an old chicken coop, already torn down. The boards turned out pretty good in several shots. We got lots of mileage out of that old chicken house."

Back to Jean's first shoot at Sturges's house.

"After I got to see Lena in action in the kitchen, I thought, 'I'm not going to be so worried,' " said Liles, "because Lena was not the most precise person when it came to measuring." Unless she was putting the eggs, shells and all, in the pound cake. But Lena could eyeball a recipe and know if it suited *Southern Living*—you had to give her that.

"One of the most vivid memories I have of the photography we did that first week," said Jean, "is of a marble pound cake. We set part of the batter aside and stirred melted chocolate into it and sort of drizzled it in and kind of swirled it around in a pan. Then when it bakes, and you turn it out and cut it, each slice has these nice swirls. So we had it set up on the dining room table, where Taylor was going to take his photographs.

"I remember this swirly, red-and-white fabric Taylor was styling for the shot," said Jean. "While he was doing that, Lena brought the cake back to the kitchen and set it on a stool. She turned around for about thirty seconds. Remember that little puppy dog she had? He went over and took the biggest bite out of that cake. He was so careful doing it. He didn't knock it over. Well, that didn't stop us, because we just whacked out a big cut and shot the picture.

"I was supposed to work only three days the next week," said Liles, "but Les Adams decided Oxmoor House wanted to publish an outdoor cookbook, and they needed it immediately. [The mercurial Les Adams, whom you will meet later.] Lena told him she needed a grill installed at her house. And I started full-time. So I never missed a beat. I guess I was making about seven thousand five hundred dollars a year."

"How long did it take you to understand Sturges, and how did you manage to get along with her?" asked Logue.

"I was lucky," said Liles, "because I was older than many of her other victims. And I had taught school several years. And I had grown up cooking and spending time in the kitchen. I think she accepted all of that, and I worked a lot."

"You never felt fearful, weepy, the whole nine yards?"

"I probably should have. Maybe I didn't have sense enough. You know, I was interested in her. I genuinely liked her. I guess I kind of felt sorry for her, too, and maybe that was the thing that clicked with her. And I would offer to do things for her. Especially at the end, when she was in the hospital. She'd had the mastectomy, and then in December of 1974 they discovered the bone malignancy.

"In fact," said Jean, "I first encouraged her to go back to her doctor. She had some tests run. She wanted to know the results immediately. And he did not want to give them over the phone. This was on a Friday. I knew she had been to the doctor. I offered to stop and buy her a newspaper on the way home. She told me, 'I think I have cancer.'

"She was really in a bad way," said Jean, "crying and very upset. So I volunteered to stay with her that night. And take her to the doctor Saturday morning. I had my little Karmann Ghia. I picked up her dry cleaning. And took her to lunch at Joy Young's where she liked to go. Her suspicions were confirmed. Her doctor told her she had bone cancer. I mean, she wanted the news straight. She asked me to come in the office. She wanted me to hear it, too."

Nobody ever met Mr. Death more straight on than Lena Sturges.

"I remember she called Beth Carlson and Dixie Snell," said Liles, "and told them. She told Dixie, 'Jean took me to see Dr. Lee today. She just folded me up in that Karmann Ghia.' "

"She was pretty heroic," said Logue. "I remember a scene that Tony Silver shot in the first documentary of *Southern Living*. He set up a picnic scene with the editorial staff at Lane Park, near the Birmingham zoo. That was when Farmer Seale told how he grew up in a boardinghouse in Selma, and they had an old boarder 'who would put his watch on the dining room table and eat for an hour.' And Lena was taking chemotherapy and wearing that wig, and she tossed her head back and laughed like a young girl. It was a great moment in the film. She could be a terror. But she was a gutsy lady."

So the company moved into its new building on Shades Creek Parkway, south of Birmingham, in the spring of 1973.

"Gary, you asked me my thoughts about how the new test kitchens should operate," said Liles. "I said, 'Testing is serious business. The kitchens should be a scientific laboratory.' And you said, 'Well, Jean, I'm putting you in charge of the test kitchens.' "

Lena's editorial assistant of that time, Peggy Smith, was the first employee to work full-time in the new test kitchens, and with a short break in service, Peggy is still there, testing recipes with the same enthusiasm. "We've had some wonderful and talented people on our foods staff," Liles said.

Jean was a recruiter of great editorial assistants, whom McCalla and Logue stole without mercy. Jean hired Karen Ward Baucum, who wound up as assistant to Editor McCalla for ten years. "Karen really ran the bloody magazine," said Logue. And today she is a major force, running the company benefits department.

Liles also hired Rebecca Brennan, whom Logue spirited away and then promoted to editor at Oxmoor House, ignoring the heresy that she didn't like the poems of William Butler Yeats. Another of Logue's editorial assistants, Ann Nathews, is now company librarian.

Dianne Mooney was briefly McCalla's editorial assistant and later rose through Oxmoor House to become a vice-president and one of the most creative marketers in the entire company. Kay Fuston rose from editorial assistant to copy chief of *Southern Living*. Nathalie Dearing worked her way from editorial assistant to managing editor of *Cooking Light*. Lynn Carter rose from the copy desk to managing editor of *Southern Accents*. Carol Boker moved from working on the copy desk to running it. Sylvia Martin came as an editorial assistant and became one of the magazine's star photographers. So did Beth Maynor and Mary-Gray Hunter. Beverly Morrow came as an editorial assistant and became an outstanding photo stylist, working with Charles Walton. Bari Love and Cyndi Maddox made the same climb to travel writers. Lil Petrusnek also started as an editorial assistant and helped develop and then run the *Southern Living* House Plans Service, a million-dollar profit center. Angela Scott, from the same start, became *Southern Living* research director.

Upward mobility, promoting from within, equal opportunity for talented women has been one of the strengths of *Southern Living* and Southern Progress. McCalla and Logue, looking back on their years, get the biggest kick out of the successful careers of the young people who when they came to work at Southern Progress had never seen the inside of a publishing house, and are now running it. Much of the great spirit of *Southern Living* you could find in such editorial assistants as Polly Stroud, Karen Paris Smith, and Janice Noles, who still does the Travel Calendar begun by her pal Dixie Snell those many years ago.

Sandra Day was Jean's first Assistant Foods Editor. She was followed by Marilyn Wyrick, who was gifted but soon left to be married back in Texas. Diane Hogan joined the test kitchen staff in 1978 and remains there to this day, doing valuable work. Jane Elliott was a rare thing among the foods editors: she was not only talented but very quiet. Getting a word in edgewise among the foods editors took force of character.

Deborah Garrison Lowery came aboard in 1982 and today is a Foods Editor at Oxmoor House. Martha Hinrichs was a capable early director of the test kitchens, and was followed by Lynn Lloyd, "who was just dynamite in the job," said McCalla. Kaye Mabry Adams for years set high standards directing the test kitchens and has climbed through the ranks to be an executive editor of *Southern Living*.

"Continuity was a great strength of the Foods Department," said Mc-Calla. "We could call on many years of experience and deep knowledge of our readers."

Liles and McCalla both remember with some alarm a lunch in the new test kitchens with President Emory Cunningham, a year after moving into the new building.

"Gary asked, 'What percent of the recipes we publish come from our readers?' " said Liles. "My reluctant answer was, 'Only 25 percent.' Gary was shocked."

"I think it sort of went over Emory's head," said Gary. "He didn't comment on it. All I said was, 'We'll do better.' I hadn't been paying close enough attention."

"I felt we could organize ourselves and attract more reader recipes," said Jean. So she began to publish a small editorial box in the food section, requesting favorite recipes from readers. "One month, readers sent in four thousand four hundred and sixty-four recipes. Back then, we paid three dollars for each recipe that passed the kitchen test and was published. Today it's ten dollars, and they get a copy of *Annual Recipes*. And, of course, they get twenty-five *Southern Living* cards with their recipe printed on them."

"Those cards are the best promotion we ever came up with," said Mc-Calla. Neither he nor Liles remembers whose idea it was. "Don Cunningham always wanted a pack of those cards when he made an advertising call," said Jean. "Readers gave them to family and friends, spreading the word of *Southern Living*."

During Jean's twenty years with the magazine, readers submitted more than five hundred thousand of their best-loved recipes for possible publication in *Southern Living*. In the twenty-two years McCalla edited the magazine, it published over twenty thousand of those recipes. After the first few years, nearly all of those recipes came from readers. And the food section under Jean Liles became the cornerstone of the magazine and of the book division, Oxmoor House.

Things didn't start out lavishly. "I remember in the early seventies, we had one full-page color photograph each month in the food section," said Jean. "At Christmastime, we'd get two pages of color, and maybe the cover.

"We surveyed our food audience in 1976," said Liles. "We asked them how they used the March issue. I remember the big food story that March was onion soup. [Of course, Liles remembered that; it was on the tip of McCalla's tongue.] We had a terrific response to the questionnaire. We found we had accomplished cooks who were cooking from scratch, and beginning cooks, and readers who didn't cook at all. It was obvious we needed to publish a careful balance of recipes. In our planning sessions—the food staff was the first on the magazine to have monthly planning sessions—we'd ask: 'What's seasonal, what's quick and easy?' We learned we needed more step-by-step stories. One of the first of those was how to make egg rolls. Every story couldn't be a dessert story, though Southerners do have a sweet tooth."

Sturges was not well enough to go to the Pillsbury Bakeoff in February, 1975, and sent Liles in her stead. "The bakeoff was in San Francisco. It was the biggest trip of my life at that point," Liles said. "They had a two-day seminar for foods editors. Then a man won the twenty-five-thousand-dollar first prize with a torte cake. I noticed a man also won the grand prize this year," said Jean, "and it paid one million dollars. Imagine that?"

The *Southern Living* Foods Department of 1972 could have used a few of those bucks for operating expenses. "I remember when we moved to the new building on Shades Creek Parkway," said Liles, "Britt Butler did not want us to buy any new dishes. And I can remember hauling dishes from home when we would have to do a luncheon for an advertising group. I also hauled from home napkins and tablecloths, and I was the maid to wash and iron them, too."

"Hell," said McCalla, "we operated through those early years on just 50 percent of the national magazine average of editorial costs. We were putting out a full column of editorial for one hundred and seventy-three dollars." *Fortune* magazine at the time was spending some $2.37 a word for editorial.

"McCalla could have saved money on Napoleon's retreat from Mother Russia," said Logue.

By 1975, Lena was deathly ill. "I went to see her in the hospital every day at lunch, after taste-testing," said Jean. "She was afraid the hospital laundry would lose her things. I lived in an apartment without a washer/dryer. But I got her laundry done. Then I'd go back to the office. We began to get hundreds of letters, in addition to the thousands of recipes. And I felt obligated to answer every letter. I took them home with me, and on planes, and even on jury duty. They might ask, 'How can I roast a pig for my garden club?' or say, 'My mother-in-law brought me two bushels of cucumbers—how do I make pickles?' or, 'My husband threatens to divorce me because I've lost his chocolate cheesecake recipe. Help!'

"I learned a lot about our readers from that mail," said Jean. (One thing she learned was that readers hated to cut up their *Southern Living* to save the recipes; as we shall see, that discovery was to earn the company millions of dollars every year.) "I learned not only what our readers cooked, and how they cooked, but who was doing the cooking, the wife, the husband, or the kids. But so much was happening, I don't know how I survived."

Lena Sturges, tough ranch lady from Kerrville, did not survive, though she clung ferociously to life until January, 1977. She went home to Texas to die. Her hard-earned stock in the company would later bring a windfall into the lives of her much-loved sisters and nieces and nephews.

President Emory Cunningham gave McCalla a mandate to find "the best qualified Foods Editor in the country." (But at a reasonable salary, of course.) "I started looking," said McCalla. "In about six months I'd gotten ninety résumés. Many of the applicants were working on newspapers. Most of those editors didn't have test kitchens. Many of them just published handouts from the food companies and went on boondoggle trips. I didn't find anybody I wanted to hire.

"Finally," said McCalla, "I told Emory, 'Look, this girl has been running the damn thing for a year. And has done a great job. And all the time looking after Lena, who was dying.' I said, 'Let's give her the job.' And Emory finally agreed." No company ever made a sounder, more profitable promotion of an employee.

"Of course," said Logue, "as time passed, McCalla did learn to say 'young woman' instead of 'girl.' But one thing McCalla did not have to learn was how to take care of his own people. *If you look out for them, they'll look out for you*, was his motto." Logue remembered, "McCalla squeezed every dollar out of management that he could every year for deserving employees. His editorial assistant was always the best paid in the building. He even helped teach Don Logan, future company president, the art of 'taking care of the troops.' "

The book division, Oxmoor House, was already in the cookbook business when Jean became Foods Editor. In 1970, Oxmoor published *Our Best Recipes*, a collection of the first five years of recipes to appear in *Southern Living*. McCalla won't soon forget the printing of this book, for which he wrote the introduction. "Tom Ford, of the *Southern Living*

Art Department, had designed the book cover, and Kingsport Printing in Tennessee was having trouble with the reproduction of it," he said. "Oxmoor House was holding thousands of Christmas orders, and time was running out. Art Curl and I chartered a small plane and flew through an awful thunderstorm. I told the printers to select enough covers to fill the Christmas orders and junk the rest and reprint. We got home about midnight. We were glad to get home alive."

Our Best Recipes in 1970 was very much a success, and Oxmoor published two sequels. But any one-shot book has a limited life, and you have to find a new set of buyers for each book, which in direct mail is expensive.

The creation of those three cookbooks, under Lena's aegis, got off to a rocky start.

Logue remembered this tall, thin young woman with hair as dark as an eclipse, and eyes darker than that, rushing into his office cubicle and falling into a chair, and not saying a word, and putting her head on his desk and commencing to weep, not cry, but *weep*. He'd seen her in the hallway but had no idea who she was.

"You got a name?" said Logue, when the weeping tailed off a bit.

"Betty . . . Ann . . . Jones," she said in separate gasps.

"Why are you so cheerful? You been looking at the company financial statements?"

"I have to do a cookbook with Lena Sturges and she just threw me out of her office."

"I'd put my head back down and cry some more," said Logue.

"Jones laughed instead," remembered Logue. "There was some hope for this child. I said, 'Hell, Sturges will come around. She'd like to see her picture in a cookbook. But, dammit, don't ever let her see you cry or you'll never get it done.' She didn't. And she did get it done. Jonesey was a trip. Only person in the building who could out-cuss Orville Demaree. She would have been a great baseball manager in the Southern League, if she could have just learned to chew tobacco." Jones ran the direct marketing many years for Oxmoor House. And she was smart and capable. Logue always got a great kick out of her and her vocabulary, which masked a sentimental bent.

Logue and Jones were once innocent observers of the most awful accidental circumstance any young man could ever find himself in. They'd flown into O'Hare Field in Chicago, working on some direct mail project for Oxmoor House. It was in the post-Vietnam days, and thousands of young soldiers could be seen in the airports. There was this red-haired, freckle-faced young kid, obviously home from basic training, waiting to claim his bag. There to meet him was his girlfriend, as innocent as the absence of makeup on her young face. And with her were her proud parents, just as eager to hug the boy as was the young girl. Bags began to be lifted up on a conveyer belt and spit out onto a carousel that turned in a circle. The boy spotted his duffel bag and turned to get it, but the bag ripped on the conveyer belt and spilled out his clothes and shaving kit, and, oh goodness, about twenty round, golden packages of Trojans rattled and some of them rolled on end, and the young soldier leapt on the carousel but they were tumbling in every direction. Logue and Jones were too horrified for the young boy to laugh or look at the faces of his girlfriend and her parents, and took their bags and fled to the less murderous terrors of downtown Chicago. In later years, Jones left Oxmoor House and went up to Nashville and made a bunch of money selling Bibles and music boxes. God works in mysterious ways.

Jean Liles ran a tight ship. She was organized beyond anybody in the company. And kept the precise notes of a research physicist. "I'd tried to manage by the 'three *F*'s,' " said Liles, "fair, firm, and flexible. I expected every member of the foods staff to be involved in every story. I expected everybody to be there to taste test and to develop what I call 'taste memory.' If we were testing a chocolate pie, and we'd published a similar one three years ago, we needed to remember the taste of it so we wouldn't repeat the same recipe."

When Jean came to the magazine, Sharon Watkins of the copy desk had put together a single editing sheet for recipes for the foods staff to go by. "We added and added and added pages until it became a very substantial editing notebook which the whole magazine goes by now," said Liles.

It was a lucky thing for McCalla that Jean Liles was so talented and so organized. (And still found time to make advertising sales calls across the country to the foods industry, and especially in Chicago when Scott Shepherd ran that office.) Her relatively small staff produced all the foods material for *Southern Living,* and later took on the creation of all foods copy for *Progressive Farmer.* And by the middle eighties, *Southern Living* was publishing large special sections of food and entertainment: "Summer Suppers," "Holiday Dinners" (which once ran to seventy-two pages), and "Breakfasts and Brunches."

In addition, Jean's young staff, working with free-lancers, helped produce a line of remarkably successful cookbooks for Oxmoor House, including: *Outdoor Cookbook, The Party Cookbook, The Illustrated Cookbook, The Southern Hospitality Cookbook,* and *Dinner and Supper Cookbook,* and all of these books were published by 1979 when Jean's food staff was not only young but small.

The Southern Living Cookbook, published in 1982, was one of the most ambitious of the foods staff's efforts. It required enormous test-kitchen work and the near full-time service for the better part of three years of star Assistant Foods Editor Susan Payne. *The Southern Living Cookbook* was a great success, selling three hundred thousand copies over several years. Liles has often said if she were going off to live on an island and could take only one cookbook, it would be this one.

Susan Payne, a bright young woman with an unsinkable personality to match Jean's, was on McCalla's short list of candidates he considered capable of replacing him when he retired. After Jean Liles took early retirement in 1992, Susan chose to move to a full-time career with Oxmoor House.

Of course, the grandmother of all cookbooks created by the *Southern Living* foods staff was, and is, *Southern Living Annual Recipes.* Begun in 1979, the annual cookbook is made up of all the recipes published each year in *Southern Living.* It's indexed three ways: by ingredient, by month of publication, and by recipe title. Readers whose husbands are about to divorce them for losing their favorite chocolate cheesecake recipe cannot help buying it in these eighteen existing volumes. *Annual Recipes* without question is the single most valuable book title in American publishing, selling more than one million copies *every year.* Not even Stephen King can knock out a new horror story every year.

Don Logan in 1977 moved from the computer fulfillment division of the company (Akra Data, now known as Media Services) to take over the management of Oxmoor House, which had fallen on hard times. Logue was still the editor-in-chief of Oxmoor House, but was back on the magazine in exile until Logan could figure out how to make the book division profitable again. Most critically, Logan was searching for ways to marry Oxmoor House more closely to *Southern Living,* which he correctly identified as the central engine of opportunity.

Jean Liles not only never failed to read all the letters from her readers, but she never failed to understand them. Company research had shown that most *Southern Living* subscribers saved every copy of their magazine. And Jean's mail told her that readers "hated to cut up their copies" to save the recipes.

"I remember you, Gary and John, and myself and Don Logan spent a lot of time thinking about how we could package our recipes and get them to the readers in a book," said Liles. "We'd done it in the three cookbooks that were five-year collections. But we were trying to think of a way to package the recipes every year."

"In the early days it took five years of recipes to make a book," said McCalla. "By 1979 we were publishing over twelve hundred recipes a year, more than enough for a book a year."

Logue said, "The big question was, could we get the dang thing done in time for the Christmas season, and still get the December recipes in it?"

"The only way to do it," said Liles, "was to lay out each month's recipes in separate chapters, then we could have the first eleven chapters set in type while we rushed December into print before that month's magazine was even published. There was no way we could put all the breads together or the desserts together, so we identified recipes by food category in one of the three indexes."

Neither Liles nor McCalla nor Logue could remember who came up with the title *Annual Recipes*. Logan said you couldn't credit it to him. Like Jean, he remembered the idea for the book coming out of many discussions among the four of them.

McCalla agreed to put food on *Southern Living*'s December cover that 1979, so that the same photograph could be used on the jacket of the first edition of *Annual Recipes*. He didn't guarantee to do it every year thereafter, but *Annual Recipes* proved so popular that it carries the same jacket photograph to this day as appears on *Southern Living*'s December cover.

The idea for *Annual Recipes* was not overwhelmingly popular with everyone, remembered Logan, sitting in his corner office on the thirty-fourth floor of the Time-Life Building, habitat of the president and CEO of Time, Inc. Logan said, "Our direct mail consultant Dick Benson thought it was 'a terrible idea.' He said, 'It's not a book at all. These people already have these recipes. And you can't sell it.' "

"Other than that, Benson was optimistic," said Logue.

Logan was prepared to go against the opinion of the Old Master of direct mail. "There were you two, and Betty Ann Jones; there were seven or eight of us; we talked to Jean Liles, and she knew her readers; and we

all agreed to publish the book. Our first ads for *Annual Recipes* emphasized we knew the readers didn't like to cut up their magazines to save
the recipes."

In fact, the headline for the first two-column ad in the June, 1979,
Southern Living read: "Before you clip the recipes from this magazine . . .
there is something you ought to know," followed by: "Every single one
of the recipes appearing in *Southern Living* will be conveniently compiled
in a beautiful and durable hardcover collection. So you will always be
able to find the exact *Southern Living* recipe you want—when you want
it—in seconds." The ad worked, big-time.

Tom Angelillo, who was to succeed Logan as director of Oxmoor
House and later as president of Southern Progress, remembered the first
ad, in the June, 1979, *Southern Living*. "It was a black-and-white ad, and
it pulled six thousand orders," said Angelillo, who in those days worked
for Akra Data and helped fulfill those orders.

"We ran a series of ads in the magazine," said Logan, "and by that fall
had fifty-six thousand orders, before the book was published. I remember
setting our original print order. Our projections showed that we needed
two hundred and forty-two thousand copies. I went over to tell Vernon
Owens, and we rounded it up to two hundred and fifty thousand. And,
of course, we sold them all. We ultimately sold in excess of a half million
copies of that first title. We kept selling that 1979 book for five years
while selling new editions every year."

Annual Recipes, now selling its million copies a year, remains one of
the great engines that power the book division, Oxmoor House, which
by the mid-1990s was a greater profit center even than *Southern Living*.
If Jean Liles hadn't read and understood her mail from her readers, Oxmoor House would surely be a different and lesser beast. Since the overwhelming success of *Annual Recipes*, almost every home magazine in
America has tried the same annual recipe formula in a book. Not one of
them has been able to make it work, not even the magazine cousins at
Sunset.

Liles's same attention to her mail ultimately provoked the launching of a
highly successful new magazine. Logue sat in on a meeting in which Jean
spoke of a significant change in the food habits of *Southern Living* readers. She said they were sending in many more recipes that called for fewer
calories, less fat, less *cholesterol* (that word that was soon to influence

America's eating habits). Jean proposed to McCalla a column in the foods section on lighter food.

Logue went back to Oxmoor House and wrote up a one-paragraph description of a book based on Jean's report. Oxmoor, under Logan, would describe five or six book ideas in a four-page letter, and concept-test them with *Southern Living* readers and book buyers. Logue couldn't think of a title for the book. He called up Oxmoor's Foods Editor, Ann Harvey, and asked her, "What would you call a cookbook that only included lighter recipes, if you couldn't call it a diet book?"

Harvey said, without hesitation, "Not a very good idea."

"Very funny, Harvey. Give it a few minutes and call me back."

She called back in less than five minutes with a two-word suggestion: *Cooking Light.*

"It's grammatically undefendable. I love it," said Logue. The concept test jumped off the Richter scale of predicted success.

Meanwhile McCalla had approved Jean's request for a column on lighter food in the magazine, and was looking for a name to call it. Logue, being naturally sneaky and knowing that if the magazine published a column by the same title as Oxmoor's cookbook they would sell a huge pot of cookbooks, said: "McCalla, why don't you call it 'Cooking Light'?" He eventually did. And the original column, under another title, actually came out in January of 1982, before the cookbook, and has run for eighteen years. The "Cooking Light" column was first edited by the talented Susan McIntosh. The entire company despaired when she gave up her magazine career to free-lance and raise a family. Susan was succeeded by Helen Anne Dorrough, a significant talent who later followed her medical doctor husband to Denver to be close to the snow skiing and the kayaking. The *S.L.* column is now called "Living Light."

Every year since 1983, Oxmoor House has sold a huge quantity of its annual *Cooking Light Cookbook.* The reason annual books were so profitable and became the nucleus of Oxmoor's success was that you did not have to find a new buyer—a very costly process—for each year's book. Last year's subscriber simply gets a written notice that she will be mailed this year's book unless she doesn't want it. It's a multi-million dollar system.

The *Cooking Light* book and column were so popular that Don Logan proposed a new magazine called (you guessed it): *Cooking Light.* One of the strengths of Southern Progress is to take a successful idea and package it in a dozen different directions. McCalla, who grew up working in the oil patch, says old wildcatters know it's a hell of a lot more profitable to drill where you are already pumping oil.

Jean Liles, Martha Johnston (who at the time ran the *Southern Living Cooking School*), and Kathy Eakin of Oxmoor House served on a three-person editorial panel to define the new magazine, which Logan launched without an editor or a publisher. Eakin ultimately became its first editor, followed by Doug Crichton. And Jeff Ward came over from *People* magazine to distinguish himself as the first publisher. *Cooking Light* magazine today has more than a million subscribers, and is, in fact, the largest food/life-style magazine in the country.

A word of advice to young editors from the Jean Liles school of management: *Read your mail, kids.*

11

Tasty Images

If you measure the editorial space in any given issue of *Southern Living*, you will find that it is split almost fifty-fifty between text and photography.

"McCalla's greatest strength was his knowledge of photography and understanding of the visual impact of the magazine," said Logue. "He was not a shabby writer, but he wrote too short. Sometimes he didn't write at all, coercing one of his buddies, who shall remain nameless, into writing his bloody column. Let me back up a minute," said Logue. "McCalla's greatest contribution was adapting the *Sunset* formula to our own magazine, and keeping the editors—all of us from time to time hell-bent on heading off into some new direction—on the straight and narrow path to Travel, Gardens, Homes, Food, and Southern people doing positive things. But McCalla knew photography and good design."

Nowhere in the magazine was the visual impact more important than in the food section. If it didn't look edible, you were in trouble with McCalla. And photographers had to do it without gimmicks. The food was served and eaten after it was photographed. No glycerin spilled over it for fraudulent effect.

The one and only Taylor Lewis, of course, set the original standard for food photography in *Southern Living*. McCalla tried repeatedly to catch up with Taylor and get a few quotations for this book. He finally reached his widow. It seems a couple of years ago Taylor, who had had a heart attack, fell dead while playing tennis. He was in his early sixties. Taylor was an original, and especially behind the camera. His images helped shape the magazine that *Southern Living* was destined to become.

A young photographer, Bert O'Neal, joined the magazine staff in 1974 and introduced McCalla to Jerry Drown, a talented free-lance photographer from Atlanta. Bert himself did some nice work—shooting blueberries, melons, home canning, a picnic in Austin, Texas, even a cover story on "Backpacking in Daniel Boone Country"—before leaving for a life as a stockbroker, the only profession more alarming than the magazine business. Bert never told McCalla he was color blind until years later when he was investing McCalla's retirement nest egg. "I hope it's the color of money," said Logue. For the next several years, Jerry Drown shot most of the magazine's lead food photography, including each year's Christmas cover from 1977 until 1981. "Jerry's work was excellent," said McCalla.

One day in March, 1988, Logue was hanging around the office at lunchtime, which was a very great aberration of habit, and a tall, dark-haired young man came by looking for McCalla. His name was Walton. Charles Walton. He might have been a model for Hathaway Shirts (that was before he grew a beard like Mephistopheles'). He was carrying a tiny sample of his work—in fact, one plastic sheet of thirty-five-millimeter transparencies.

"I'm not your man," said Logue, "but let's see what you've got." He threw the twenty slides on a light box, expecting not much. He was wrong. The one extraordinary slide he remembers was of a tube of lipstick raised to an art object. "Hey, this stuff is over my head," said Logue. "You better come back and see McCalla."

"He had that one sheet of slides," remembered McCalla. "Damn, they were terrific." McCalla made the decision on the spot to hire him.

Walton worked with Jerry Drown for a while. Then he took over the role of food photographer for the magazine, at a time when it was going to all four-color. "There is not a better food photographer in the country than Charles," said McCalla. "And he can shoot anything. His country ham stuff, shot on location, was sensational." Jim Bathie and John O'Hagan, both gifted photographers, also did good work on the magazine's Regional Foods series, as did Mike Clemmer.

Beverly Morrow Perrine proved a brilliant and longtime stylist of Walton's food shots, pillaging department stores, warehouses, attics, rummage sales, flea markets, and the kitchens of friends and enemies to come up with an ever-changing selection of props for the photographs. It's astonishing to realize that in some years Walton and Morrow would style and shoot over four hundred food photographs for *Southern Living*, including, over the years, many, many covers. Their imagination and their end result rarely flagged.

Dressed up, Walton looked like your ordinary Jaycee. Not so. He moved not only to his own drummer but to his own rhythm section. He took a vacation to Italy and stayed in the flat of a working Communist family. His photographs of their spare, Spartan quarters could hang in a museum. After shooting all day on the Cajun food story, driven nearly mad by the outsized scale of the twenty-pound redfish, Walton drove up to Joe Bar pulling the damned fish on a rope behind his Volkswagen. Once, on his own nickel, Walton bought an elaborate Thanksgiving dinner, from turkey to pumpkin pie. He borrowed an equally elaborate table setting, from china to silver to glass goblets. He had the entire meal prepared and set up as formally as a State Department dinner at the Jimmy Hale Mission in downtown Birmingham. One of the homeless guys there turned out to be a former magazine executive and helped him set it all up. Walton seated the men and struck the most astonishing Thanksgiving photograph you have ever seen; it would have done justice to the jacket of a novel by Dickens.

A young features editor, Mark Childress, whom Logue recruited from the *Birmingham News* at age twenty-two, wrote the Cajun food story. It was the first regional coverage for New Orleans Chef Paul Prudhomme, who within a year would be a guest chef in the White House, with his photograph on the covers of national magazines. Mark's story made blackened redfish so popular the government had to limit catches of the once-unremarkable fish. And now chefs across America blacken everything from guilty fish to innocent chicken. Childress stayed on the magazine for four years and wrote some of its most memorable stories. He went on to become a successful novelist, living in Costa Rica overlooking the Pacific Ocean. One of his novels is entitled *Crazy in Alabama*, a phrase he might well have siphoned from his years on the magazine. Later in this narrative, he will share a few memories from that rich time.

Some of the other foods stories that McCalla looked back on as being among the magazine's best, with photographs by Walton unless otherwise indicated, include:

"Cornbread like Mama Used to Make," written by Margaret Chason Agnew in September of 1985. It started out: "Johnnycake. Hoecake. Ashcake. Cornpone. Spoonbread. Corn sticks." The poor reader was starving already. Margaret has pressed on to a free-lance career, and collaborated with another former *Southern Living* editor, Catherine Hamrick, in writing *The Husband Hunting Handbook*. God help any unsuspecting male caught in the aftermath of this "dangerous" book, which is a lot of fun and, experts say, very sound. "Their own husbands never had a chance," said Logue. "It was like shooting quail on the ground."

Susan Payne wrote "A Chocolate Fantasy" in February, 1989, and it still keeps readers up at night with visions of "this rich, brown confection" stirring their souls and their appetites. "Summer Comes Up Okra" was the memorable work of Deborah Garrison Lowery with photographs by Bathie. The poet James Dickey, in a book for Oxmoor House, called it "the divine fact of okra."

Linda Welch visited the mountains to search out such Appalachian wonders as apple butter. John O'Hagan did the photography, which was excellent. O'Hagan himself would remind you of a younger Peter Sellers, and he does secret and wonderful impressions of *Southern Living* personalities, including a marvelously devastating imitation of one-time garden editor Dr. John Floyd. And he could capture McCalla in full oath in a photographic pick.

"Breakfast at Brennan's" was actually written by Lena Sturges herself, with a little editing help from her friends. And Taylor Lewis captured that New Orleans restaurant on film as no one else ever has. Someone on the magazine questioned the "appropriateness" of some of the more unusual breakfast dishes in the story for the "staid" *Southern Living* audience. "Damn right, something's wrong," said McCalla; "where's the snails?"

Marilyn Wyrick, before she fled back to Texas, wrote "Where There's Smoke, There's Barbecue," one of the magazine's many, many stories on that blessed Southern phenomenon, and one of the best.

Margaret Agnew invaded Wyrick's territory to write "Mexico Comes Alive with a Party." An Austin, Texas, hostess entertains "with all the flair and feel of Old Mexico." No subject in the history of *Southern Living* has proven more elusive than the entertainment story. It's damn near impossible to shoot people having a good time who are concerned about the camera shooting them having a good time. The magazine pulled it off a few times, including this one.

Good Lord, McCalla's favorite food stories could go on for volumes. Here's one more: "Our All-Time Best Desserts," researched and written by Dana Adkins and Susan Payne, shot by Walton, styled by Beverly Morrow Perrine in December, 1990. It began: "Here we present you with 25 favorite dessert recipes from the 25 years of *Southern Living*."

One of those twenty-five recipes is the only recipe in Jean Liles's twenty-year tenure that received *more* than a perfect score in the test kitchen. That would be a "Triple Layer Chocolate Cheesecake." Taste it and you'll have no doubt why the woman's husband was about to divorce her for losing the recipe.

"This cheesecake was my all-time favorite," McCalla said. "The kitchens fixed it every time we had a special occasion."

Earlier, at the end of the last chapter, the *Southern Living* Cooking School was mentioned. It came into being originally as "the *Progressive Farmer* Cooking School." It was the brainchild of *P.F.* Advertising Manager Ted Bjork.

"I couldn't believe a traveling cooking school could help us," admitted Emory Cunningham. "Ted did. I was pretty stubborn about it. It took him months, but he finally convinced me to try it. I think more than anything else I wanted to get him out of my hair and let him see if it would work." The idea of the cooking school was to have a traveling team of young women who would demonstrate cooking techniques to paying audiences around the South. Exclusive usage of individual foods products in the recipes would be given to food companies, which would agree to place advertising in *Progressive Farmer*.

"Ted set up a date for the cooking school in Cullman, Alabama," said Emory, "and, behold, it was successful. We got quite a bit of advertising in *Progressive Farmer*. I had long felt that our food editorial and market story was a whole lot better than the food advertising we were getting in *Southern Living*."

More food advertising in *Southern Living* would mean a great deal more profit for the company than increased food advertising in *Progressive Farmer*. And Emory knew it would give Oxmoor House many more recipes to include in cookbooks—specifically, *Annual Recipes* after it came along.

"I asked Ted one day if he would be willing to let *Southern Living* have a cooking school," said Emory. "He finally agreed, so we moved it to *Southern Living* and picked up food lineage." And the magazine picked up additional food pages and reader recipes.

The *Southern Living* Cooking School did suffer growing pains. "Jean and I received complaints from readers who attended the early shows," said McCalla. "We heard they almost had a disaster in Baltimore. About half the people walked out. I said, 'Jean, let's go to Little Rock and see what's going on.' We did. It wasn't very professional. Half the people did walk out at intermission. I went to see Emory. I told him the show was a disaster. Ted was angry with me. I told him if the cooking school was going to have *Southern Living*'s name on it, by God, it was going to be good."

Cunningham and McGuire brought Martha Johnston in to run the cooking school, and she soon had it performing as slickly as an off-Broadway production. Each year, some thousands of people pay to attend the cooking school performances throughout the South. Many are sold out and tickets scalped like an Auburn-Alabama football game.

Cunningham said that he "stayed after" Les Adams at Oxmoor House to publish an annual collection of *Southern Living* recipes, but that Adams "didn't believe it would work. And he told me, 'We've tested that thing, and it failed miserably.' " Logue was editor-in-chief of Oxmoor House from 1974, and Les never mentioned an *Annual Recipes* concept to him or to McCalla. Logue wrote all the first concept tests at Oxmoor House, but they came into being only under Don Logan. The only records of a direct mail test for *Annual Recipes*, or a similar concept, come after Don Logan took over Oxmoor House in 1974.

"Certainly one of the highlights of my twenty years," said Jean Liles, "would be when we had the Cooks Across the South visit the company for our Twenty-Fifth Anniversary Super Jubilee. We sent out a long questionnaire to readers whose recipes had been published in the magazine. We chose twelve women, from their twenties to grandmothers, and from a true cross-section of society. They came in April, 1990, and spent three days with us.

"We took their individual photographs and published them in the magazine with a group interview," said Liles. "We had a catered dinner. And the next day they divided into groups and tested recipes in our kitchens for an hour. We toured Birmingham, the botanical gardens, the entire city, and ate at the Summit Club. Their last night we placed beautiful silver trays from Bromberg's in each of their rooms. Susan Dozier, Helen Anne Dorrough, and I heard them screaming, and we rushed up, thinking somebody was ill. They were in the hallways taking pictures of each other with their trays. It was like Christmas."

Liles said, "They are still my pen pals. They've become like a sorority. They even had a reunion in Birmingham in 1992. John Floyd took them all to dinner. Rubelene Singleton from Scotts Hill, Tennessee, sometimes calls me for suggestions when she has to cater some affair, and she comes back each year for Table Scapes at the building. Laura Faulkenberry always sends me greetings at special times during the year. They were elite cooks, these women, but their love of *Southern Living* was typical of how our readers felt about the magazine."

Jean was concerned about a *S.L.* subscriber at the very moment that she was remembering the women of the Super Jubilee. A reader from Fort Walton, Florida, had called her to say she was coming to the famous University of Alabama at Birmingham Hospital for surgery. She made Jean promise to come see her. She said she didn't know anybody else in Birmingham. Jean was trying desperately to catch up with the woman, as if she was one of her own kin.

"Each reader seems to believe the magazine is only published for herself," said Logue, "and that is one of its great charms. As McCalla says, you can always find something in it from within a few miles of your home. And the readers consider our editors to be personal friends."

McCalla and Logue saw many kids go on to be editors, and art directors, and chief photographers, and department heads, and vice-presidents. They consider it to have been a miscarriage of justice in an otherwise just company that Jean Liles was never made a vice-president. "It's as if the Queen had never knighted Sir Laurence Olivier," said Logue.

Don't expect Liles to complain. When she was retiring in 1992, Editor John Floyd said, "Would you do me one favor? Stay involved in *Annual Recipes*, since you've been involved in it all these years." Liles said, "Sure." And she enjoys the part-time work, which gives her freedom to spend time in her condo at the beach with her husband, a very successful lawyer.

"Any regrets?" asked Logue.

"I always felt, when the company was sold to Time, Inc., it would have been nice if a little money, a little tribute, had been paid to those of us who hung in there and were dedicated to the cause," she said.

"It would have been a good thing, wouldn't it?" said Emory Cunningham, when told of Jean's sentiments. "I never thought of it. I had so much I was trying to do. I should have thought of it. I wish I had done it."

"Emory called me in his office once," remembered McCalla. "This was before the company was sold. He said, 'We are going to have a little stock offering for key employees. Talk with some of your key people.' I talked with Jean, a few others," said McCalla, "but the stock offering never came about."

"No regrets," repeated Liles. "I decided, after I had worked for a quarter of a century, to wrap it up, so I could enjoy other things I had never had time for. And, guys, who will ever have more fun than we did?"

12

Call for Philip Morris

Back to late summer, 1969. McCalla was in a dangerous position. He'd gotten what he'd hoped for, the editorship of *Southern Living*. Now it was up to him to publish a magazine that successfully revolved around the home and the hometown. What he didn't have was an editor who could carry the homes pages, urban design, historic preservation, neighborhood restoration, etc., to the design levels they had to achieve for the magazine to distinguish itself.

If McCalla looked at the clippings of ninety foods editors before promoting Jean Liles, he and/or Logue looked at the work of at least that many design editors. Nobody's stuff was impressive enough to provoke even an exploratory interview.

McCalla had agreed to speak to the annual Creative Writers' Conference at his alma mater, the University of Oklahoma. Looking for a lead on a design editor, he swung by the office of Dr. Joe Holland, who headed up the School of Journalism.

"Joe told me there was a guy writing for the *Oklahoma Journal* in Oklahoma City who had once been enrolled in the School of Architecture," said McCalla. "Joe liked his stuff. The guy's name was Philip Morris. I gave him a phone call that day." He caught Morris entirely by surprise.

"I didn't know the magazine," recalls Philip, sitting on his deck that is semi-enclosed with an arbor and antique cypress shutters, giving it the feel of an open-air extension of the house interior.

To know his home is to know Morris. It's a small L-plan house, built in 1928 and "vaguely English," with a contained garden that wraps the side and back. The hall/living room is underfurnished, with two over-stuffed chairs flanking a shoulder-height, rough-cut stone fireplace. Over the fireplace is a large original print by Canadian artist Brian Kelly, a vigorous sketch of a Provençal or Tuscan road extending up a hill into the distance. Anchoring the other end of the room is a five-by-six-foot reproduction of Nolli's celebrated century plan of Rome. In the event you haven't guessed the owner's interest in architecture, cities, and the cultural landscape, the room also includes a display of antique architectural prints.

A strong axis extends from the front room through a dining room/library, past a breakfast room into the kitchen, giving the sequence of small rooms some drama and flow. Between the dining room and kitchen, outside a set of French doors, "an imaginary cross-axis" is created by a dramatic forced perspective view of the Tuileries gardens that hangs inches away on a wooden screen fence. Painted for outdoor placement, this four-by-six-foot commissioned work is based on a seventeenth-century print. Philip Morris eats, sleeps, and writes design in all its timeless manifestations.

"What did you think when you met McCalla?" asked Logue.

"I didn't know *any* magazine editors," said Philip. "I didn't know what one was supposed to look like."

"Good thing," said Logue, "since you were meeting with Gary and then me."

Morris in 1969 was twenty-nine years old, a slim guy with blond hair that he wore brushed forward, making him look very much like the character Illya Kuryakin in the old television series "The Man from Uncle." To this day, Morris swims seventy-five laps three times a week and has grown slimmer if anything.

He was raised in Kansas City, Missouri, one of seven brothers and sisters, and took an English literature degree in 1962 at Rockhurst, a small Jesuit college there in Kansas City. "I enrolled in architecture at the University of Oklahoma," said Morris, "mainly to hide out from my family, because what does an English major do for a living? I hung out there for a while, and one day applied for a job at the *Daily Oklahoman*, which is in Oklahoma City and is the big newspaper in the state."

Morris said, "They brought all us cub reporters into a room. They asked each of us what we were interested in writing about. I said, 'Design.' I can still see the other reporters looking at each other like, 'What the hell is that?' I did my regular news assignments and then my design reporting on the side. I started digging up people, met my first landscape architect, explored urban design, which turned out to be my lasting avocation. I was covering suburban towns and developing my design stories in the Sunday paper, which in those days had plenty of space; they would print just about anything I did."

The *Daily Oklahoman* was owned by the powerful Gaylord family, and E. K. Gaylord himself was very much alive and kicking. "I loved the crusty old newspaper reporters on the paper," said Morris. "They would say, 'You think anybody is going to tell E. K. anything? He's *thirty-seven years older than the state*.' E. K. was cooking around eighty-plus in those years and still running things, and his son was in the wings, getting older and older."

"You left a newspaper whose owner lived to be over a hundred," said Logue, "and wound up on a magazine whose owner lived to be over a hundred. Must be a lesson in there somewhere. Maybe it's *Rich owners live longer than poor hired hands*."

"Another similarity," said Philip, "is that Mr. Gaylord and Mr. Eugene Butler were tiny little men. The newspaper moved into a new building in downtown Oklahoma City, and they were testing the helicopter pad on the flat roof. So we were all standing around the landing pad, and the helicopter came down and almost blew E. K. off the roof. I mean, they caught him just before he went over.

"Those were the big urban renewal days," said Morris. "I. M. Pei came into Oklahoma City to draw up an urban renewal master plan. It was a great plan, but it tore the city down, and they never put it back. It was a real education for me. I. M. Pei had probably the best urban design firm in the country. Their ideas for the city were flawed, but the experience was an introduction for me to design at a really high level. I hung out with his people and learned a lot from them. It really got me hooked on the idea of writing about design."

Morris remembered, regretfully, "A friend of mine kept saying, 'Don't kid yourself. They—the editors—are not serious about design.' Sure enough, after two years, one day they said, 'We want you to forget about the design stuff and cover fires and the police like any normal reporter.' And that's when I went to Europe," said Philip, "a reasonable response. I had sixty dollars when I landed in London, and no way back."

"Yeah," said Logue, "for years after Gary hired you, he would be interviewing some serious young applicant for a job and ask him, 'Have you ever had to sell your clothes to get back from Europe?' If that sort of recklessness worked for you, Philip, he thought it might help anybody. McCalla's other favorite questions to some young college graduate, eager to show off his straight 'A' transcript, which Gary had no interest in seeing, was: 'Have you ever been arrested?' Or: 'Did you ever spend the night in jail?' Once an applicant realized these happenings might be in his favor," said Logue, "you'd be amazed what funny stories would spill forth. In truth, McCalla and I both felt if you didn't have a spirit of adventure, *Southern Living* wasn't the place you needed to be. Which accounts for a lot of wonderfully eccentric characters who have flourished on the magazine. And that's still true, I hope."

"I got a little advance from my brother," said Morris, "and headed for Paris, then Germany. Once you got to Germany, they grabbed you off the street to work. So I would tend bar, wait tables, mainly at American military officers' clubs. I wasn't looking for permanent work. I just wanted to stay alive. I'd do a stint of work and then head to Italy in the spring, or to London. After two years, I came back home, selling my clothes and a few other things along the way."

A new paper had sprung up in Oklahoma City, the *Journal*. Morris signed on. "It had a very small staff," he said. "I was covering City Hall."

So in the late summer of 1969 Morris agreed to meet with McCalla for lunch at the old Skirbin Hotel in Oklahoma City. He brought along some clippings of his design coverage.

"What did McCalla say to you?" asked Logue.

"I don't remember," said Philip, laughing. "I think he mainly just talked. Told me he was from Oklahoma."

"That's McCalla, tell you as little as possible and let you hang yourself," said Logue.

"I wasn't worried if the *Journal* would survive," said Philip. (It didn't.) "I felt strongly about design and cities and what was happening on the street. I was concerned that I would be able to write about that, whatever else I did. I talked to a few people. My brother and sister-in-law had seen *Southern Living*, and they were impressed."

"Thank goodness it didn't take a great deal to impress them," said Logue.

McCalla brought Morris's clippings to Birmingham and gave them to Logue. "I turned around and walked back to my office," said Logue, "and twelve minutes later, I walked into McCalla's office and said, 'Get your butt on the airplane and get this guy by the throat because we have got to have him.' "

McCalla got on the telephone instead. Morris agreed to visit. He had never been to Birmingham. But he had seen Mobile. "When I came back from Europe," he said, "I hitchhiked through Mobile to Houston to get a job as a teamster on a freight dock. I worked for about six months. I didn't want to go home broke. I hadn't written home, and my family thought I was dead."

"What were your impressions of Birmingham, 1969?" asked McCalla.

"I think my response to Birmingham was somewhat unusual," said Philip. "I had been in Europe, and I missed a lot of the civil rights unrest. So I didn't have this image of a violent place. I must say, when I came to interview, it was a pretty dirty town. I know I stayed at the original Parliament House. I remember you two didn't show me the old building," said Morris, laughing.

"Oh, hell no," said Logue. "We drove you through Mountain Brook. Took you up to The Club. I remember you said you 'weren't sure you could live in Birmingham.' And I said, 'Look, you don't have a choice because we have got to have you.' I said, 'You don't have to *live* here. You just have to land here and write your stuff. You can live all over the South.' I didn't know, Philip, that I was outlining your professional itin-erary for the next twenty-five years."

Morris had to laugh at that reality. In truth, no come-to-town new citizen has done more for the city of Birmingham in the last twenty-five years than Philip Morris. He was a co-founder of the Friends of Lynn Park. He helped raise the millions to renovate and rename moribund Woodrow Wilson Park into the vital Lynn Park that now anchors 20th Street in the heart of the city.

Philip has been a longtime president of the Birmingham Historical Society. He recently wrote a popular history of Vulcan, the cast-iron god who stands on Red Mountain and looks down on the city. Philip's book is meant to help push the city into raising more millions to restore the largest cast-iron statue in the world to its original condition when it appeared in the 1904 World's Fair in St. Louis.

Morris also was a founding board member of Horizon 280, which helped preserve some of the character of that much-trafficked artery south of Birmingham. He served on the Jefferson County Planning and Zoning Commission, the Sculpture Committee of the Birmingham Botanical Gardens, and the Art Committee of the Birmingham Airport, and was co-organizer of "Go to Town Birmingham," an urban design forum, and "Destination Birmingham," a tourism forum.

Along the way, Philip was named a Harvard Loeb Fellow and studied for a year in the Graduate School of Design. He's a member of the board of directors of the American Architecture Foundation and the Southern Arts Foundation. In 1994, Morris was presented the Alabama Humanities Foundation Award for his lifetime contribution to the state. If Philip didn't much like the looks of the city he found in 1969, he's hung around to help alter the town immeasurably for the better.

McCalla and Logue kept after Morris until he gave up and joined the magazine. The two of them now agree that Morris was "the most important, the most critical addition to the staff in the history of *Southern Living.*"

"He gave us great design awareness," said McCalla.

"And civilization," said Logue; "we already had two semi-talented barbarians, you and me. I remember one of the first things Philip did was go out to Texas and meet the great San Antonio architect O'Neil Ford, who told him, 'Don't ever write down to readers about design.' It was great advice. Philip never did. When some architectural term was needed, he used it. If he had to define it, he defined it. And Philip knew outstanding design when he saw it. And he could capture it in words and see that it was captured in photographs. And he could do it in a hurry. Philip is the only person I have ever known who thinks out what he is going to write and sets it down in complete sentences with no need to change a damn thing. It's spooky."

"Philip gave us style and design credibility and we could not have become the magazine we became without him," said McCalla. "Of course, Jean Liles was equally important in building our Foods Department, and I say again, food built the *Southern Living* empire."

Morris was aboard. Now he had to see the old company headquarters building at 821 North 19th Street. He stood across the street, and his three-word comment became instant corporate lore: "*Vintage cotton gin,*" said Morris.

"I actually thought the old building had a lot of potential," he said, sitting on his deck all these years later. "I had been working in this modern newspaper building of the 'sealed building era.' . . . Not one window. It was horrible. It had a blue carpet and a reflective ceiling, so it always looked as if it was about to rain. I liked the old newspaper warehouse on 19th Street."

Morris remembered, "I didn't meet Emory Cunningham on my first visit. But you two took me to lunch with him at the Downtown Club my first week on the job. I remember walking across the park and John took me aside and said something like this: 'Say what you believe. Be yourself. Don't worry about Emory. He's the president. But he doesn't edit the magazine.' As soon as John said, 'Don't worry,' I started worrying," said Philip. "I thought, 'I'm going to say something, and he'll call me a pinko commie, and I'll be out of here.' Well, I found out reality was the reverse of that.

"When we sat down and started talking," said Philip, "instead of my having to apologize for my interest in good design, and urban design, Emory was pushing in the same direction, the opposite of what I had expected. And here I was talking to the president of the company. At the *Daily Oklahoman*, the administration was on another floor and a world apart from the newsroom. But the real surprise to me," said Philip, "came after I'd only been here a few months. Emory asked me to help him find an architect to design the company's new headquarters building. I couldn't believe it."

"And you pointed him toward Jova Daniels Busby in Atlanta," said Logue.

"I'd been over in Atlanta looking at houses Henri Jova had designed," said Morris, "and we subsequently published several of them. Actually, Henri had me helping him carry a rug into his offices, which were in Colony Square, which Henri, of course, had designed, and he'd done a beautiful job of it.

"Emory wanted to choose a local firm to design our building," said Philip. "Remember, at that time most of the architectural talent had gone to Atlanta because there wasn't any real opportunity in Birmingham. Today it's different."

McCalla said, "I remember, Philip, that you and I and Emory got in the car and drove around Birmingham all one day, looking at new buildings. We went into one building to visit the CEO, and we had to go through a *fire door* to get to his office. And a glass curtain on the west wall kept snapping and popping like a bowl of Rice Krispies. It was a total bust. I think that did it for Emory."

"Yes," agreed Philip. "He told me to tell Henri Jova to call him. Emory kept saying he wanted something like the Ford Foundation Building in New York."

Emory remembered those discussions. "I was talking to Roger McGuire about the new building I envisioned. Roger said, 'The next time you go to New York be sure and see the Ford Foundation Building. It's made out of material you ought to use on our building.' So I did. I saw immediately what Roger was talking about." The material was steel that would oxidize into a reddish-brown warmth that would fit comfortably into the trees. "Philip," said Emory, "put me on to the architect, Henri Jova."

But before Philip could be concerned about a new building, he had to attack the existing homes pages in *Southern Living*. "Gary put me in a room with stacks of *Sunset* magazines and said, 'Read these and absorb them.' I had never seen *Sunset*. But it was pretty easy to pick up what they were doing, both in terms of language and content.

"Simultaneously, I was going through the damn photo files to see what we could salvage. We were headed into winter and without much chance to get out and shoot. There wasn't much photography we could use. We had reams of stuff, but so often we had one photograph which was waiting on another to be complete. I told our homes photographer, Bob Lancaster, 'From now on we will shoot two of everything.' "

Morris remembered one set of mystifying photographs. "We had this array of Birmingham women standing by their mantels," he said, "these impressive looking dowagers, these intimidating women *looking right at you*. What on earth could you do with that?"

Morris said, "We didn't start out working with interior designers. *Sunset* did not do interior design. So that came later for us. We began by working with architects. I just looked in the yellow pages. I found this guy, and we did his house on the Eastern Shore of Mobile Bay. It would still be a very nice house in the magazine."

On that first trip to Mobile in February, Morris and Lancaster shot forty stories, shocking McCalla. "All of it was black-and-white photography in those days," said Morris, "but we soon began to run the homes lead in color. Some of the stuff we did in Mobile we wouldn't do today, of course, and some of it never ran. But it was a start."

That first trip also introduced Morris to the rituals of working with the absolutely professional and portly Bob Lancaster. "It was like traveling with your grandmother, you know," said Philip. "Once you established where you were going to have lunch, it helped matters. That was Bob's highest priority. And he only liked to eat vegetables, so you couldn't just grab something. I learned that the longer I delayed lunch, the faster and faster Bob would work. I was really a photographic assistant. I carried Bob's damn bags most of my career." If the meticulous Lancaster ever absolutely missed a shot, no one can remember it. Very soon Morris was writing and producing over two hundred columns a year.

He agreed with McCalla's decision to build a staff to shoot the magazine's own photography. "The free-lance architectural photographers all wanted to shoot the glamour stuff. None of them wanted to shoot the bloody closets," said Philip.

It didn't take Morris long to understand that the total contemporary *Sunset* look was not right for *Southern Living.* "I began to get the feeling that to serve this region a diet of only contemporary things was not a good idea," said Philip. "I remember getting a letter from a woman who lived in a historic house, which was beautifully reproduced on her letterhead. And in this beautiful handwriting she said, 'I'm sorry I'm dropping my subscription because your houses *have too many sharp angles.*' " Much laughter from McCalla and Logue. "You know when I looked at what we were doing, there *were* a lot of sharp angles in those houses," said Morris.

He said, "I used to go up to the Furniture Mart in North Carolina and try and help our guys drum up advertising. I met this fellow at Thomasville Furniture. He just said point-blank, 'Why don't you do interiors?' I said, 'Well, we don't use color, we really hadn't thought about it, we're not sure, and so on. He said that many more people are going to redo a house than build a house. I knew he was representing the furniture industry, but those were sound statements.

"After I'd been on the magazine about two years, we finally started looking at interiors. We approached interiors with the same purpose we'd approached architecture, which was problem solving," said Philip. "Interiors really do solve problems. And they made sense for us. We were turning away from *Sunset* and toward serving our own region. We were looking for interiors that had traditional roots but had some freshness also. We played that theme again and again. We weren't interested in any designer who had gone off the deep end.

"We did a house in North Carolina by a wonderful interior designer, Harvey Gunter. He had gone to the Parsons School of Design. Harvey collected small versions of furniture; he had tables on top of tables, as far as you could get from clean contemporary design. I think it was Harvey's partner who came up with the phrase to describe their basic client. I'll say it quickly, the way he did: *Junior League–Georgian.*

"It did capture the *Southern Living* style, and we used that phrase many times," said Morris. "Among basic Georgian stuff that we published, there was always a painting or something fresh that you could talk about. So we were portraying what people wanted and felt comfortable with. We always wanted to be a little upscale, but not out of the question."

It's funny to remember that the magazine in those days put a sort of ceiling of about one hundred thousand dollars on the price of a house it would feature. Some of those houses today resell for one million dollars. Morris would often shoot a vignette in a house that would be far too elaborate to feature in its entirety in *Southern Living.*

And sometimes the house he scouted would prove a total disaster, and making his escape was a matter of much diplomacy. "I killed off Bob's family many times," said Morris. "I would take a look at the place and say, 'I'm going to have to send my photographer home; there's been a death in the family.'"

Louis Joyner, a graduate architect, came aboard the magazine in 1973 as a photographer, and ultimately succeeded Morris as design editor. Once in a photo-pick session, Joyner, possessed of a dry wit, gave a two-word description of an unfortunate image on the screen: "Subject failure," said Louis. And that unhappy phrase has been uttered in photo picks many times through the years.

Diplomacy itself occasionally failed, however careful the Homes Department. "A woman in Texas once sent us scouting photographs of her house," said Morris. "It was a very sterile, commercial-looking building. I passed a note to Louis. I said, 'This thing looks like a branch bank, and we're just not interested.' Somehow, when Louis sent back her photographs, *my note went with them,*" said Philip, wincing at the memory. "The lady wrote me one sentence: 'I believe this belongs to you,' and enclosed my own note."

"I hope you sent her a cookbook," said Logue. "God, we should have sent her a test kitchen."

It didn't take long for Morris to practice his life's obsession, urban design, be it new or historic. "We did 'The Vamp of Savannah,' " he said. "Savannah, Georgia, was just turning itself around. That was my introduction to historic preservation, because there was no preservation in Oklahoma. The story was a combination of urban development and preservation. We did Savannah in the well of the magazine, and our homes lead was a house on Jones Street. We had a good response from Savannah, and it was important, because preservation in the early 1970s was a battle zone. They didn't know then that it was also a great investment. We didn't present it as controversial. We just said, this is the way it is."

Whenever possible, Morris would formally pose the people who had made it happen in the renovation of a historic district, or a small town, or a neighborhood. "It made heroes of them in their own community," said Logue. Morris agreed: "Yes, we wanted to recognize the people who made these things happen."

After Savannah, he did "Upright, Uptight, Victorian Renovations" in New Orleans. "In the Garden District," said Philip, "really neat architecture. The architect spent twenty-seven thousand dollars to redo his house of three thousand five hundred square feet. The writing was so simple and direct." And problem solving. *Southern Living* began to discover its own design voice.

"I think we began to establish our independence from actual national thinking," said Morris. "The national thinking through that period was 'Regionalism is dead, our buildings should be built in international style, it's only sentimental if you respond to local tradition.' "

Morris said, "I went to the Home Builders Convention each year in Houston. I went to a party at the house of architect Clobis Heinsmith. He still practices in Texas. At the party, I met this editor of *Architectural Record*. He found out I was from the South. He said, 'Oh, I hate to be invited to go talk in the South. They always want to talk about regionalism. There is no regionalism.' He said it in the most arrogant way."

"Did you hit him?" asked Logue.

"No. But mentally it firmed up the idea that we're going to say something different. And I remember we got these scouting photographs of a new house in Huntsville, Alabama. It was this rectilinear cube that stepped down this hill with these cumbersome ugly bays. I took the photographs into Louis Joyner. It was a watershed moment. Louis and I had been talking about our design direction. I said, 'Louis, this looks to me like a Midas Muffler Shop. And we're not doing any more of this stuff.' We had been gradually moving away from it. It wasn't two years later we did a pure Greek Revival 'Idea House' in Mississippi. We were way ahead of what was happening in architecture. We were postmodern before post-modern was cool. We didn't invent anything; people were doing what we considered good regional architecture, contemporary takes on regional, traditional forms."

Morris had not been on the staff a year before he researched and wrote "The Southern Seacoast—Keeping Its Balance." It ran as a cover story with a rare gatefold image and was one of the seminal stories on the environment in the history of *Southern Living*. Gerald Crawford shot the photography, including the gatefold cover. Typical of the magazine, it approached the destiny of the South's 2,500-mile coastline from the point of view of constructive solutions. "For thousands of miles of South-ern seacoast, the future is just beginning. Beneficent neglect of the past gives way to a new concern that man's increased activity not destroy the delicate naturalness of coastal lands."

It was not an antidevelopment argument. "We included the better coastal developments," said Philip. "It's amazing how little we knew in those days about the seacoast. Swamps were considered wastelands. I think South Carolina pioneered the protection of sea oats, the one plant that holds sand dunes together."

The story had a powerful influence in every Southern coastal state. The Texas state legislature was about to vote on a bill offering protection of its own seacoast. A copy of that issue of *Southern Living* was placed on the desk of each legislator. It didn't hurt. The bill passed.

There is hardly a city in the South that sits on the water, be it an ocean or a river, from Selma, Alabama, to Baton Rouge, Louisiana, that hasn't had its innovative treatment of its waterfront in *Southern Living*.

Morris is particularly proud of his early story "The Great Neighbor-hood Revival." Featured were New Orleans' Lower Garden District, Jacksonville's Riverside-Avondale, Atlanta's Ansley Park, Little Rock's Quapaw Quarter, Raleigh's Oakwood, Durham's Trinity Park, and Mo-bile's Oakleigh. "We had the shotgun house from Mobile on the cover," said Philip. "The important thing was communities were no longer only trying to save a single building but a whole neighborhood. They weren't just trying to preserve history but to protect the entire neighborhood from commercial encroachment."

And then there were the small towns. "Mary Means of the National Trust invented the Main Street program," said Morris. "Her daddy was an Atlanta architect." The program recognizes outstanding work by small towns in keeping or restoring their character. It began twenty years ago, and *Southern Living*, under Philip, became a willing accomplice. In one issue in 1984, the magazine featured Staunton, Virginia; Tarboro, North Carolina; West Point, Mississippi; Georgetown, Texas; and Fayetteville, Arkansas. "We did them as surveys," said Morris. "We wanted to create a sense of movement, of something bigger going on. I remember Tarboro. It was one of my favorites down toward tobacco country, a sweet place that had done everything right."

Philip said, "What these small towns didn't do was more important than what they did do. I remember the banker Allen Tartt, from the little town of Livingston, Alabama. Allen had a wistful sense of humor. They'd had a consultant in from Mobile. 'You know we never built the monorail,' said Allen. I said, 'The what?' This consultant had advised them they needed a *monorail* from downtown Livingston—population 1,200—to their empty industrial park, which is still empty.

"But the craziest thing that did happen, happened in Rock Hill, South Carolina," said Philip.

"Careful," said Logue, "my wife went to college at Winthrop."

"One of these consultants convinced Rock Hill it had to become a mall in order to compete," said Philip. "They totally enclosed Main Street in this giant box. Of course, it immediately died. And was empty. It looked like the Twilight Zone. Now they have taken the son of a bitch off and restored Main Street. I want to finish my career putting together a book of examples of small towns and what they have done to keep their character. There are some wonderful examples."

In 1990, Philip compiled and wrote the introduction to one of Oxmoor House's most beautiful and significant visual books, *Southern Places*. It captured the physical essence of the South and represented the work of many on the *Southern Living* staff.

There has never been a greater champion of Southern cities than Philip Morris. Or a more alert critic of their successes and their foibles. Sitting on his deck, the day he met with McCalla and Logue, he was excited over the re-energizing of downtown Fort Worth, Texas. "They've done some extraordinary things," said Philip. "They've got a multiplex cinema right downtown that is drawing huge crowds. They have a new opera house.

They are trying to attract a big bookstore." Morris burns with the same enthusiasm that lit his fires in 1969.

Logue said, "I always enjoyed the stories we've published of cities restoring their great old motion-picture theaters, like the Fox in Atlanta. Remember the grand old theater in one city had fallen into the clutches of an adult movie operator. It created a bit of a stir around town when we casually dropped into our story the fact that the building was owned by a local church. It was one of the more rousing reactions we've had from a restoration story."

The titles alone of some of Morris's most memorable stories capture the thrust of his career: "Don't Just Save the Past, Use It" ('74); "Five Southern Towns Change and Stay the Same" ('78); "Building with, Not Against the Land" ('78); "Shaping Livable Southern Cities" ('80); "Making Cities Beautiful Again" ('85); "Houston's Monument to Civic Art" ('88); "The Revival of Town Planning" ('94); and perhaps the finest city story, words and photography, ever published in *Southern Living*: "Pennsylvania Avenue, Making an American Place" ('87).

"John O'Hagan took the terrific photographs of Pennsylvania Avenue in one afternoon," marveled Morris.

In an average year, Philip will make as many as thirty major speeches on design to a great variety of audiences. They range from the Atlanta Midtown Business Association to the Historic Mobile Foundation, to the Texas Historical Commission, to the Junior League of Nashville, to the University of South Carolina, to the Asheville (N.C.) Federation of Garden Clubs. Morris doesn't go to hear himself talk; he goes to make a difference in the design integrity of the South. Probably no other single design voice has had as much influence in the region in the last quarter century. These days Morris operates as editor-at-large for the company, contributing to *Southern Living* and writing an architectural column and garden design for *Southern Accents*. His work has already surfaced to good effect in the new magazine *Coastal Living*.

Philip was quick to point out that Louis Joyner was the first magazine journalist to capture the now-internationally celebrated Seaside development on the coast of the Florida Panhandle.

"Louis discovered it," said Morris. "He said, 'We found this crazy thing down at the Gulf Coast.' And he shot the first street under construction and got real low to the picket fence, and the folks at Seaside will tell you people showed up with the magazine, saying, 'Where is this place?'

Louis made it look like it was completed." Since that story, no major design magazine in America, or Europe, has failed to cover Seaside.

Morris said, "The developer, Robert Davis, and the husband/wife architects, Andres Duany and Elizabeth Plater-Ziberk, rediscovered the idea that you can make a community of architecture, a community of houses, not just houses on lots. It's the most important movement in community architecture in the last half of this century."

It's also a smashing success. Morris said, "They ran their streets perpendicular to the beach front. They narrowed the streets, brought the houses close to the street, created a civic realm by putting major features at the ends of streets, gazebos or pavilions. A town is a town. So the interior land is valuable. Duany told me five years ago that interior land at Seaside was selling for one million dollars an acre. It has just been a revolution in terms of what they have reintroduced to the world. Again, we didn't invent it. But Louis discovered it."

The power of *Southern Living* to influence the awareness of good design in the landscape was never more evident.

"We did the *Sunset* bit in the beginning," said Morris, "but we went far beyond what *Sunset* ever did."

In the 1970s, the magazine was bankrupt of garden design. "We weren't doing any," said Philip. "We taught you how to plant something, but no design. Bob and I started picking up garden photography on Fridays, literally on our way to the airport. I would call landscape architects. We could do it quickly. If we didn't like the damn stuff, we didn't have to use it. We were starting to cover landscape architecture at the very time the profession took root in the South. I'm actually most proud of that. There were only two landscape architects in Birmingham when I moved here in 1969."

"We also had only two bookstores," said Logue. "You can't count them now."

"As time went on, you would find landscape architects in smaller cities like Knoxville, as well as in Atlanta and Birmingham," said Morris. "I think we really helped, because a lot of people didn't know what a landscape architect did."

"We even hired one," said McCalla.

"Two," said Morris. "We interviewed Glenn Morris and Norman Johnson. They were both so interesting, Emory said hire them both, which we did, which was pretty darn amazing."

"Both were great characters," said Logue. "McCalla would get on

Glenn for wandering up and down the halls taking up everybody's time. But it was his curiosity that made him restless. He was curious about everything and wrote very well. He wound up doing stories on rock climbing, how sand dunes are formed, all manner of things as well as landscape design. I hated it when he left.

"And Norman could throw twelve stems across a crowded room, and they'd make the most smashing flower arrangement you could imagine. He wrote in the strangest way I've ever known," said Logue. "He'd write down phrases and then come back and link them together and make sentences. He was full of good ideas." Now Norman is a successful landscape designer in Birmingham, and Glenn lives in North Carolina and writes free-lance articles for various Southern Progress publications.

Morris recruited bright young people and helped them evolve into journalists. One requirement: a passion for design. Katherine Pearson had never written a sentence for publication when she was recruited from a utility company in Georgia in February, 1974. "I remember she came into my office one day," said Logue, "and asked me, 'How do you learn to write?' I said, 'Get a sheet of copy paper and put it down like you were writing home to your mother.' Katherine didn't need any help from me. She became an excellent writer." Later Pearson was the editor of *Coastal Living*. Katherine took a few years off to get a degree from the Parsons School of Design before she was recruited back to the company.

Another Morris favorite was Carol Engle. "Carol was never a great writer," said Philip, "but she could bag the subject matter. She knew exactly what a *Southern Living* house was. She made her first trip to Louisville. I was supposed to stay with her the whole week. I could see Carol knew exactly what she was doing, and I just left." Carol later married a dentist and moved to Florida, but has done the occasional free-lance piece.

Shelley Tichelli and Julia Hamilton Thomason had a genius for clever and practical projects for the home, as did Deborah Hastings and Andy Hartley. "I always felt we had a good climate for people to flourish in," said Morris.

Linda Hallam, a bright young woman who writes as rapidly as she speaks, followed in the talented tradition of *Southern Living* Homes Editors before moving on to *Better Homes & Gardens*. Then Julia Hamilton moved back to Birmingham and took over the job, also in the talented tradition of *S.L.* Homes Editors.

McCalla and Morris launched a program of "*Southern Living* Plans."

It continues to feature, and offer for sale, original house plans by leading Southern architects. A typical plan was "the Highlander . . . inspired by the raised cottages of the Southern coastal region and by the comfortable, country farmhouses of the interior South." Lil Petrusnek grew up running the program, which is not only a service to the readers but has become a large profit center for the magazine.

Southern Living began building "Idea Houses" in the 1970s, one of the first being a house in San Antonio designed by O'Neil Ford and staff. Houses have been built in collaboration with the Brick Institute of America, and today the magazine builds as many as one hundred custom houses each year, all across the South. Tens of thousands of readers pay to visit these Idea Houses, which are then sold to the public.

"I remember when we moved into the new building in 1972," said McCalla, "Emory called me in and asked how many people I would ultimately need to produce the magazine. I thought about it and decided not to hold back, and put down thirty-five people. And now there are over a hundred on the *Southern Living* staff.

"In the late seventies, as the magazine grew so fast, we nearly doubled our editorial staff from forty-eight people to eighty," said McCalla. "That gave us the talent and the time to improve. And the 1980s were our glory years."

"And we had the freedom to follow our instincts," said Logue.

"Yes," said Philip. "I remember when McCalla was out." (At one point McCalla was out drying out in a highly successful battle with demon rum.) "Frankly," said Morris, "having spent that month with Emory when Gary was away—that month seemed like a lifetime—I never realized before how much Gary had buffered us. I never realized how important it was for Gary to let some of Emory's ideas go in one ear and out the other."

"Well, I gave Emory several excuses to fire me over the years," said McCalla, "and he never did. I don't know why."

"I can tell you why," said Logue. "Check the subscribers' renewal rate. You were putting out the best-loved magazine in America. Emory had great instincts but they didn't always translate to specific editorial ideas. I think one of Emory's strengths was he would push his platforms, but he didn't insist on them, and he would back away, and his instincts for the overall magazine were good, and for what our role should be."

"Oh, yes," said Morris. "Emory's instincts were very important. They allowed me to be serious about this stuff, design. But I'm glad Gary was there to buffer us. And I always thought John was the great coach."

"Yeah, and McCalla was our UN Peacekeeping Force," said Logue, "except he was more likely to stir things up than settle them down."

In truth, Philip himself and Caleb Pirtle never did exactly "gee and haw," Caleb with his folksy ways and Philip coming from a more sophisticated and serious-minded intent. Luckily, they were usually traveling in different states. Remember what Tallulah Bankhead said when asked if she believed in separate bedrooms: "No, separate cities, dahling."

Logue startles an innocent mermaid at an editorial conference.

McCalla, a genuine Choctaw, often startled job applicants when he appeared in full headdress.

Bob Lancaster is legendary for his immaculate homes shots and his profound lunches.

Charles Walton proved to be the boy genius of food photography.

Ralph Marks adds the finishing touches to his portrait of an All-South Football Team.

The *S.L.* photography staff of the early 1980s. *Front row, left to right:* Sylvia Martin, John O'Hagan, Lisa Simonton, and Susan Chandler. *Back row:* Mike Clemmer, Charles Walton, Bruce Roberts, Beth Maynor, Geoff Gilbert, Mac Jamieson, Mary-Gray Hunter, Bob Lancaster, and Van Chaplin.

Talent stacked on talent. *Front row, left to right:* Associate Copy Chief Louise Mimbs and Senior Writer Dianne Young. *Second row:* Art Director Donovan Harris and Managing Editor Bill McDougald. *Back row:* Senior Writer Steve Bender and Copy Chief Isie Hanson.

The editorial conference dance team from the mid-1980s: *Front row, left to right:* Kay Fuston, Rebecca Scoggins, Linda Askey, Wanda Butler, and Cheryl Dalton. *Second row:* Donovan Harris, Charles Walton, Darryl Moland, and Clay Nordan. *Back row:* McCalla and John O'Hagan. This dance team's antics rivaled the musical *Springtime for Hitler*.

From a tiny handful in 1967, the *Southern Living* editorial staff had grown by the 1980s into a rousing, gifted crew of more than a hundred.

Tough guys who danced to the music of the advertising wars. *Front row, left to right:* Jim DeVira, Emory Cunningham, Smith Moseley, Roger McGuire, and Jerry Jehle. *Back row:* Bill Nauman, Don Cunningham, and John Ruffin.

Don Cunningham tells—one more time—the Wide-Mouth Frog Joke.

The best magazine advertising sales force in America in the 1970s. Jerry Latzky, of course, stands up front in his open-collar shirt and sandals, with professional Irishman Mike Fitzgerald directly behind him. Smith Moseley (*left*) and Orville Demaree are the front row bookends.

Cunningham and DeVira are both tall, but they don't always see eye to eye.

A sign of coming up in the world: Southern Progress's first new building on Shades Creek Parkway.

Logue reviews some of his infamous rejection letters on the occasion of his twentieth anniversary with the company. Helen Logue has a laugh, as do Don Logan (*left*) and Tom Angelillo, two very popular presidents of Southern Progress Corporation.

Dixie Snell gets a hug from the top man, Emory Cunningham, on the occasion of her twentieth anniversary with the company.

Direct mail guru Bill Capps celebrates some good circulation news with McCalla (*center*) and Logan.

Sold to the strong bidder, Time, Inc.: one company, Southern Progress, for $480 million, whence the laughter. *Sitting, left to right:* Emory Cunningham and Southern Progress Chief Financial Officer Vernon Owens. *Standing:* Don Logan; Time, Inc., President Dick Monroe; Southern Progress Associate Financial Officer Jim Nelson; and Time, Inc., magazine chief Kelso Sutton.

Henry Grunwald, editor-in-chief of Time, Inc., who hates t-shirts, nonetheless is a good sport at a *Southern Living* editorial meeting soon after the sale of the company.

John Floyd (*left*), one of McCalla's old boys, replaces him as Editor of *Southern Living*. Bill McDougald moves up from the Gardens Department to become Managing Editor.

Southern Progress's new, new building on Lake Shore Drive in Birmingham.

Southern Progress Corporation President Tom Angelillo and the new vice-president in charge of SPC editorial, Jeanetta Keller, visit the *Southern Living*–Opryland "Idea House" in Nashville. The changing of the guard at the company is now complete.

Once more to the good times! *Left to right*: Vice-President for Travel Advertising Bud Flora, Gary McCalla, Jim DeVira, and John Logue engage in a toast as time moves inexorably on.

13

Circulating Around

Sam Baldone heard everything, saw everything, remembered everything. Like the pharmacist in *Madame Bovary,* he was the ideally positioned observer. All those years he ran the *Progressive Farmer* mail room, then jousted with labor at the Oxmoor Press printing company, and finally became the jack-of-all-trades running every sort of errand for management at the newly named Southern Progress Corporation.

It's nearly impossible to interrupt Sam. And you learn more if you don't.

"Yeah, I seen and done a lot of things, but I never got no stock," said Sam, who made his own nest egg buying old houses and fixing them up and renting them out. He also contracted to keep the company's building cleaned at night, and helped send his son through medical school with the extra money.

A short, happy, powerful man with dark eyes that didn't miss much, Sam joined Progressive Farmer in November, 1946. "Mr. Jeff Newton said we had 'a twelve-million-dollar company,' " said Sam. "He said, 'We take in six, and we spend six.' " Newton went on to become the company treasurer.

Sam remembers when Vernon Owens first interviewed for a job in

1948. Later, Vernon became the company's chief financial officer. "Vernon came down and said, 'Mr. Dugger wants me to talk to you.' Hell, I just had a job in the mail room. We talked, and I kept grabbing them bundles of mail. Mr. Dugger passed word to me to come up there and see him. He wanted to know what I thought of Vernon. I knew he wasn't coming to work in the mail room.

"I said, 'He's tall, and he's a big boy, and you like them big boys, and he's a University of Alabama graduate.' Mr. Dugger said, 'Well, that's enough.' . . . Anyway, Vernon stuck and did a big job for Progressive Farmer.

"He wanted to follow in the footsteps of Fowler Dugger as general manager," said Sam. "And Fowler Dugger wanted him, because I saw the letter when Mr. Dugger wrote to introduce Vernon as his follow-up. If we ever had a gentleman that worked for Progressive Farmer, it was Mr. Dugger. Well, they had one of those meetings in the auditorium in the old building. I'm picking this up from Pop Rogers [circulation manager].

"Everybody was going to get introduced to Vernon," said Sam. "But President Gene Butler said, 'I hadn't cast my vote yet.' He didn't want to move Vernon from his job. Mr. Butler said he didn't want to overlook Emory Cunningham. He was up there in Chicago selling advertising. He got real good at selling. And if you meet him today, he ain't quit selling. At that time, Paul Huey—advertising manager—had a heart attack and died in Barbados, and he was a big wheel. Mr. Butler insisted they move Emory back to Birmingham.

"Vernon quit," Baldone said. "He was mad. But he got glad and came right back. He pouted for a couple or three days. But there was a little friction there between him and Emory. Dr. Copeland used to be the referee between Emory and Vernon. That was his job. Hell, they had shouting matches upstairs on Shades Creek Parkway. But they halfway got along. They were old enough and smart enough to understand their positions.

"Emory didn't pull no punches," said Sam. "He put that number fourteen shoe down, and he wouldn't move it."

Baldone had a special friendship with Cunningham. They had a long-running argument about who was the older. Sam admitted, "Emory's really thirteen months younger than I am. But we used to argue about it." Sam built the closet for Emory's hat and coat in his office in the old building. And he put in strip heaters in the new building on Shades Creek Parkway to keep Emory's feet warm. "I remember telling him it would take a lot of heat because his feet were big. I joked with him now and then," said Sam. Emory saw to it that Sam got the contract at a fair price to get the company building cleaned at night.

"When they got ready to sell Oxmoor Press, they began to cut back, and I got laid off," said Baldone. "I went to work for Associated Cleaners. In the meantime, I wrote Emory a letter, and got them to give me a leave of absence plus my vacation. And then two weeks before that was up, Britt Butler came back from Alaska. He called me up and said, 'Your time is about to run out [to keep his job and his pension]. Come on over here,' said Britt, 'and just go on down to the mail room.' " Sam said, "Otherwise, I would have been out."

The company would hardly have been the same without Sam Baldone.

"Vernon knew numbers," said Sam. "He was smart with the pencil. I always got along with him. When he'd get mad and bawl me out, most of the time he was right. When he asked you a question, don't bullshit him, tell him the numbers right. Because he'd come back and check you. I learned that a long time ago.

"Vernon liked Jim Nelson," said Sam. "He encouraged Nelson to go to school, and he did. Nelson run a good set of books for Vernon, and when you satisfied Vernon and you done what Vernon told you, Vernon would take up for you. Nelson was good. But he was never a mixer." Nelson succeeded Don Logan as president of Southern Progress when Logan moved to Time, Inc., in New York. Nelson now works for Logan in Manhattan.

Oh, Sam remembers Britt Butler. "He would buy that cheap Scotch tape. You would pull it, and it would break. Y'all weren't there when he bought them cheap pencils. You put them in the pencil sharpener, and the damn lead came out the other end. He used to save all this string. He had a ball of string THIS BIG at his desk and every time he'd get a piece of string, he'd wrap it around it. And we had this little offset press for office work. Britt would call up some of these ink companies and talk to them and ask if they would leave a sample. They would do it. They would be thinking of selling *Progressive Farmer* drums of it. Well, Britt got those samples forever; he never did buy no ink.

"Britt drove an ol' pickup truck," Sam said. "One time he went to the airport to pick up Mr. Butler and Charlie Scruggs. Charlie told me they didn't have no seat for him. He had to ride in the back of the pickup with the suitcases, and he was hot about it. 'Damn editor of a damn magazine, and I'm riding in the back of a pickup truck,' he told me. I said, 'Charlie, nothin' wrong with that. Hell, you're workin' for *Progressive Farmer.*' "

In the early days of *Southern Living*, Roger McGuire once flew back from Texas with a top executive from the Dallas advertising agency Tracy-Locke. McGuire spotted President Gene Butler on the plane. Getting off and getting their luggage, McGuire stalled every way possible, because he knew the president of the company was about to climb in the cab of a sorry old pickup while he was trying to convince this advertising heavyweight that *Southern Living* was the magazine of the New South.

One thing Sam hasn't forgotten about Britt Butler. After Sam wrote the letter to Emory, it was Britt who gave him his old job back in the mail room.

"My first recollection of Roger McGuire," said Baldone, "was when I'd be cleaning the building, sometimes I would bring my grandson D. J., and McGuire would be in the Administrative Department lots of nights. He used to like to talk to D. J. because D. J. had learned all these dinosaur names, and he used to question D. J. about them. I never did get the story on why McGuire quit."

Baldone has some rich memories about the old building, which saw its share of hanky-panky over the years, even under the very proper water tower labeled THE PROGRESSIVE FARMER. "We built Pop Rogers this huge office," said Sam. "It had a little sectional couch in it. Pop called me one morning, mad as he could be. There was strong evidence somebody had done made out that night on his couch. And Pop said, 'What the hell are you gonna do about it?' I said, 'The first thing I'm gonna do is clean this damn place up.' "

Then there was the young agricultural editor who was discovered one night with a female employee in the most awkward of circumstances. McCalla and Logue remembered the incident. They believed the young man might not have lost his job if they hadn't been on top of the big, formal company conference table. It wasn't the sort of collaboration the founding fathers had in mind when they first commissioned that table into being. McCalla and Logue thought the young woman, in her choice of partners, showed a poverty of imagination.

"We used to sit outside and wave at the gals coming to work," said Sam. "There was one who never waved back. We called her 'Miss Stuck Up.' We had a photographer, we used to call him 'the Green Hornet.' We had nicknames for everybody. One of the guys found these pictures in the photo lab. The Green Hornet had done taken these pictures of this girl sittin' on a stool, and all she was wearing was *just beads*, not even any shoes. It was her, 'Miss Stuck Up.' "

On a grimmer note, Baldone can remember in the postwar years when money was tight and "Mr. Dugger cut everybody's pay 10 percent. But he couldn't cut the crafts because they had contracts," said Sam. "I was president of the Birmingham Mailers' Union at the time. And I went before them and said, 'Look, these people are in trouble. And we need to help them.' And we were the only ones that voluntarily laid off for three days or four days. But come Christmas, they sold more ads and paid us for all the days we laid off. Mr. Dugger had lost his voice box, but he was fair and honest and pretty damn smart."

Baldone remembers the secret comings and goings when Time, Inc., was negotiating to buy the company. "I went out to the airport one time to pick up the guy they dealt with so much. Dick Monroe. A nice guy. And they come over in that plane at Airport One. And we got in Emory's new Mercedes, and Mr. Monroe said, 'Sam, whose car is this?' I said, 'This is a company car.' He said, 'Well, we drive Chevrolets up in New York.' I said, 'Well, hell, I wouldn't want to drive anything up there better than a Chevrolet either, 'cause y'all always gettin' fenders bent.' "

Sam said, "I knew what he was saying. And he said, 'How much did this car cost?' And I said, 'Mr. Monroe, I have no idea.' Of course I was the one who signed for it with the sticker on the window. I knew exactly what it cost. I was not telling them Yankees nothin' to get me fired."

Baldone worked long enough—forty years—to receive *two* company watches. Emory played a trick on him and put a Mickey Mouse watch in the box the second time but quickly came across with the real McCoy, a Rolex. When the company became profitable, Cunningham decided that if you were going to give somebody a watch, give him one he'd like to have. It was also his decision to keep fresh fruit in baskets for the employees on every floor of the company buildings.

By the end of Sam Baldone's career, if there was anything in the building that needed handling, he handled it. "I got to helping Dr. Copeland do all that stuff for Emory," said Sam. "One big thing in the fall was to have a big party in the morning and go to Legion Field for a football game. I learned how to hire policemen for the police escort, and make arrangements for the bus, and call the caterers.

"So one Friday evening, Dr. Copeland called me up before this big party. Alabama was playing somebody. And Cope said, 'Sam, nobody in this building knows this but you, and don't tell nobody. I'm going to the

Auburn-Georgia game tomorrow. Emory gave me two tickets.' He said, 'I going to the game, and I'm not coming back.' I said, 'What do you mean?' He said, 'Well, I've been wanting to retire because I want to go teach at the University of Georgia at least for a couple of years. And every time I bring it up to Emory, Emory ignores me. So I'm not coming back. I've already written a letter to Emory, and when I leave I'm going to put it on his desk.' "

Sam said, "I was scared to death I was going to do something wrong. I'd gotten the police, everything goin'. And then Emory the next morning said, 'Sam, come here. Where is Cope?' 'Hell, I don't know.' And then he came back again. I wasn't going to mention the letter. I said, 'Didn't you give Cope two tickets to the Auburn-Georgia ball game?' Emory said, 'I didn't think he was going to leave until after he got the party over.' I said I didn't know."

So Dr. Copeland, the ultimate company man, eased away into the night to avoid his last confrontation. Sam survived. The party was a big hit.

Nobody had his hands on the pulse of *Southern Living* more securely than Bill Capps, who ran the Circulation Department from the early 1970s into the 1990s. Capps, a large athletic guy, quick with a quip, was famous for his sweepstakes promotions, for his terrible poems written on the retirement of fellow workers, and for his over-the-top wit. A huge Auburn fan, Capps once put a sign on his van during a Tiger football slump: FOR SALE. VERY LOW MILEAGE. DRIVEN ONLY TO WINNING AUBURN GAMES.

Logue once dropped Capps a memo, asking him to give a report at the *Southern Living* editorial meeting on "Circulation and the Cardiovascular System." Capps and his sidekick Buddy Floyd showed up in white intern jackets, wearing stethoscopes, with all manner of circulation-medical charts. Their presentations were right out of the old comedy team Bud Abbott and Lou Costello.

In 1968, Capps answered a blind ad Jim Moon had placed in the Birmingham newspapers. Capps's beloved father worked for the post office. "I cheated," said Bill. "I called my dad and found out whose box number it was in the ad. I wrote a letter saying I wanted to apply for a position 'with Progressive Farmer.' Turned out Moon lived a half block from me.

He was so intrigued that I found out whose ad it was that he came to my house to see me."

Moon worked in advertising promotion, and was a good Catholic guy with six or eight kids. When the old building was sold he bought the huge old conference table as his dining room table. (It was more storied than he may have known.) They say the good die young and so, tragically, did Jim Moon.

"Jim offered me the job right then,' said Capps. But I had to interview with Emory Cunningham and go to lunch with Roger McGuire and Smith Moseley. Roger and Smith wanted me to visit with Orville Demaree."

"The acid test," said Logue.

"I was working for Protective Life," said Capps. "I could only see Demaree early in the morning. Orville went in at 6 A.M. It was winter and dark. They didn't leave many lights on in those days. I walked past the old-timey switchboard and got on the black-dark elevator. I got off at the third floor. Still no lights. I said, 'Hello!' 'That you, Capps?' said this voice. 'Come in here.' There was Orville bent under a goose-necked lamp."

"Like out of Dickens," said Logue, not for the first time in this narrative.

"Yeah. I told him who I had met with. And he said, 'I don't know what those sons of bitches told you, but I'm getting ready to tell you the real scoop.' I liked Orville," said Capps. "He would scream and yell. He and Smith Moseley used to get into screaming matches. Orville really thought he ran the sales force. He said *Southern Living* had all kinds of opportunity, but the mainstay of the company was *Progressive Farmer*. He was sold on *P.F.* He said, 'If you work hard, this is a good place to work.' "

Capps came aboard. With no office. "Moon put me in the office with him," said Bill. "He smoked these godawful cigars. I sat at a drawing table on a stool with no back. See, I was actually helping our artist a lot; they found out my degree at Auburn was in ad design. Smelling those cigars, my back hurting, my head, after a month I couldn't take it. I moved out in a big room with typewriters all around me. I was also writing copy. There was too much noise. So I built me that office out of filing cabinets."

"First time I ever saw you, you were buried in there," said Logue.

"Emory came in and told me I was gonna get fired if Britt Butler came up there and started asking who moved those files. Sure enough, Britt came up. I said that I did it. That they were going to build me an office but think how much money I had saved, and boy, that's all it took," said Capps. "Emory came over and said, 'You're gonna go a long way.' "

"I know how you felt. I had to build our editorial offices with ten sheets of plywood," said McCalla.

How did Capps move into the Circulation Department? "J. L. Rogers didn't work real well with John Tosarello, his young assistant," said Bill. "J. L. went to Emory and Emory went to McGuire and McGuire said, 'We've got a young fellow who might be good over there.' That was me."

"I remember Tosarello," said McCalla. "He barely got here when he opened up a night club in downtown Birmingham. That got Dr. Nunn's attention." There was some trouble, and Emory remembered the police showing up in his office. Nothing came of the trouble, but John was a city boy in deep country at Progressive Farmer, and was actually ill and didn't know it. "Once John got on medication he really became okay," said Capps.

"J. L. didn't fire Tosarello," Capps said. "He told me it was a sort of foregone conclusion John would quit if they brought me in. That was the way they did things back then. The first trip I took with John to New York to meet suppliers, we no sooner got on the airplane than John said, 'I've got me another job. I'm leaving. You're gonna have all this crap.' "

Tosarello's greatest contribution was introducing the company to direct mail consultant Dick Benson. The acerbic Benson, who walked with a cane and dripped with sarcasm, had been one of the founders of *American Heritage* magazine. With help from Art Director Irwin Glusker, he had invented many of the modern direct mail techniques for selling magazine subscriptions. If you didn't believe it, you could just ask him. But it was true.

Glusker, the only living American artist to have a sculpture in Central Park, and former art director of *LIFE*, was to design two of Oxmoor House's finest visual books: *A Southern Album*, with introduction by Willie Morris, and *Southerners*, with text by Charles Kuralt. Glusker also designed Oxmoor's eighteen-volume *Southern Heritage Cookbook Library*. "I don't know who is America's second-best designer of books," said Logue. "Glusker has retired the trophy as the best."

"We could not have done what we did in circulation promotion without Dick Benson, or somebody who played the role he did," said Emory Cunningham. "He would come into my office and order me to do this or that. He ordered me to send Bill Capps—he called him a kid—'Send that kid'—I believe, to Kansas City. There was some direct mail genius there who was old and sick, teaching direct mail. We sent Bill up there. Bill picked it up and I thought did a real good job of it."

When *Southern Living* was launched, Circulation Director Pop Rogers was dead against direct mail, and Benson's presence and knowledge helped Cunningham insist on selling the magazine in the mail, rather than have sheetwriters selling it door-to-door as *Progressive Farmer* had been sold for generations.

"Pop Rogers was a great, great guy," said Capps, "a grandaddy type. The first day I was in circulation, Mrs. Lucille Cater pulled me aside. She'd been Pop's secretary thirty-something years. Frances Mobley had been with him over forty years.

"Mrs. Cater wanted me to know a secret that J. L. didn't want anybody to know," said Bill. "Every afternoon he took a nap on the couch in his office. She said we had to protect him and keep him from being disturbed because he'd had a heart attack two years before, and 'He didn't want his wife to know.' I swear," said Capps. "Harold Dobson was working for Pop then, running field sales, and got him to the hospital. Pop wouldn't let 'em tell his wife. They told her he was out of town. I swear. Pop stayed in the hospital a week or two and went on home.

"Of course, he had another heart attack," said Capps, "and I got him to the hospital and really saved him, or he would have died in his office. I heard something stirring in his office, and I told Mrs. Cater it sounded like Pop was up. I walked in there, and he had this really gray look on his face. He said his arm hurt, he'd 'slept on it funny.' And I said, 'Uh-uh. We're going to the hospital.'

"He didn't argue," said Bill. "Jack McCain was coming back from lunch. He had a bad leg. I left him with Pop and went to get the van. We took him to Carraway Hospital. Boy, they slapped him into intensive care. I slipped in to see him, with those tubes running all into him. The only thing he said was 'Don't tell my wife.' My dad knew J. L.'s brother [a distinguished Birmingham lawyer]. I called him. He said he would handle it, that he would tell Pop's wife."

Capps said, "J. L. never did actually retire. He was off a whole year. And then he died [January 24, 1973]."

"Nobody could afford to retire at the old company," said McCalla. "They didn't have the money to fund an adequate retirement program. Everybody worked till they died." The Progressive Farmer Company began its first modest retirement program in 1944. One of Emory Cunningham's great contributions to the company was to launch a state-of-the-art retirement plan. But it was only possible because of the tremendous profitability of *Southern Living* and then of Oxmoor House.

Capps had been working in circulation only for a brief time, and suddenly he had responsibility for *Southern Living*. By 1974 he also took over circulation for *Progressive Farmer* from Jack McCain.

"Jack got crossways with Vernon Owens," said Bill. "It had something to do with reader demographics. Vernon was against what Jack wanted to do. It would have cost money. Jack wrote about a ten-page memo to Emory, and that really killed him with Vernon. Jack was a great guy. We were close friends. He told me after he was let go, 'I don't want you to be associated with me because I know how it works around here. So when I leave, I leave.' I didn't see him for three or four years. He went to work for *Writer's Digest* but came back to Birmingham and died.

"About that time," said Capps, "Emory decided we had gotten all the help we needed from Dick Benson. But Pop was dead. Tosarello was gone. I was green behind the ears. I didn't know what I was getting into in circulation. I went to Emory, and I said, 'Let's keep Benson on.' Benson doesn't know to this day I saved his consulting job."

This day of our conversation was February 21, 1996. "Is Benson still living?" asked McCalla. "Oh, yes," said Capps. Before the weekend was over, Benson had died, and Capps, Emory, Don Logan, and Tom Angelillo were flying to his funeral.

Capps said what he learned most from Benson was "how to evaluate the results of a direct mail test, how to understand the test results, and then figure how to roll out the direct mail campaign. And I got a lot of exposure through him to other magazine people that I wouldn't have gotten. Circulation people help each other; we're not competitive.

"I let the last field sales people go, the 'sheetwriters,' the carney types," said Capps. "McCain recorded a bull session among those old guys in a motel room in Mississippi. They were drinking Jack Daniel's and telling old stories. It was absolutely hilarious. One of those guys would get him a set of crutches and drive up to a farmhouse and sit on the horn until somebody came out, and he'd tell them he was wounded in the war, and hell, he hadn't been old enough to be drafted. But he'd get the sympathy vote and sell them a subscription to *Progressive Farmer* and life insurance and all that stuff. I wish I had that tape."

What was the true story on how *Progressive Farmer* converted subscribers to the newly launched *Southern Living*? Did the company really ask these readers if they wanted to be converted?

"They took two hundred thousand *P.F.* subscribers and just converted them," said Capps. "If you subscribed to *P.F.* and had a city address, suddenly you got *Southern Living*. If you complained, then they sent you *P.F.* again. Of course, it got mixed up and a lot of people wound up getting both magazines. And on about the second direct mailing, they sold some ninety-two thousand new subscriptions for an introductory price of *one dollar* each. The regular price was *two dollars*. When I got there in 1969, the introductory offer was only *a dollar fifty*. We were still pulling 10 percent on some lists, which was remarkable."

Capps still gets a chuckle out of how *Southern Living* was mailed that first year. His dad told him at the time, " 'If Progressive Farmer hadn't been such a good customer of the Birmingham Post Office, they would never have been able to launch *Southern Living* the way they did.' They mailed it illegally almost that whole first year. They didn't file for a separate second-class permit. They just mailed it like it was an edition of *Progressive Farmer*," said Capps. "It even carried that line on the cover: 'An Edition of *The Progressive Farmer*,' but it wasn't mailed according to the rules. Back then the postmaster's salary was based on the amount of mail that went out. *P.F.* was his biggest customer in Birmingham. So anything *P.F.* wanted to do they could because they basically paid his salary."

Capps said that *Southern Living* made its first one million dollars of promotion profit in 1971. Of course, it had lost over $120,000 in circulation promotion in 1968.

"The magazine had a long way to go but was pretty well departmentalized by 1971," said McCalla. "I think the readers had a better idea of what they were going to get."

Capps said, "We grew in circulation every year. No other magazine could talk about that to advertisers. There ain't a magazine in the world that will ever have our kind of growth and show a profit while doing it. Most new magazines have to buy subscribers at a huge loss." *Southern Living* was able to attract new subscribers at a clear profit, making it a true money machine. The magazine today has over three million subscribers, most of whom pay twenty-eight dollars for a year's subscription. A single copy sells for $4.95 on the newsstand.

Southern Living reached one million subscribers by 1976, and turned a promotion profit of $6.8 million. By 1983, that promotion profit was $27 million, and it has gone up exponentially every year. (Remember that promotion profit is above what it costs to sell subscriptions; it does not include the cost of producing the magazine. But neither does it include advertising profits.)

Capps always said the magazine's editorial content had to sell the renewal. At advertising sales meetings and editorial meetings, Bill would never quote the *Southern Living* renewal rate, no matter how often he was asked.

"I wouldn't tell it because Emory didn't want me to and because the rate varies according to magazine practices," said Bill. "Take *Reader's Digest*. They used to claim 70 percent renewals. But they didn't tell you how many of those renewals were at cut rate. If you wouldn't renew at first, they'd make you many cheaper offers. We didn't do that.

"Now we had to replace an awful lot of subs in the early years of the magazine," said Bill.

"Readers couldn't figure out what the hell the magazine was about," said McCalla.

"By the middle and late seventies, and in the eighties, our renewal rate was in the 65 percent range," said Capps. That would put it at the very top among American magazines. "And we didn't sell cut-rate renewals. I remember I went two years without a raise. So I wrote Emory a letter, pointing out that I handled circulation for *Southern Living*, *Progressive Farmer*, and [now defunct] *Decorating & Craft Ideas*. All together, in 1983, circulation accounted for forty-five million dollars in cash flow. I got a raise."

Capps said, "But the honest-to-God truth is I did my best job on *Progressive Farmer*, keeping that income up, making that son of a bitch survive with the farm population going down. I was busting my butt on *P.F.*, but nobody ever realized it because it was so overshadowed by *S.L.*"

McCalla said, "Early on, I remember Mr. Butler said he 'hoped the money would hold out until we got *Southern Living* profitable.' "

"And we did that," said Capps. "Do you remember that Mr. Butler smoked *every other month?*"

"I'd forgotten that," said Logue. "He'd smoke a month and lay off a month. The tobacco industry would love to use him today as a witness to the question 'Is tobacco addictive?' "

"That was the kind of discipline he had," said Capps. "And he lived to be over a hundred."

Emory Cuningham never liked sweepstakes as a gimmick to attract subscribers. (A company's direct mail solicitation offers a sweepstakes prize, of, say, twenty-five thousand dollars, and other lesser prizes, all to be drawn at random. By law, a person does not have to subscribe to win.) Emory remains skeptical of their effect even today, though admits he gave Bill the go-ahead to use them all those years. "Bill said the sweeps were just an 'action device' to get them to open the envelope," said Emory. "I felt like sweepstakes were kind of reaching out beyond the natural level of our circulation. I felt we could find upper-income people who felt like Southerners, and we could mine that vein and not get out of it. I didn't want to get on newsstands for the same reason. We did a little bit because we needed to identify newsstands we could sell to in case we got in a bind. But while I was there you didn't see a lot of newsstand sales."

"I knew something other magazines didn't know," said Capps. "People who subscribed with us in a sweepstakes campaign renewed just as well as the ones who subscribed without sweepstakes. It was the editorial content that renewed them. And we were converting 10 percent of newsstand buyers into subscribers. All through those years. Nobody outside our company believed that." Today, *Southern Living* is sold widely on newsstands, even in cities on the periphery of the South.

Capps preferred to write his own circulation copy. "We were always testing nonsweeps against sweeps," he said. "I shared this nonsweeps package at a department head meeting. Roger McGuire wanted to know where the copy was written. I said, 'In New York.' He went on a tirade, about how he knew New York, how we had gotten a lot of criticism about things produced in New York. He went on and on. I said, 'I wrote it in LaGuardia Airport while I was waiting on a plane.' Emory cut his eyes around to McGuire, and McGuire's mouth fell open, and everybody broke up laughing.

"McGuire didn't understand me," said Capps, a rare comment about Roger. "He thought I was a little wild. Did things off the wall. Was a riverboat gambler. Well, I did. I was. Once I went to Dick Benson and pointed out that we were paying the return postage on big sweepstake mailings for people who answered, No, they didn't want to subscribe. That was three-fourths of the people who answered. I told Benson, if we didn't pay *any* return postage, I believed the 'Yes' people would pay their own, that if we lost any it would be the Nos.

"Dick said to spread out twenty thousand mailers and test not paying the return postage. I did. But I reversed it. I didn't offer to pay return postage for millions of potential subscribers, and I kept offering to pay it for twenty thousand. I warned Vernon Owens what I was doing. He said,

'I hope you know what you are doing.' If it had failed, it would have failed big-time. But it didn't.

"I took the responsibility. I just took it," said Capps. "I'm risking millions, and one day Britt Butler tells Mrs. Cater she has to get three bids on a forty-dollar electric pencil sharpener. I went in the department head meeting, and I said, 'We've got our priorities all screwed up.' Emory said, 'What's the matter?' I said, 'I'm trying to order a pencil sharpener, and I've got to get three bids. And I just spent a million dollars ordering lists, and nobody questioned whether I ordered the right lists or not.' Emory turned to Britt and said, 'Get him a pencil sharpener.' We weren't out of the meeting until 4:30. But I had a pencil sharpener on my desk by the next morning." Good ol' Britt.

Asked what he believed happened to Roger McGuire, why he left the company so early in his career, Capps said, "His health, of course. The diabetes. And I think Emory was putting a lot of pressure on him. Vernon didn't like McGuire. They didn't get along. They butted heads. McGuire knew zero about numbers. McCalla and I used to push for a higher percentage of advertising in *Southern Living*, because it made more money. And Roger would always go the other way."

That was true. Although he worked in the business end of the business, McGuire was always the idealist. A lot of people in the company loved him for that reason, even while often disagreeing with him.

Emory Cunningham himself insisted on keeping the magazine's advertising percentage per issue one of the lowest in the industry. And do realize that every time you remove an editorial page and substitute an advertising page, the gross money goes straight to the bottom line. *Southern Living* in the 1980s consistently ran about 53 percent advertising, and that was a full 10 percent less than most magazines.

"My relationship with Emory was good," said Capps. "I would stay up all night working on my damn budgets to please Vernon Owens, and I got along with Vernon, and many didn't. I worked at the numbers, the budget, and he appreciated that. But I could walk into Emory's office and get a decision. If I'd say, 'I think we ought to raise the subscription price,' then he'd say, 'What does the subscriber get out of it?' I finally got smart, and Gary and I would get together before we went in there. And we'd say Gary was going 'to be doing this and that for the reader.' "

"Once we went to a better grade of paper," said McCalla. "We doubled our editorial staff in just a few years, adding a great deal of needed talent. At one time we published more recipes than any magazine in the country. And we did get around to doing bonus editorial pages that Emory gave us." More about those later. Finally, McCalla took the magazine editorial pages to all four-color in the 1980s.

"Many times," said Capps, "Emory just flat out didn't know what I was doing. But at direct mail meetings [DMA], I ran into a lot of publishers. Emory was more knowledgable about circulation than any other publisher I met at those meetings. He knew what made it tick. Most publishers did not.

"There were times," said Bill, "when I was putting ten million pieces in the mail and I was the only one picking out the lists we rented. In the early years, if the president of the United States had been shot or some other tragedy had occurred the day our mail dropped, I'm not sure we could have survived the loss of a couple of million dollars or more. My job was always in jeopardy."

In the early years of *Southern Living*, he was not alone.

14

"Since You Looked at Jesus, You Ain't Looked Twice at Me"

Meanwhile, back at the magazine, the Foods Department and the Homes Department were on the road to righteousness. Caleb Pirtle's leaving had created a vacuum in the Travel Department that was not readily filled. And it would be years before the Garden Department realized its potential.

Happily, Karen Lingo was growing into quite a travel writer. "I used to mail my copy to Jerry Flemmons [the Fort Worth travel writer], and he would make comments and suggestions and bawl me out," said Lingo. "He always told me, 'Write for yourself. You don't have to please anybody else.'"

"No better advice was ever given," said Logue. "I remember when you first met Flemmons on a cruise story you were doing."

"There was this sea of people waiting to get on the boat," said Lingo, "and I saw this one tall man, standing above everybody else, his hair slicked back, and his sunglasses on, looking it all over like Mr. Cool. It had to be Flemmons. He looked down at me and said, 'Who are you, little girl?' He also taught me, 'You only write as well as you read.' And he wrote the funny story about 'Francisco the Paraguay guitarist' who tried to beat his way into my cabin on that cruise."

"Flemmons didn't miss much," said Logue, looking over his reading glasses. "And he wrote for us the best European travel section I ever read, anywhere." Flemmons in later years survived a heart transplant and, though retired and ill, was still one of the fine travel writers in America and a great friend of *Southern Living* until his death in 1999.

While Lingo was learning her profession, McCalla brought in a very good writer. Blame Logue. He'd seen this writer's work in a city magazine. McCalla also agreed to move the writer's lover. It was the first lover the magazine had moved, though not the last. He drew the line at moving the writer's horse. After the writer's first couple of trips, McCalla called Logue into his office and threw down the writer's expense account. "We just moved the goddamn horse," he said. Out went writer and lover and horse.

Along in there, Karen Lingo took seven weeks' leave to join her then-husband, who was in the military at Okinawa. "Part of it was vacation and part of it was unpaid leave," said Lingo. "When I came back I felt horrible, because the Travel Department was in shambles."

Not so long afterward, McCalla and Logue brought in Les Thomas, a versatile writer from Texas, to be Travel Editor. He came recommended by Flemmons and was, in fact, then writing for the *Fort Worth Star-Telegram*. Thomas possessed a wit as dry as a parched July creek in West Texas. He was only the size of a modest front door of a significant building. He once reached the finals of the Texas Arm-Wrestling Championship, having put down at least one of the Dallas Cowboys' biggest, fiercest, most brutish linemen. But Thomas was, and is, a truly nice and gentle guy and a great asset to the magazine.

"I remember the first time we three talked," said Les. "We went to the Birmingham Country Club. I thought we'd be having lunch there every day. It took me a while to realize it—and I still think it's true—but the common denominator y'all were looking for above anything else at *Southern Living* was people who were eccentric.

"You could run into all kinds of strange people out in Texas," said Thomas. "I knew one guy who had a German staff car and who believed in the Kennedy conspiracy theory, and I knew a guy who believed that people from outer space were doing cattle mutilation. We had one guy on the city council in Austin who shot his garden hose. He thought it was a snake. At least he hit it. There was a guy in a little West Texas town who owned part of the high school football field and got mad and put a barbed wire fence across the twenty-yard line. Flemmons himself once went five years that I know of without wearing a necktie. They were all amateur eccentrics, compared to my colleagues on *Southern Living*."

Logue said, "I always thought, being fairly quirky himself, one of McCalla's great strengths was he had a tolerance for a variety of personalities." Which was a good thing for Logue, thought Logue.

"Had to take a hostage once in a while," said McCalla. "We had a photographer who spent two hundred dollars calling his girlfriend from the motel telephone. I thought he ought to be able to find a girl where he was."

"That wasn't his girl; that was his wife," said Les. "She was running away with another woman."

"He shoulda called collect," said Logue.

"It was different, coming from the *Star-Telegram* to *Southern Living*," said Les. "At the newspaper you could never talk to the publisher. I got to the magazine, and I could not only talk to him, I could argue with him. I'd written this story about Texans vacationing in Colorado. I got into a hot argument with Emory Cunningham, the president, about doing stories on Colorado. I've got to hand it to Emory. If I'd been in his shoes, I would have probably fired me. It was pretty big of him not to."

"He was probably afraid he would have to arm-wrestle you," said Logue.

"Another thing that was different about magazine writing," said Les, "was the long lead time. You just wrote it up and waited for disaster to hit. If we wrote about a desert, it would flood. If we wrote about a riverboat, the river went dry. You know we picked that photograph out of the files of what looked like the perfect family at the Rose Festival in Tyler. Turned out the man left his family and ran off with his boyfriend."

Les admitted, "The people loved you if you were from *Southern Living*. We were doing a story on a train ride. And the town of Hugo, Oklahoma, turned out to meet us. That's the town, you know, where all the old circus people, the carnival people are buried. When the photographer and I stepped down, the whole town said, 'Where do you want us?' "

A year or two went by, and McCalla came to the conclusion that Les's ability to write stories as tall as he told them could do the magazine more good attracting readers in Texas and the Southwest than his large presence in an office in Birmingham.

Les set up camp in the state capital of Austin. "I think it was like serving sixteen years in the trenches of World War I," said Les. "*Texas Monthly* magazine had their territory staked out, and we had ours, and the only way you could get killed was to get out of your own trench and run over to the other side. They were so doggone different from us; we were only fighting them really for circulation and advertising, not over subject matter.

"Texans aren't prejudiced against anything or anybody in particular," said Les. "They just think they are better than anybody else."

Thomas said, "It wasn't until John Connally got into office as governor that he set up the state tourism department, and Texans really began to understand the potential for travel. In the old days, there was a liquor store in the Alamo." Now four or five million tourists a year visit San Antonio and the Alamo and the other restored Spanish missions, not to mention the reclaimed river running through the downtown. And no publication in America could touch *Southern Living* in telling the Texas travel story.

Thomas couldn't leave the table without a last story. "The best airplane ride I ever went on was when Roger McGuire got us into covering this rodeo and Western Celebration in South Texas. I hate rodeos. When I worked for the newspaper, we spent twelve hours a day for ten days out there in Fort Worth sweating to cover 'em. Photographer Geoff Gilbert and I kept thinking of reasons to get out of there. An oilman who was helping put on the celebration said he would be glad to have his pilot fly us to Dallas in his Lear Jet because he had to fly the Dallas Cowboy cheerleaders back anyhow. The whole time we were on that plane, I kept praying, 'Let this thing crash.' It would have been the highlight of my life to have my friends pick up the paper and read that Les Thomas went down in a plane today with three Cowboy cheerleaders. Except I knew the paper would read: *Three Cowboy cheerleaders survived a plane crash today in which one unidentified travel writer was hurt pretty badly. Photo by Geoff Gilbert.*"

Beginning in March, 1978, Karen Lingo was running the Travel Department. Karen, like Jean Liles, was organized to the tips of her toes. She started Travel's annual and monthly planning sessions and brought Flemmons in as an outside voice. It's doubtful that any one person has been down more city streets, or around more town squares, or across more mountains, or down more rivers, or seen more festivals, or shopped more arts and crafts boutiques, or spoken to more governors' conferences, or made more friends in the American South than Karen Lingo, who has been at it since 1967. Joining her staff as an assistant editor was another young Texan, Gary Ford, who'd worked at Callaway Gardens in Georgia.

In 1983, Logue was hand-carrying the editorial message to the good advertising folk in Detroit, as he did for about twenty-three years. He'd asked Lingo to add up the miles the travel writers had covered in the last year. This was her inventory:

"Wrecker (rental import broke down): sixty miles. Pony and trap, in Ireland: six miles. Helicopter: two miles. Hot air balloon: twelve miles. Greyhound bus: thirteen hours. Tour bus: one thousand miles. 1932 Ford: four miles. Train (counting bullet train in Japan): two hundred and fifty miles. By foot, hiking trails, etc.: nine hundred miles. Ship, across Atlantic, around Caribbean: By days, we're looking at twenty. Plane: five hundred thousand miles. Car: three hundred thousand miles." The good folk in Detroit were impressed, especially with the rental import breaking down.

Karen remembers the early story she wrote about Amtrak. McCalla looked at it and called her in. "Did you ride Amtrak?" he asked. "When I was in the ninth grade," she said. "Go ride it, and then write it," said McCalla.

"I flew to Orlando," said Karen. "I got on the train and rode it to New Orleans. I spent the night. I rode it to Houston and spent the night, and rode it to Fort Worth. I felt I knew what it was like to ride Amtrak and flew home. Everything else I've ever written, I've done it or seen it. That's the strength of our travel coverage."

Asked what stories she was particularly proud of having written, Karen said, "I think I wrote a good story on the Shenandoah Valley. I was there to research it when the apple blossoms were in bloom. Another time we had an emergency and you guys called me off my vacation in the Cayman Islands, in February, to write a story on Kiawah Island in South Carolina. That was dedication. I got up before daybreak and went out on the beach at Kiawah. It was cold as all get-out and the most gorgeous sight I have ever seen in my life. The entire beach was littered with conch shells, and as the sun was rising they glowed orange. It was one of my favorite stories. I'm kind of like Flemmons. He never thinks he writes anything good."

"Flemmons would be the first to tip his Texas hat to how many good things you've written," said Logue.

"The travel industry is different from any other thing I've ever known," said Lingo. "You remain friends long beyond what you are working on together. You come across somebody years later, and they remember you. One of our writers will say, 'I saw old So-and-so out in West Texas, and he said to tell you hello.' And I'll say, 'My God, I was afraid he might be dead.'

"I used to go to governors' conferences on tourism," Karen said, "and we'd make an accordion foldout of everything we had published in the past year on, say, Texas, and it would go around the room twice. *Nobody* covers the South like we do."

McCalla said, "I once told Don Cunningham that sure, *National Geographic* might do seventeen pages on Old Salem, North Carolina, but that would be once in a lifetime. We'd do two pages, and we'd be back next year."

"People want *to have an experience* when they travel," said Karen. "They want to do something or see something they can take back and remember the rest of their lives. I've been extremely fortunate, stumbling into my own life, going in and hiring myself. I've got a sneaking suspicion the two of you played a big part in any accomplishments I ever had at the company. And Caleb was encouraging. I wouldn't have wanted to do anything else."

And what are her favorite places in the South?

"I love the Big Bend country in Texas," said Karen. "Baltimore. I love Baltimore. The crab cakes. I love the Blue Ridge Mountains in North Carolina. I wouldn't mind living around Eureka Springs, Arkansas. Or up in Kentucky, near Lexington, that's gorgeous country. But I like Birmingham, I like living here. If I didn't live here, I'd probably live somewhere around Dillsboro, North Carolina, just west of Asheville."

"We'll know where to find you if we ever start up another magazine," said McCalla.

After Lingo hired him, Gary Ford plugged along as a good, solid, unremarkable travel writer. Years passed. And suddenly he flowered as a prose stylist. In 1982 he wrote a ten-page piece, the second-longest to appear in the magazine, "The South Burns for Barbecue." Ford hit every imaginable barbecue joint, from pork to beef, from mustard sauce to tomato sauce, from chopped to pulled to sliced barbecue, from the high-rent district to the low-rent district. He cut a smoky trail across the South. The story was a smash hit. It has been anthologized perhaps more times than any other staff-written piece, and appeared in *The Encyclopedia of Southern Culture.*

Ford also wrote a distinguished and moving "Journal" about his annual Christmas trips home to Texas over the years and his parents' Christmas Day anniversary.

Gary, ultimately, was named Travel Editor of *Southern Living.* The magazine's reputation in the travel field has never been stronger.

Dianne Young recently joined Steve Bender as one of two Senior Writers at *Southern Living.* She holds other responsibilities, but also concentrates on her own writing and nurturing the writing of other staff members. Young has come a long way since 1974 and her days as a part-time assistant in the Production Department. She had graduated from Cornell University in English and anthropology and realized "I was going to be unemployed for the rest of my life." She was tipped off by one of her good friends that there might be an opening at *Southern Living.*

She began by working for Bill Proctor, who ran the Production Department. "We referred to him as 'Paper Clip Bill,' " said Young. "He was the most anal-retentive human being I have ever met. He gave us a procedure for where to fix a paper clip: it had to be two inches from the left-hand side of the page. So we used to do little things to irritate him. He kept his own paper clips lined up by *size* in his desk drawer, so we would link them all together. He hated to have cabinet doors open, so we would leave them all open. We may have been responsible for tipping him over the edge."

"I do remember the time he got down on his knees and prayed for me in my office," said McCalla. "I said, 'I appreciate your doing this. I know I need it.' "

"Sounds like Nixon and Kissinger to me," said Logue.

Proctor, in his own exacting way, coped with the production manager's job, which is a diabolical one, until he was succeeded in 1977 by Clay Nordan.

"Clay was really great in that job," said McCalla. "He was organized and could juggle a multitude of responsibilities. And he never panicked. The only time he ever bothered me was when he had a real problem."

Nordan is now managing editor of *Southern Living,* which in its many manifestations now produces over six thousand editorial pages a year, including eighteen special sections (for example, four quarterly magazine "Living" sections: North Carolina, Tennessee, Texas, and Georgia), not to mention free-standing, single-subject magazines in travel, foods, homes, and gardening. Counting the twelve annual issues of *Southern Living*, Editor John Floyd's staff now publishes thirty-eight free-standing magazines a year as the company works ceaselessly to extend the *Southern Living* presence in the market-place. Clay Nordan manages the production of all these publications with astonishing composure.

"Early on, before we had built a professional staff, McCalla would, from time to time, erupt out of his office with a look of panic on his face," said Logue. "I knew he had made the terrible mistake of reading the raw copy that collected in his 'In' basket. I'd say, 'McCalla, don't read that stuff. It hasn't been touched by human hands. It's liable to throw your heart off.' Then we'd have to fix every bloody non-sentence."

Young abandoned the copy desk to get her masters in journalism on a full scholarship at the University of Texas. "I enjoyed it," she said. "But it was a wasted two years. Sharon Watkins and Kathy Boozer on the copy desk had already taught me everything these good people could teach me about journalism."

Dianne was working in the public information office at Austin College in Sherman, Texas, and she got a call from Karen Lingo. "She said Caleb Pirtle had left and did I want to 'try out for a job' in travel? I thought about it less than two seconds. Sherman, Texas, was a dry county. I did a couple of stories, and I've been back on the magazine ever since." She's written travel. She's written the magazine's "Outdoors" column. She's edited the "Southern Journal" page. She's edited the "Book Review" page. She's edited and written the "Southerners" profiles.

McCalla and Logue looked back over a quarter of a century of issues of *Southern Living*, and it was formidable how many of the best stories had been written by Dianne Young. In picking a set of all-time features, they chose among them her 1989 piece on the South's seven National Seashores, photographed by Geoff Gilbert.

"When I came back to the magazine, nobody wanted to cover Florida," said Young. "I said, 'Hell, I do.' It was December and cold. They also gave me Kentucky. People in the South use the magazine as the bible for their travel. You go anywhere to research a story, and they open any door, roll out any rug to help you."

Her own favorite stories? "I did a thing on 'Old Time Music Rings in the Hills.' And I did the one on catfish, 'Netting a New Image.' I won two Lowell Thomas Awards for those stories. And they were fun to do." Young's moving story on the Arlington National Cemetery was voted by the editorial brass to be the best story to appear in *Southern Living* that year. And it was one of the best ever to appear in the magazine.

"It's been an interesting life," said Dianne. "I've been lucky, the people I've worked for, the people I've learned from. We've had a host of good writers. I think *Southern Living* is now a well-written magazine."

"And you haven't had to live in a dry county," said Logue.

"Maybe now we're approaching the Edgar Allan Poe era," mused Mc-Calla.

In the year 1980, Logue noticed the writing of a young reporter in the *Birmingham News*. His name was Mark Childress. McCalla agreed his stuff was more than promising. Mark agreed to come by for an interview, but said that he had already accepted a job with the *Charlotte Observer*, a very fine Knight-Ridder newspaper.

Childress was twenty-two. He looked seventeen. McCalla liked his stuff and liked Childress, too. Logue said, "The third week you are up there covering the courthouse, you will already be repeating yourself. We'll set you loose in sixteen states and see what kind of trouble you can get into."

Childress stiffed the *Observer* and was immediately the finest writer who ever wrote for *Southern Living* and one of the finest to write for any magazine. He had as much nerve as he had talent. He would stand up to McCalla, and McCalla liked that, so long as you backed it up with your work.

"Two weeks after I started at the magazine," remembered Childress, "I went to the editorial conference near Austin, Texas. I was the new kid on the block, anxious to make a good impression. My method of doing this consisted of perching myself on the edge of a cocktail table. At the moment the welcome party reached its height, the glass tabletop cracked and crashed to the floor, bringing the party to a dead halt, and landing me on my butt at the center of a circle of my new bosses."

"McCalla knew at that moment we had a winner," said Logue.

Childress remembers "shoehorning a story in the magazine about an African-American woman who ran a ground-breaking alcohol rehab center in Little Rock. Great story," said Mark, "except that it appeared opposite an ad for Smirnoff vodka: 'It's Bloody Mary Time!' Whoops."

Childress also remembered a night on Avery Island, researching his landmark story on Cajun food that first made Chef Paul Prudhomme famous outside Louisiana. "We set up a lovely outdoor shot," said Mark, "but the bugs were so thick that night on Avery that we must have sprayed five pounds of Raid on that food to get a decent shot. Otherwise it would have been delicious. That night we ate Burger King.

"We spent two weeks driving Prudhomme around the Cajun country," said Childress, "eating in little country cafés and stores and his sister's and aunts' homes, where for once the Southern Livers were ignored. Paul, on the other hand, was treated as actual royalty. Those were the best ten pounds I ever gained."

Childress said, "Of course my strongest memory is of the story that photographer Mike Clemmer and I did about the commercial fishermen in the South ['On the Face of the Sea—Reflections of the Fishermen']. The South occupies about two thousand seven hundred miles of coastline, and Clemmer and I were assigned to travel the length of it, interviewing and photographing fishermen for a piece that detailed a supposedly dying way of life.

"Sounds glamorous. Right? Not. Fishermen don't work out of places like Palm Beach, more in places like Apalachicola and Bayou La Batre, where you can find their boats at the ends of weedy lanes.

"Most of the fishermen we met were initially suspicious of us. *Southern Living* was their wives' favorite magazine, but they couldn't understand quite what we were up to, since commercial fishing is about as unfeminine an occupation as there is. I think they thought we were from the DEA. Still, we met some great people, and after their initial suspicions wore off they clasped us to their collective bosom."

Childress still shakes his head to remember, "Now, photographers like the light in the early morning and late in the day. Which meant we met a lot of boats at 3 A.M. to prepare for dawn shooting. We also quickly learned that diesel fuel is the fisherman's biggest expense, so they didn't just go out for a few hours' fishing. These were two- or three-day trips.

"After ten months of shooting and interviewing, we thought we had everything we needed. We showed a tray of great stuff to McCalla, who said: 'What else you got?' His famous damn question.

"He insisted we had to have some Texas fishermen," said Childress. "By this time, having spent months trying not to be seasick, we were a bit weary of the story, and we decided to find the worst-looking fisherman we could, as a kind of revenge. We brought back a set of lovely pictures of the sorriest-looking fishing crew in history, and McCalla pronounced the story finished," said Childress. "I'm still proud of that piece."

It was thirteen pages long, holding the indoor record for length in the magazine. An ironic thing, Clemmer took thousands of excellent photographs of the fishermen and their working boats. Childress picked up a camera and knocked off a couple of shots. McCalla picked one of them for the cover of the magazine.

The story won that year's National Maritime Award for journalism, succeeding previous pieces by the *New York Times* and *National Geographic* magazine. Childress accepted the prize at a banquet in St. Louis for two thousand people.

He also wrote a timeless narrative, looking for the "Places of the Man," Robert E. Lee, the houses he lived in, the fields he fought over, the places he loved that are still in existence.

And he wrote an essay on blacksmiths, "Wrought in Iron," that McCalla and Logue count among the all-time feature spreads to have run in the magazine, with photography, again, by Clemmer.

One day Logue took Childress to lunch at Wanda June's. He said, "Don't come back to work this afternoon. This is the day you start your first novel." Childress, for years now, has been one of the few American novelists able to sustain body and soul with the sale of his novels. He has published five. His novel on the life of Elvis Presley was a No. 1 bestseller as far away as Germany. It was titled *Tender* in this country and *Elvis* in Germany. His best-selling novel *Crazy in Alabama* was made into a movie in 1999, directed by Antonio Banderas, starring his wife, Melanie Griffith, with a screenplay by Childress himself. He has moved from a house in Costa Rica overlooking the Pacific Ocean to Manhattan, but remains a friend and occasional visitor to *Southern Living*.

One day in November, 1973, a manuscript came uninvited "over the transom" onto the desk of Editor Gary McCalla. He read it. Not something for *Southern Living*, but a free-lance gardening story, a rarer thing than a talking house plant. He liked it. He handed it to Logue. Logue liked it. It was well written by a chap named Fred Bonnie. Odd thing, he lived in Burlington, Vermont.

Oxmoor House was looking for a guy to put together the definitive *Southern Living Gardening Book of the South*. And the magazine could use all the gardening firepower it could muster. The new Garden Editor, H. T., had a problem: deadlines. They terrified him. Beth Carlson, God bless her, was putting together most of the gardening pages, including the "Letters to the Garden Editor." They weren't getting any in those days, so she was making up gardening questions she knew the answers to. (These days the magazine draws thousands of garden questions a year, all of which are answered in person if not in the magazine.)

McCalla invited this Bonnie to visit Birmingham. Logue met him at what is now the Radisson Hotel on 20th Street. Bonnie at the time was a slight but wiry young guy with a shock of dark hair. He spoke English and French interchangeably and had been "the most interested student in Chinese history" at the University of Vermont and had taught in the Berlitz School of Language in France.

"Just the man we needed to write Southern gardening," remembered Logue.

"Logue was drinking gin and tonic," said Bonnie. "He found out I was a writer, had published two short stories as well as two free-lance gardening pieces. We didn't talk business. We talked about Flannery O'Connor and Eudora Welty. We talked about Truman Capote and William Faulkner and, my hero, Erskine Caldwell, and Katherine Anne Porter. We talked about Harper Lee, and Logue asked me, 'Do you think you'd be interested in moving to Birmingham?' I remembered the grim look of the unreclaimed Sloss Furnace, and I said, 'Maybe I could do some free-lance work for you.'

"We talked about Larry McMurtry and Harry Crews and William Styron and James Dickey and Marjorie Kinnan Rawlings, with more gin and tonic. Logue said, 'How about moving to Birmingham?' I said, 'I'll think about it.' We talked about Thomas Wolfe, and William Price Fox, and Annie Dillard, and then we talked about my writing and his writing. He had a couple of novels in the works. More gin and tonic. It was winding down toward 1 A.M. Logue said, 'How about coming down to Birmingham and working for us?' I said, in a rather slurred voice, 'I think tha's a goddamn great idea.' "

Bonnie said, "The next day I met Mr. Gary McCalla and Mr. Les Adams, director of the book division. I met the charming and animated Dixie Snell and the charming and animated and motherly Beth Carlson, the good-looking Karen Lingo, spoke French with Mary Whitfield and Philip Morris, who, like me, had been exposed to Jesuit education. I met my first Texan, Caleb Pirtle, and photographer Gerald Crawford." Bonnie agreed to come down the following June and go to work on the definitive Southern gardening book.

"Logue drove me to the airport," said Bonnie. "He seemed a whole lot more serious than he had been the night before. He looked straight at me and said, 'Don't let me down.' A hard chill of reality whistled through me. I realized this was serious business."

"And Bonnie, one of the most talented, most musical, most intelligent, most gifted linguistically, most unswervingly eccentric people ever to step in the door at *Southern Living*, never did let us down," said Logue.

Fred and his fiancée, Ellen, had been as far South as Nashville once before, in an attempt to sell two country songs they had written. The titles were: "Since You Looked at Jesus, You Ain't Looked Twice at Me" and "I Never Was Lonely Until I Met You." Hard to imagine Nashville passing on those titles.

Fred drove into Birmingham "the day Shelby County Sheriff Red Walker arrested his opponent in the election coming up the next Tuesday, along with two reporters from the *Birmingham News* and the probate judge of Shelby County, along with some other people, charging them with conspiracy to murder him," he remembered with great glee.

"Later I found out the reason he arrested the probate judge is he is the only county official who can arrest the sheriff," said Fred. "That was exactly the kind of scenario I was hoping to find in the so-called 'New South,' because one of my primary reasons to move down here was to see how Southern life translated into literature. And here it was happening in my own ears."

Bonnie went on to publish over fifty short stories in serious literary magazines and several hardbound collections of those stories. Two of the stories came out of the life of Gary McCalla, including the time his commanding general in France, after the big war, ordered him to come up with a nickname. He told McCalla, "All the great generals had nicknames, Patton was 'Old Blood and Guts.' I want a nickname, Lieutenant." It was a supply outfit, so McCalla came up with the nickname General "Lifeline" Woodward, who somehow never got to be as famous as General "Blood and Guts" Patton.

McCalla's other memorable caper in the Army was to talk his general into sponsoring a French frog in The Celebrated Jumping Frog Contest of Calaveras County, California, an event made famous by a young Mark Twain. McCalla recruited a famous French perfume to sponsor the frog, and a French airline agreed to fly him over to America. Unhappily, the muckraking French newspaper *Figaro* got wind of the enterprise and published a wicked cartoon of American Army colonels trying to round up a wild frog, with the nasty observation that "the American Army obviously has nothing more to do in Europe than catch frogs."

General "Lifeline" Woodward could see his military immortality evaporating in laughter. "Lieutenant, you get us out of this ——— frogjumpin' business by dark or you are in deep ——— trouble." There went the best-smelling frog in the history of the Calaveras County competition.

No sooner had Bonnie hit Birmingham and his assignment had changed. He was to write a series of paperback gardening books, rather than the one big complete *Southern Living* gardening book.

Working with material that included what H. T. was producing for *Southern Living*, Bonnie soon produced a string of polished paperback gardening books.

Calamity. The Lane brothers of *Sunset* magazine and books—Emory Cunningham's deadly rivals—called to protest that material had obviously been lifted from their magazine to be included in Oxmoor's books, which were in direct competition with their own books.

Cunningham was justifiably angry and embarrassed. Fred Bonnie was not at fault. H. T., under the pressure of deadlines he could not meet, had been lifting illustrations and copy from *Sunset* magazine. The Lane brothers, happily, didn't realize the material had first reappeared in *Southern Living*, from which Bonnie picked it up for Oxmoor's books. The Lanes were determined to stop the sale of the Oxmoor gardening books, and they did.

McCalla had run H. T. by Emory Cunningham before hiring him, because he had had such wretched luck with past gardening editors. Emory was not impressed. Afterwards, he cautioned McCalla not to hire the man. But H. T. was bright, well educated, and he wanted the job. McCalla and Logue should have listened to Cunningham.

In fact, Oxmoor's entire, ill-advised string of eighty paperback "how-to" books was doomed to ultimate extinction. The profit margin was just too thin. *Sunset* itself has never been able to generate a serious profit from its own excellent line of paperback instruction books.

Emory told McCalla to fire H. T. immediately. He did. H. T. was not a bad guy. He was just over-matched by the challenge. He later became head horticulturist for a major American city, and fell dead at a terribly young age.

McCalla called Bonnie in. "I need a Garden Editor. I need one today.

And you are the only show in town." As Bonnie remembered, the timing was terrible for McCalla, who was headed into the hospital that day for heart bypass surgery, which proved successful.

Bonnie said, "I was the last of the mavericks to become a department head at *Southern Living*. I can't imagine the magazine ever hiring another person to write garden copy who didn't have a degree in horticulture."

Fred's memory of McCalla never fades. "He was a short, sort of round-shouldered guy, and had a way of looking at you with a scowl that was actually a smile. So much of McCalla was punctuated by laughter. Short spurts of chuckle.

"He pretended to be one of the most conservative people that ever walked the face of the earth," said Fred, "and, in fact, he was one of the strangest. He had done everything. I used to tell him the reason he had done so well at *Southern Living* was because he had a way with us paranoid creative types. McCalla seemed to like me because there was never any prodding needed to get me to turn in stories. Each month, I'd walked into Gary's office. He'd be sitting there with Sharon Watkins, the copy chief, and I would show him story after story. And his first question would be, 'What's Southern about it?' And his second question, 'What else you got?'"

Bonnie proved a marvelous recruiter for the magazine. On a trip to Florida, he met a delightful young graduate in horticulture and entomology, Lois Trigg. McCalla hired her on the spot, and her knowledge and energy and lively Latin spirit (she was of Cuban descent) enriched the garden pages over the years. "Only problem with Lois," kidded Logue, "she was always on the side of the bugs." She married the magazine's talented garden photographer Van Chaplin and now free-lances out of their home.

Fred set out to improve his own knowledge of horticulture, enrolling in classes at the local Jefferson State Junior College under Dr. John Floyd, who had gotten his undergraduate degree from Auburn and his doctorate from Clemson. Fred also took a photography seminar and went on to shoot dozens of gardening layouts for the magazine.

Fred said, "The spirit at *Southern Living* in those days, I have to tell you, was really, really wonderful. It was not at all unusual for John Logue to come out of his office and start telling crazy stories, and McCalla would come out of his office and start telling crazier stories, and Phil Morris would come out and Caleb Pirtle would stick his head out, all telling stories. It was a great, great time. Great time."

Bonnie said, "McCalla once gave me the bizarre challenge of hiring my own boss." Fred introduced Dr. John Floyd to McCalla and to Emory Cunningham, and John consulted some on the care of the trees and shrubs in the company landscape around the new building on Shades Creek Parkway. McCalla liked Floyd's organized approach to getting things done. He broached the subject to John of coming to work as *Southern Living*'s Garden Editor, an ill-fated position in past years. Floyd was interested. Emory suggested to McCalla that John "might be happier where he was," in the academic community. And there is little doubt that Floyd was on the fast track to becoming somebody's college president, with his ability to write government grants and raise money.

This time Emory was wrong. Floyd became the magazine's Garden Editor and proved from the first day to be brilliant at it. "The color in the garden pages became the glory of the magazine," said McCalla, who in 1981 moved the garden section to the front of the magazine, just behind the Travel South section. The material was that powerful. And the move freed up more space for homes and food, after the center pages, or "well," of the book.

The truly nervy move McCalla made, without permission of President Emory Cunningham or Publisher Jim DeVira, was to move the Food Department from the center of the magazine to the last pages of the magazine.

In the beginning of *Southern Living*, all advertisers fought to be as far forward as possible in the magazine, on a righthand page. They didn't at first buy into the fact that *Southern Living*, under McCalla, became highly departmentalized, and that it made absolute sense for travel advertisers to be up front in the travel section, and gardening advertisers to be in the garden section, and homes advertisers in the homes section and food advertisers in the food section.

Roger McGuire and then Jim DeVira and their sales staffs gradually convinced advertisers it was more important to be in the proper department than to be as far forward as possible in the magazine. McCalla also felt the magazine "drizzled off" in its back pages. He moved its most powerful section, food, to the back. Luckily advertisers bought into it, and so did readers. McCalla never got one complaint from a reader about food moving to the rear of the magazine.

Back to the Garden Department. "I knew John Floyd was going to be tough," said Logue, "when he assigned his editors and photographers to shoot spring dogwoods for the next year. They shot. And at color pick,

John flashed up the damndest dogwood stuff we'd ever seen. Beautiful stuff. John said, 'Well, it's not bad. But it's not complete. We'll put it off and do dogwoods next year.' In the past, we would have killed an honest citizen for the photographs that now 'weren't complete enough.' "

Floyd recruited Linda Askey to the garden staff in 1979. She did a tour of duty on *Southern Accents,* and is presently Garden Editor of *Southern Living.* No question she is one of the most gifted writers in the company, and from time to time steps out of the gardening pages to lend her graceful sentences to other subjects. In selecting an all-time series of features published in the magazine, McCalla and Logue could not leave out "The Art of Brookgreen Gardens," in Myrtle Beach, South Carolina, written by Askey. She also wrote memorable stories on Queen Anne's lace, and rhododendron, and "Wildflowers Worthy of the Garden," and foxglove, and phlox, and even bald cypress, and too many other subjects to call up here.

No magazine in the country has two finer writers in one department than Linda Askey and Steve Bender. Bender wrote such garden classics as "Old Roses Find New Friends," and "Loosestrife Is a Sure Thing, a Perennial Every Garden Needs." His wit and his language set all his stuff apart.

Floyd also recruited Bill McDougald, who succeeded him as Garden Editor, then became managing editor of the magazine, and now runs its Homes Group Department, responsible among other things for the Idea Homes built all over the South. The garden section, under Floyd, grew from the weak link in the magazine to one of its true strengths.

At the editorial-sales conference at Amelia Island, McCalla designated Fred Bonnie as official ambassador to the Sales Department, "which meant," said Bonnie, "I was to infiltrate their quarters and steal some of their booze as they had a lot more than we did. I believe I managed to heist about four or five gallons of their best stuff under McCalla's smiling approval.

"Well, I myself fell into the rum and tonic and stayed up most of the night drinking with more seasoned drinkers than myself," said Fred. "I think I got one hour's sleep. I had to make an editorial presentation first thing in the morning. My head felt like a train wreck, my mouth and throat were so dry I could hardly speak. I looked every bit as bad as I felt. Word had spread of my then-legendary behavior of the night before. So the mere fact that I was able to walk into the conference room earned me a standing ovation."

The ultimate free spirit, Bonnie admits that he chafed somewhat under the more strict regimentation over the Garden Department by Dr. Floyd. John once left him a note that he was to be in the office by 8 A.M. and that lunch hour was just that, one hour. Bonnie, a volatile writer, especially when angered, wrote back the ultimate insubordinate answer, which Floyd took to McCalla and Logue, who despite every effort at professional composure, broke into laughter.

Bonnie was about to bring out his first collection of short stories in 1979. His publisher made a big fuss over him in Ottawa, Canada. He admits today he was full of himself. And he got a highly erroneous tip from a photographer who was being fired from the magazine that he was to be fired next. He was not about to be fired. McCalla and Logue had a weakness for Bonnie, who could sing "Heartbreak Hotel" in German wild enough to make Elvis Presley rise out his grave to join in the chorus. So, Fred decided to quit "and become a full-time writer, as Erskine Caldwell had once done."

Logue tried to talk him out of it. "Remember, Caldwell ate turnips for a year."

"McCalla ran into me in the men's room," said Fred, "and he asked if I really wanted to leave. I realized I wasn't about to be fired. But I was committed to leaving. McCalla said, 'You don't have to work the three months' notice you gave. When a corpse has been around too long, it starts to stink.' " McCalla could always be counted on to turn the poetical phrase.

Bonnie went on to get a fine arts degree from the University of Alabama and has another collection of stories in the works and at least two novels. He's remarried, and he and his physician wife have settled near Birmingham, and already Bonnie has thrown a homecoming party, with McCalla and Logue and Fred swapping lies like old times.

Back again to the Garden Department. John Floyd not only knew horticulture, but had a command of money and budgets and a strong streak of ambition which sustained him through a number of jobs within the company, including a couple of years in exile in advertising promotion, which made him management's choice to succeed McCalla when he retired March 31, 1991.

15

Shooting Stars

The *Southern Living* experience is meant to be a visual one. "Photography really made the difference in the success of the magazine," said Mc-Calla. "The more I've looked at it, the more it seems perfectly clear that we didn't make a lot of progress in a subject area until we had good photography. And we didn't really have a great magazine until we had great photography.

"Up until the famous, or infamous, July, 1967, issue," said McCalla, "we were just getting by with John McKinney covers and a bunch of ten-dollar photos. Beginning with the fall issues of 1967, we began to use a great deal of free-lance photography from Bruce Roberts and Taylor Lewis and Gordon Schenck. And Jeff Hunter shot the September cover story on riding the river to Tennessee football in Knoxville.

"As we've talked about, Taylor's four-color spreads of pecan pie, rice, an oyster roast, and his portraits of restaurants, such as Perdita's of Charleston, raised our standard of food photography to a new level. But the rest of Food in the sixties was usually illustrated in some inane fashion, the *Progressive Farmer* way of that era, or with Bob Simmons' swipe file. It was a good thing Lena Sturges was looking for some guidance in those days. I guess she thought I knew what I was doing in the area of food photogaphy."

"Yes, and you never cried before lunch," said Logue.

McCalla said, "Free-lancers Bruce Roberts, and to a lesser extent, Gil Barrera of San Antonio set the standard for travel photography in the early years. And fortunately Gerald Crawford was a fast learner as a travel photographer. I think, and I always thought, that one of the major reasons for *Southern Living*'s success was that we showed the beautiful side of the South: beautiful scenery, beautiful gardens, beautiful homes, and a few beautiful people. One of the important strengths we talked about in promoting the magazine was our large and truly talented photographic staff. We usually had sixteen or seventeen staff photographers. We always said we were second only to *National Geographic*, a nonprofit outfit, in our number of full-time photographers, and that's including all the big national magazines. That's how important photography was, and is, to us."

McCalla said, "Schenck did some fine architectural work for us in the early years, until Bob Lancaster came aboard. And Bob was a trip you've already experienced. I don't think our gardening people really caught on to photography until John Floyd came along. Fred Bonnie did some good step-by-step things. Luckily, Phil Morris and Lancaster kept us in the garden design game until John built a strong photographic team.

"I think the role of photography in *Southern Living* boiled down to this," said McCalla: "whatever subject we were publishing, until it *looked good* in the magazine we were in trouble. *Southern Living* is a visual experience and an emotional experience, to go along with its practical information and its more lyrical writing.

"Photography was always important to me. I wanted a camera from the time I was just a kid, but we couldn't afford it. I finally got a cheap one about the time girls came along, and I forgot photography for a while."

"I bet you did," said Logue.

McCalla helped work his way through the University of Oklahoma shooting for a man named Mel Newsom, who had a studio just north of the campus. "We shot everything, from fraternity and sorority parties, to Oklahoma football, to all the candid shots in the university yearbook, to strippers. I shot a lot of party stuff," said McCalla. "We also processed the black-and-white film. Some weekends we'd shoot twelve to fifteen parties. I was going to school full-time, and usually working forty to fifty hours. Toward the end I was making two fifty an hour, as opposed to the fifty or seventy cents which was typical then."

"Yeah, McCalla, you could always make a buck," said Logue.

McCalla served in France as a lieutenant in the Army, and he advanced his knowledge of photography along the way. First, he had to march through downtown Metz to celebrate Armistice Day, November 11, 1954. "We were sent downtown to parade with the French. They left their overcoats in their barracks. We had to leave ours on our buses, to show that we were as tough as they were." McCalla had already proved that in eighty-eight boxing matches.

Gary wound up as an assistant to Captain Paul Cook in the Public Information Office in Verdun. General William R. ("Lifeline") Woodward had fired Cook's former assistant. It was Cook who turned up years later in South Carolina and tipped off McCalla to his first job with *Southern Living*.

"I found out how important photography was," said McCalla. "Our command was not one of the major commands in Europe, but we were able to get as much coverage in *Stars and Stripes* and *American Weekend* as the big commands did. We did it because we had good photographs. We had a good photographer, a guy named Kondred, who was a little hardheaded. On Memorial Day, I was up in a little church balcony and decided that there were picture possibilities looking down toward the altar. Kondred came up and said, 'No way.' I said, 'Shoot it anyway.' The picture wound up as the cover for the Memorial Day issue of *Stars and Stripes*.

"We had a terrible dearth of photography when we started *Southern Living*," McCalla said. "John McKinney would go up to North Carolina to shoot the outdoor drama *The Lost Colony*, and he would shoot two versions of the same photograph for the cover and get nothing for the inside pages. That was typical. Dr. Alexander Nunn was always talking about 'more copy,' but photography seemed to be incidental in his thinking, in the company's thinking.

"It didn't take Phil Morris long to realize that 'if we didn't have usable pictures, we didn't have a story.' And the only way you can get pictures in advance of the seasons is to plan your photography a year in advance."

During those first years the main burden of photography fell on freelancers, an erratic proposition at best, and on staff photographers Gerald Crawford and Bob Lancaster. McCalla intended to move to all staff-produced photography as soon as he could hire the necessary talent, but in 1969, the best photographers in America were not lining up to move to Birmingham, Alabama.

By 1978, Crawford had left, and McCalla needed an image maker and chief photographer. He and Logue set out for Charlotte, North Carolina, to talk journalism's best people photographer, Bruce Roberts, into abandoning his free-lance life for a career with the magazine. It wasn't an easy sell.

At the time, Roberts shot for all the big national magazines—*Sports Illustrated*, *Time*, *People*—you name it, he shot for it. He'd had the covers of *Look* and *LIFE* in their heyday. *Time* once sent him to cover presidential candidate George Wallace for an entire summer campaign, risking his life in an old two-engine prop plane leaking oil all over the American landscape, and taking hundreds of photographs. In the end, *Time* used only a couple of mundane shots of Wallace they picked up from some other photographers along the campaign trail, souring Roberts on the experience and helping the cause of McCalla and Logue.

Bruce had originally started out on the *Tampa Tribune* as a cub reporter. But he got the tide charts backwards one day and stranded fishing boats on sandbars for a hundred miles. Editors encouraged him to concentrate on photography, which was America's and *Southern Living*'s good luck.

In 1978 Bruce had about seventeen books in print. He'd done a series of "ghost" books throughout the South, and he specialized in capturing locations beloved by travelers, such as Old Salem and the Outer Banks of North Carolina. But his ex-wife, a fine writer, had done the text to most of those books, and in the divorce settlement, the copyrights went to her.

McCalla and Logue waged their recruiting campaign long into the night. Roberts finally surrendered and agreed to join the magazine.

Roberts is a rather formal guy in his Clark Kent glasses and good manners, but he is possessed of an unsinkable enthusiasm for the next shot. No assignment is too small, too trivial, too ordinary to pique his curiosity. And he is a true master at the art of photographing people under any conditions of light, or dark, or rain, or in any circumstances of great joy, or disappointment, or tragedy.

Roberts' first *Southern Living* cover was done as a free-lancer in 1966. It was a "Singing Christmas Tree," composed of more than one hundred members of the Charlotte, North Carolina, Choral Society. His second cover was of the Abington Theatre, with half the townspeople in costume.

Bruce is at his absolute best capturing an ordinary moment in an extraordinary manner. He spent the day with a barefoot, freckled-face boy of ten in the small tobacco town of Maxton on the coastal plain of North Carolina. "If I ever saw an all-boy boy, it was Mike Sneed," said Bruce, who once edited the weekly newspaper in the town. Bruce shot him holding a turtle, the boy's freckles exploding in all directions. He shot him tossing up a ball in the town square, and checking out the family mailbox in the town post office, and blowing on a dandelion, and wading in the river with his dog, and climbing in an old barn, and fishing with his buddies, and exploring an old haunted house, and looking out from inside the town clock at time running backwards.

All the photographic essay needed to be forever timeless was Mark Twain to write the essay rather than John Logue. It was shot in black-and-white, and Logue in truth misses black-and-white in the proudly all-color *Southern Living*.

Roberts struck so many grand photographs for the magazine it's impossible to even hint at a summary of them. He is particularly proud of the James River houses he shot in Virginia, and of the photographs he made of Williamsburg, and of the shoot he did of the Brazos River in Texas for the story by Les Thomas. He also remembers with affection capturing a fifty-year Alexander family reunion in Louisiana, and every face was alive and a separate image, and the images together were a visual tapestry of America of the last half century.

Bruce rose not just to the grand occasion as a photographer, he rose to *every* occasion. But as Chief Photographer and manager of the random lives of a wildly independent stable of photographers, he was less than scintillating. In fact, he was miscast. In truth, the whole world is miscast in that role. Photographers, God bless 'em, are like killer bees, hard to get your hands around. McCalla finally released Roberts from that responsibility so that he could practice his art full-time in the Southern landscape.

There is more than a little wanderlust in Bruce Roberts, not unlike in the photographer character played by Clint Eastwood in *The Bridges of Madison County*. What's over the next hill is a wonderful obsession for him. He took early retirement in 1992, shot every lighthouse standing in America and published six hugely successful books on the subject, and was soon headed for British Columbia to do his seventh book on those manned lighthouses.

Bruce even moved to his beloved Outer Banks and with his wife opened a Lighthouse Gallery on Nag's Head. The gallery was built from plans for a lighthouse keeper's own house that he got from the National Archives and adapted. He sells all manner of lighthouse memorabilia, including antique books and even jewelry. He still shoots free-lance, and his work often appears in *Southern Living*, and his spirit is still contagious.

That same spirit of adventure seems to inhabit all good photographers, certainly those who have made their mark at *Southern Living*. Charles Walton you have met. And Bob Lancaster. And Gerald Crawford. And Bert O'Neal. And Mike Clemmer.

Here are some snapshots of photographers not previously discussed who have made their marks in the pages of *Southern Living*:

John O'Hagan joined the magazine as a lab technician, but quickly shot his way out of the darkroom. John shot for Homes and Gardens, and did the memorable Pennsylvania Avenue shoot with Phil Morris. He photographed an eight-page story with Carole Engle on furniture reproductions for the home, "Out of the Past, Made for Today." It was a knockout with readers and with McCalla. He also captured the National Archives as few have, in the story "Keeping the Dreams of a Nation." John now shoots for the book division, Oxmoor House, as well as the company magazines.

Sylvia Martin joined the magazine in 1979, with an art degree from the University of Alabama. She started in the Garden Department, and the flowering kingdom never had a more talented interpreter. Perhaps the most versatile photographer in the company, Sylvia has shot for every department.

Some of her enduring shoots were: "The Rice Coast, a Vanished Southern Culture," in 1983; "Dahlias Win Big in Autumn," in '84; "Eastern Morning Rises with the Sun," in '80; "Peonies Do Grow in the South," in '86; and "A Shady Terrace in a Sunny Garden," in '86. Sylvia secured her reputation by photographing Oxmoor's critically successful coffee-table book of flower arranging: *Elegance in Flowers*.

Geoffrey Gilbert was one of the best photographers the magazine ever had. He came from Washington, D.C., where he covered the White House for a daily newspaper. Some of Geoff's lasting travel images included: "The Jewels of the Southern Shore," in 1989; "Oldtime Music Rings in the Hills," in '84; "Catfish: Netting a New Image," in '84—all three of these stories with Dianne Young. Also, "The West Still Lives in Fort Worth," in '79, with Les Thomas; and "Fishing Fall's Outer Banks," in '81 with Glenn Morris. Jumping across a ditch in Texas, Geoff ruined his knee, which brought on an operation. Then came a second operation, then an operation on the other knee, then a back operation. Finally he was unable to continue to work, which was a great loss to the magazine.

Cheryl Sales Dalton joined *S.L.* from Biltmore House in North Carolina. McCalla remembers, "When I interviewed Cheryl all we talked about was music." Her photography was as winning as her personality. She worked in Homes and Travel. Some of her best work included: "Richmond, the Renaissance City," in 1989 with Karen Lingo; "Savannah, a Plan Preserved," in '87 with Ernest Wood; "Lighthearted at the Beach," in '87 with Linda Hallam; and "By Master of Louisiana Style," in '88 with Hallam.

McCalla was looking for a November cover in 1990. "Nothing overwhelmed me," he said. "I wanted a home with a fireplace. Cheryl and Carole Engle found what we needed. In Nashville—'Personal Touch at the Mantel.' I thought it was probably the best cover during the twenty-fifth anniversary year. And it proved what I always thought of Cheryl and Carole: they were great."

Frederica Georgia was another North Carolinian, recruited this time by Bruce Roberts. Frederica became the magazine's first Southwest photographer. Her slide show of Texas at the Texas Governors' Conference on Tourism was a smash hit. Some of her notable shoots: "Louisiana's River Plantations," in 1984 with Pat Zajac; "Remembering the Texas Rangers," in '83 with Les Thomas, which featured one of the most striking photographic spreads the magazine ever published; "Learning the Ways of the Desert," in '84 with Les; "East Texas' Woodland Wonderland," in '84 with Cyndi Maddox; and "Mardi Gras in New Orleans," in '84 with Cyndi. "She was a damn fine photographer," said McCalla.

Mary-Gray Hunter was one of the surprises of the Photographic Department. She and Sylvia Martin and Beth Maynor had the grandest smiles in the building. Mary-Gray worked for the Garden Department, but shot many other things before leaving the company to work with her husband in their own studio. Some of her best work included: "The Art of Brookgreen Gardens," in '86 with Linda Askey; "Plain or Fancy, Gates Make the Garden," in '89, a shoot she shared with Van Chaplin; and the two also collaborated on "Tulips with Design in Mind," in '85.

Mac Jamieson was another of the North Carolina photographic mafia. He specialized in homes but shot many different subjects. A few of his best: "The Missions of San Antonio," in '83 with Mark Childress;

"Baskets Trace a Southern Folk Tradition," in '84 with Phil Morris; and "Listen to the Endless Rhythms of Jackson Square," in '83 with Childress. Having left *S.L.*, Mac and his wife have been restoring an old rock schoolhouse for over ten years as their primary home. Patience was always his strong suit.

There were others. Beth Maynor loved the out-of-doors. Shot some of everything, including beautiful stuff in the mountains and along the rivers of the South, which has become her specialty in her free-lance career. She is famous for her images of the Cahaba River near Birmingham. Louis Joyner was hired as a home photographer, but became editor of that department. Dianne Young has also done double duty, shooting many Southerners and other subject matter along the way. Art Meripol, Gary Clark, and Tina Evans have all been setting endurance records traveling the South, shooting memorable travel stories.

"All of them owe quite a debt to our photographic coordinators over the years," McCalla said, "Janet Pipkin, Rebecca Scoggins, and Nell Goff. Let me tell you, keeping up with a band of headstrong photographers is full-time work."

Ralph Mark was not a photographer. He was an astonishingly gifted illustrator, a graduate of Auburn, who could have worked for any high-profile magazine in New York City if he hadn't loved fishing the lakes and streams of Alabama.

His work spoke as loudly as Ralph was quiet. If you loved the illustrations in the "Outdoor" columns of *Southern Living* over the years, you knew Ralph at his best, capturing the plants and creatures of Mother Nature as if they were alive on the page. He also painted into life the great football players featured in the All-South pages for a quarter of a century. Mark could work in any style imaginable.

"I remember Ralph broke his arm at one of our company softball games," McCalla said. "At the time he was illustrating fall leaves for the piece on Southern trees. He took a few pain pills and finished the job before undergoing an operation to fix his painting arm. He was one of the great people on our staff, and raised two beautiful daughters and took care of his mother until she died. He was a class act."

Photogaphers and illustrators and writers, too, would be bland on the page without the imagination of an art director. Tom Ford, another Auburn graduate, joined the magazine in 1970. Tom, as Art Curl's apprentice, handled those pages that didn't appeal to Art. "Tom complained about doing the 'nits and the lice,'" said McCalla, laughing. "He almost quit a couple of times." Thankfully, he never left. At Philip Morris's request, Tom began working one-on-one with the Homes copy, resulting in a dramatic improvement in the look of the section. McCalla made Ford art director in July, 1977. "He did a great job," McCalla said. "Oh, he and I used to butt heads a lot, I think because we were so much alike. We both preferred to think overly long before making a critical decision. When we made it, we held to it. Tom would stand up for what he believed. Out of that conflict came some outstanding covers and layouts.

"The last big knock-down, drag-out that Tom and I had," McCalla said, "was shortly before I retired. He had been working at home for several months, redesigning the magazine. I wanted to see something. He said he wasn't quite ready to show anything. One thing led to another; we almost went to fist city. Afterward, I told him I did not hold grudges. Disagreements were part of the [normally] orderly process of developing a great magazine. Tom's redesign was outstanding."

Ford now oversees the thirty-eight magazine covers that *Southern Living* is responsible for in a year. His gifted protégés include Lane Gregory, Leonard Loria, and Kenner Patton, who at any one time hold critical jobs within the magazine group.

McCalla once slipped Donovan Harris onto the payroll as an "illegal intern" during a hiring freeze. He came aboard full-time in 1974, and eventually became S.L.'s fourth art director when Ford moved up to executive art director. Harris is now director of design/productions for *P.F.*.

Two other Ford protégés are now art directors of other company magazines: Susan Waldrip Dendy, of *Cooking Light,* and Ann McKeand Carothers, of *Southern Accents*.

"The color pick," McCalla said, "was basically the editing process for the selection of photographs illustrating each story in the magazine. Tom's people were always professional. They did a hell of a job with the visual look of the magazine. With the editors and photographers and the Art Department in the same viewing room selecting covers and lead photographs, we had our share of disagreements. When we couldn't reach a consensus, they could count on me to make the final decsion. We argued. But I don't think it ever got nasty. You could feel the energy in the viewing room. And when we were lucky that same energy was printed on the pages of the magazine."

Logue said, "I remember how much everybody cared about every image. Editors would explain the purpose of each shoot. The photographers would present their work and stand their ground. Sometimes it would hurt them to see a favorite image hit the discard pile. Gerald Crawford would sometimes lift a slide out of the front of a carousel if it hadn't caught the room's attention, and drop it back in to give it another showing, usually to much razzing. Sometimes an entire story would be killed for 'subject failure,' as Louis Joyner so aptly characterized it. The magazine really got edited in that viewing room. It's too bad some of those exchanges weren't tape-recorded. Future editors could profit from the passion and the insight expressed—and from McCalla's fearful sounding of *What else you got?*"

16

"I'll Buy! I'll Buy!"

If you want to know the way things were, ask an Irishman. Mike Fitzgerald is your man. As Irish as Dublin and as full of blarney as Joyce himself. Mike was there in the New York office at the beginning of it all.

"I had quit the Meredith Company. I had been in their training program," said Mike, still blond, still pulling on a cigarette, still too full of energy to sit in his substantial house on the northside of Atlanta. These days he is partners in G. Carbonara & Co., a successful advertising rep firm whose top clients have long included *Architectural Digest*.

"Meredith was paying me forty-eight hundred," said Fitzgerald, "and I was spending about ten five. This guy, this friend of mine at McCann-Erickson, told me The Progressive Farmer Company had an opening selling ads for ninety-eight hundred a year." The year was January, 1966.

"I got up to the eighth floor at 250 Park Avenue," said Mike. "I'll never forget the little reception area, sort of a pea-soup green with two old couches and one old chair but on the wall were these great Menaboni paintings. Now what happened to *them*? [Good question.] I interviewed with Bill Bentley, who was the New York manager, and I really liked him. A good ol' boy from North Alabama.

"Bentley asked me if there was anything I really wanted to accomplish in my life," said Mike. "I said, 'Yes, sir. There are three things I want to do. One, I want to drive a gun-metal gray Oldsmobile. Two, I want to have tow-headed youngsters that have a Southern accent. And number three, more than anything in the world, I want to live in the South.' And he said to me, 'Maybe those things will come true, and maybe we can help you make them come true.' And the last time I saw Bill alive, I thanked him. I said, 'Every single one of the things I asked you for came true.' "

Fitzgerald's Irish eyes clouded over. "Bentley was a great, great salesman and such a wonderful man, so proud of his family, and he was wonderful to work for. But in those days in New York, you go to lunch, you have three martinis. I mean that's just the way it was. And Bill would wear a white suit and white bucks and a skimmer hat to make sales calls, and smoke those cigars, those ever-present cigars, and tell people he was from Hartselle, Alabama." Mike did not have to say the martinis got many a good and wonderful man.

Bursting into the room a few minutes later as we talked were a couple of Mike's grown-up kids, who'd just been fishing, and they listened with Southern politeness as Fitzgerald introduced two old artifacts from the magazine dark ages.

Back to his first day interviewing with Progressive Farmer, Mike said, "I was thinking to myself, 'This could be a warm place to work,' and coming out of the corner office, all the way down from the end of the hallway, was this great big, good-looking guy. I thought to myself, 'Gee whillikins,' and he introduced himself. He said, in his Jersey City accent, 'My name is Jim DeVira, and I sell this here *Progressive Farmer*.' I said to myself, 'What?'

"I finished my interviews," said Mike, "and I felt really good, and I was going out with Jim on a call, and—this is indelibly etched in my medulla—Jim is getting files from the filing cabinet, right in front by the couch where we salesmen would sleep if we were in trouble and couldn't get home at night, or were drunk, or whatever, and out of Bentley's office comes this tiny little man, couldn't have been five feet tall, wearing cowboy boots, some sort of doeskin trousers, and a ten-gallon hat that was as big as him, and they introduced me to 'Mr. Butler.' And they were all talking in reverent terms, and I looked at this guy, and I said to myself, 'This is something out of central casting, for God's sake; here's a great big, tall guy, good-looking as a model from Jersey City; here's a midget with a ten-gallon hat on telling me about poultry farms or poultry dirt or something.' And I thought to myself, 'I'm about to get the greatest job in the world.' Two days later I got it. Ninety-eight hundred a year. I didn't know I was gonna be at that ninety-eight hundred for five more years." Much laughter.

"I had never sold a line of space," said Mike. "I had never called on an advertising agency. So they assigned me *Young & Rubicam*, which was the second- or third-largest advertising agency in the world, and said, 'Go cut your teeth on that agency.' I wound up that year, 1966, and I sold the second- or third-largest number of pages running in the whole magazine," said Fitzgerald, still beaming at the memory.

"And that Christmas, they talked about a bonus, and everyone was looking forward to their Christmas bonus, and I thought, 'A couple of thousand dollars would come in handy I'm so overspent.' I was only spending twice what I was making. And the Christmas bonus came. It was in a cardboard box sitting on my desk, and it was a ham and a bag of pecans. With a personal note from Lena Sturges on how to make a pecan pie. I almost died. I said to myself, 'I think I'm in trouble.' But I was committed then to *Southern Living*. And I will tell you—I've been doing this for thirty-two years, starting my thirty-third in January—we had the best sales staff any magazine ever assembled, because we believed in it so much. Believed in what we were doing. John, you described Southern football one day; you said, 'It's not a game. It's a religion.' Selling was a religion to us. We became addicted to this *Southern Living*.

"I can see Milt Lieberman, standing at the bottom of the escalators going into the Pan Am building, commuters riding down, and Milt stopping men from all kinds of businesses and agencies and asking what kind of dog food they bought, so we could do a campaign for Gaines Dog Food. And when he gave that presentation of 'cost-per-thousand dogs,' Ken Caffery said, 'We gave him the business because he was such an imaginative son of a gun.'

"And DeVira himself," said Mike. "He was the Jack Nicklaus of space sales. I don't know how he did it. To this day, he is the premier space salesman I have ever met by such a margin it is not close. In an early issue he sold Remington Arms and then for the third cover he sold Modess. I said to myself, 'I know these Southerners are different, but surely to goodness, there's got to be a different audience for shotguns than there is for Modess.' And he sold all those ads to Clairol. Arthur Pardhel was the media buyer at Foote, Cone, and Belding. He would play tennis with Jim, and Jim would raid our merchandising supply for dozens of tennis balls and tennis visors and rackets and stuff and take them to Arthur Pardhel, and two days later, boy, that order would come from Clairol. We ran more Clairol business than we knew what the hell to do with."

Fitzgerald picked up a copy of *Southern Living* off his coffee table, as if he could hold those long-past years in his two hands. "DeVira trained us to sell this magazine. There was never a sales call you didn't sit down and go through this magazine page by page. And then you told the market story. I meet people today I haven't seen in fifteen years, and they'll say, 'Fitz, don't tell me—the South is the biggest, fastest growing market in the country, I know, I know.' *Southern Living* still uses this same basic sales pitch, and that national magazines are under-delivered in the South, and if you want to sell a Southerner, talk Southern. Now in the old days, the media buyers' response would be, 'If there is one place we don't want to be, it's the South, because they are all backwards and don't buy anything upscale. And you got no "A" counties.' And that last fact once got me in terrible trouble.

"I had upstate New York," said Mike, "and there was a little Italian media director on Keepsake Diamonds, and we were *this close* to getting a piece of business. And he said to me, 'Your "A," "B," "C," "D" circulation is off line.' He said, 'I understand that one of the cornerstones of *Southern Living* circulation is *Progressive Farmer* expires who lived in "C" and "D" counties.'

"I said, 'That is the most ridiculous thing in the world,'" said Mike. "'I'll get an "ABC" statement and show you our "AB" circulation is terrific.' I called New York. I forget who our secretary was—that was before Lorraine Inzetta, who was wonderful. I said, 'I want you to get the "ABC" statement, and I want you to white out the numbers, and I want you to change the percentages of "A" and "B" counties.' Which she did. I gave this guy this statement on my way back from Syracuse. He was in Rochester. He said, 'This is interesting. Perhaps this will change my thinking.'"

Fitzgerald said, "Monday morning DeVira called me in. He said, 'We're in trouble.' The little Italian guy had got ahold of a real 'ABC' statement. He said we were 'fraudulently representing our circulation.' I said, 'That's impossible. The statement came from New York.' DeVira found out what I'd done. And he laughed about it. But he said, 'How the hell are we going to get out of it?' The little media director told him we were not welcome in his agency.

"I knew one of the owners," said Mike. "He was a young guy and very aggressive. I told him exactly what happened, that I faked it because I wanted the business so much. But I said, 'Most importantly, you belong in the book because in the South more girls are getting engaged. Southerners believe in formal weddings, in diamonds, and they are unlike the rest of these young people, all these hippies today everywhere else.' He said, 'I don't condone what you did, but I agree with you. Put Keepsake Diamonds in the book.' " Mike needed another hit of Scotch to salute the memory of the sale.

"But DeVira made the greatest advertising sales call I ever saw," said Fitzgerald. "DeVira asked me one day, 'What about this here Salem cigarette business? It's running everyplace, and we're not getting it. Why?' I said, 'The guy won't see me.' He said, 'Are you a seller?' I said, 'Yes, sir.' He said, 'Is he a buyer?' I said, 'Yes, sir.' He said, 'Well, isn't that the nature of this here game? You get together a seller and a buyer and youse convince him to buy *us*.' He said, 'Make an appointment. We're going over together.'

"So I finally made an appointment with this guy Jack McGrath. A wonderful Irishman. We caught a cab to the William Esty offices on 42nd Street. We went into his office, and McGrath said there were a lot of reasons Salem wasn't using *Southern Living*. He said, 'I've told Fitz this over the phone. I've told him in person. I'm going to tell you. First of all, we've got the entire South locked up. We are the number one brand in the South. Absolutely no reason to advertise in *Southern Living*.' "

Mike said, "The two of us went through our regular presentation. And then DeVira stood up and started to go through this thing of national magazines' under-circulation in the South. He told how many cigarettes, how many smokers there were in the South, how many people there were, how much potential there was for Salem smokers. He said, 'This here market has got 42 percent of this here people in the country, and you're not getting to these people. If you want to sell Southern, you've got to talk Southern.' And on and on, and by the time he gets finished, this guy is leaning out the window over 42nd Street, hollering, '*I'll buy! I'll buy! Leave! Leave!*'

"And Salem bought six or seven spreads, full-color spreads. And DeVira said, 'I'll split the commission with you.' We weren't on commission, but that's what he said. It was the single best sales call I ever saw in my entire life. He took this guy from Ground Zero, totally opposed to the magazine, to buying it in a big way."

And what about the first issues of *Southern Living*, what did Fitzgerald think of them?

"I couldn't believe it. I couldn't believe it, that first issue," said Mike. "And subsequent issues were even more unbelievable. Religious columns and little women with these skirts made out of material like little kitty cats sewed on them and beehive hairdos. Clisby Clarke, he was the account guy on Coca-Cola, Clisby said to me, 'Fitzy,' he said, 'the people reading this thing are located in the beehive capital of the world, Birmingham, Alabama.' Clisby was from Marshallville, Georgia, and he was slick, he had polo suits when polo suits weren't fashionable.

"But we kept on selling ads," said Fitzgerald. "We worked for a guy, DeVira, that in this day and age, the whole staff would quit. He had a rule, you had to make *five calls a day, plus lunch*. And that was an absolute hard-and-fast rule. And he would make *eight* calls a day. One Friday afternoon he called me on the phone, and said, 'What are you doing?' I said, 'I'm sitting here making appointments.' He said, 'Why don't you pick up your appointment book and bring it to my office?'

"I picked up the book," said Mike, "and I was shaking so bad I was shaking all over. He raised that big hand and sat in that leather chair which was sunk down with no bottom in it, and he said, 'Close the door and take a seat here.' I hand him the appointment book. He looked at it, and he said, 'Don't we have a rule here at *Southern Living*?' I said, 'What, sir?' And he said, 'About five calls a day plus lunch.' I said, 'That's right.' He said, 'Well, you take this here book, and you go back into your office and before you leave here today, you have that book filled up,' and he said, 'Don't put any fake names in it because I know *every single one* of them. I'm going to call them at random to check on it.' And he said, 'If that doesn't suit you, go there and take all of your crap out of your desk, put it in a cardboard box, and get the hell out of here and never come back.'

"I'm telling you that is a true story," said Fitzgerald, drawing on a Scotch and water for comfort all these years later. "I went back in there, and I called everyone I knew. I called everyone at Young & Rubicam and said, 'Please see me on Monday and Tuesday and Wednesday. I need dates. DeVira is going to kill me.' And that was when Jim Horton was working at Y&R, thank God. I had that date book filled up for the next week. I had doubles at ten-thirty and eleven. Oh, those were great times," said Mike, "unbelievable times."

Fitzgerald took on an Irish melancholy with the Scotch whiskey.

"There's no fun left," he said. "I can tell you, working for *Southern Living* and being involved with those people and the magazine was so much fun. There wasn't a day went by we didn't do something mischievous, or laugh. It was the end of an era, and we didn't recognize it. We did things that today would just be considered childish pranks, but at the time were hysterical. We knew DeVira was going over to Ted Bates to make a call on Rene Schneider. We made *fifteen* phone calls to Rene. She'd answer, and we'd hang up. The phone would go three, four, five rings, and De-Vira is in there trying to make a pitch, and we'd hang up and dial right back. DeVira came storming back in the office and groaned, 'That was the absolutely, goddamn worst call I ever made. The phone kept ringing. Rene finally said she wasn't going to accept any more calls.' And we were roaring laughing, knowing it was us."

So many memories rushed across Fitzgerald's face he was unable to speak for a minute—which was, in fact, a personal record of silence. "I was talking to this professor at the University of Mississippi," said Mike, "and he asked me if I was with the magazine in the early days. And I said, yes, I was. And he asked if there was any moment that really stood out in my mind. And I said there was. 'There was a sales meeting at Callaway Gardens, in Pine Mountain, Georgia, the first sales meeting. We came down. The Chicago, the Detroit offices came down. Everyone gathered around, and I said, 'We ought to have a drink.' And they said, 'Well, this is a dry county.' I said, 'I beg your pardon?' I'd never run across one. They said 'a dry county.' I said, 'DeVira, what's a dry county?' He said, 'What are you thinking of, asking me? I'm from Jersey City.' So, old Smith Moseley came over with that huge suitcase, and he had those millions of miniatures in there, and we're sitting out drinking by the pool, and that Detroit boy that Jerry Jehle hired, the salesman that was a practicing minister, he got us down on our knees around the swimming pool and said a prayer before dinner. I said to DeVira, 'When I get back to New York I'm getting my resumé out on the street. This is an insane asylum.' "

Fitzgerald laughed tears into his own eyes. "We were going to throw this Southern dinner in New York. The manager brought the menu, and it had some kind of straight chicken and something called *white asparagus*. And we wanted to make it all Southern. Well, DeVira and I grew up in very modest backgrounds. We never knew what the hell white asparagus looked like. DeVira said, 'Where do these things come from?' And the man explained it's a European technique, you just keep covering the asparagus with dirt and it stays white and grows just fine. So DeVira said, 'I never heard of this here kind of thing. What should we do?' I said, 'Why don't we call it *Charleston Asparagus*? These people will love it.' So, on the menu, that's what we called it. And we called the chicken 'Savannah Squab,' or something, and no one else in the audience knew the difference because they'd never been South, and we'd never been South either. DeVira spoke first to the four hundred people, and Jimmy's knees were knocking like *that*." Fitzgerald rattled the coffee table.

Which reminded him of his own first standing pitch for *Southern Living*. "This is a true, sentimental story, and I'd just forgotten it until about four or five years ago. I was at a sales meeting with *Architectural Digest* out in the desert," said Mike. "I was reminded of it because Jeff Peterson was the associate publisher of the *Digest*, and his father-in-law is Dewey Roberts. At the time of the New York dinner, Dewey Roberts was the single most powerful guy on the General Electric business at Young & Rubicam. He ran the business. And we went to make a presentation. Don Cunningham and Jim and myself marched up to 285 Madison Avenue, to the fourteenth floor, the conference room.

"Don turns to me and said, 'Now you are going to introduce everyone, and you are going to introduce the magazine, give 'em the basic story. Now don't worry about it, but Dewey Roberts is going to be here, and he controls the account. If he doesn't like it, the whole thing will fall apart.' So we get up there, and I'm twenty-three years old, and everyone was going to be sitting around this long conference table, and there would be twenty-five of the very, very top people of Y & R, who had an interest because Jim Horton had a great interest in the new magazine."

Mike said, "I asked the woman organizing the room, 'Do you have a podium?' And she said, 'Why do you need a podium?' I said, 'Because my knees are shaking so much and Mr. Roberts is going to be here.' Now Dewey years later is at this *Architectural Digest* sales meeting, and I started to tell him the story, and he said, 'I can tell you I remember the people who were there, and I remember loving Don Cunningham.' And Dewey made me tell the story all over again, how they didn't have a podium anywhere on the fourteenth floor, and my knees were shaking, and I'm saying, 'S-S-S-S-S-*Southern Living* this' and 'S-S-S-S-S-*Southern Living* that,' and Dewey and his wife fell over laughing, and he said, 'I loved you guys so much we'd have bought you no matter what the hell you brought up for that presentation.' And that was a lot of years ago, Godamighty."

Fitzgerald's melancholy had lifted, and his eyes were full of mischief.

"And there was the time we were going to unionize," he said, laughing so hard he had to put down his Scotch and water. "Latzky had gotten a divorce, and we were over at his apartment in Beacon Place. Steve Berezney and Latzky and myself. We decided we were going to get all the reps and start a union. DeVira was working us too hard.

"We get to the office," said Mike, "and we sent Latzky in to break the news to DeVira. Now DeVira was ready for Latzky, so somebody had ratted on us. Latzky came out ashen; he was white as a blank sheet of paper. And I said to myself, 'Oh, shit!' And I waited and sure enough, about ten minutes later, just long enough to put my stomach absolutely in knots, DeVira called, 'You mind coming down here to me?'

"I closed the door," said Mike, "and sat down, and Jim said to me, 'Uh, I've been in this here business for about six or seven years.' He said, 'I was with the Hoyst company.' And he said, 'Do you know we didn't make very much money at Hoyst, and now I got a great opportunity with this here company, and uh, this here company is known as *a non-union shop*.' And he said, 'I understand youse is going to be creating a union.' He said, 'It will be very nice, and where will you be working when you set this thing up?' And I said, 'Union?' He said, 'Don't bullshit me, I know you started this here union. There will be no more unions, and I ever hear the word *union* around here again,' he said, 'I'm going to kick your butt—right out this here window onto Park Avenue, do you understand?'

"I said, 'Yes, sir. I think I got the message. This is a non-union shop.' " Fitzgerald was lying on his back laughing.

When he could speak again, Mike brought up the occasion of the watershed speech by Dick Anderson of Young & Rubicam at the 1968 sales meeting at Lakeway Inn, near Austin, Texas. "Remember that day on the bus?" said Mike. "We went with the *Progressive Farmer* editors to visit a Red Angus farm. And they were talking about Johnson grass and some kind of 'wind blowers' and putting the hay up in round balls. And DeVira and I were sitting on that bus from six o'clock in the morning. DeVira said to me, 'If I hear one more word about this here wind throwers and this here Johnson grass . . . I'm dying here, I want to get off the bus and have a drink.' Now that's the mental frame of mind we were in when Anderson made his presentation the next night. It was the greatest single presentation I ever heard—there never was a greater one," said Mike.

"Anderson would pull out these cards. They had slices of color, angles of color. He would hold up a bright red piece and ask, 'What do you see?

Perception is reality,' he said, 'and the way you are perceived is often greater than you think you are, or than you think you are going to be.' That was the beginning of his speech 'Great Expectations,' which he gave many, many times. He told us how fabulous it was going to be for *Southern Living*."

"And that was the first time I understood, I believed, that the magazine could be, not just a success, but a *huge* success," said Logue.

So why did Mike Fitzgerald, who loves *Southern Living* to this day, leave the company, not once but twice, and the last time for good?

"There was the feeling," said Fitzgerald, "that you got to a certain level at *Southern Living* and you could go no further. It was finally obvious to everyone that the company was making so much money, and you didn't have to be a rocket scientist to know they weren't paying us guys a whole lot."

Fitzgerald said he almost left before he did leave the first time. "My salary had gone from ninety-eight hundred to thirteen thousand," said Mike. "This guy at *McCall's*, John Bell, said to me, 'Fitzy, I like the cut of your jib. I'm going to give you a good list of advertisers, American Airlines, Eastern Airlines, lots of other things. And we pay pretty good bonuses over here.' And I thought about the hams and the pecans at *Southern Living.* 'I'm prepared to offer you thirty thousand dollars.' This is 1967 or '68."

Fitzgerald said, "I went to DeVira. Jim said, 'Don't take the job, unless . . . you go back and demand a vice-presidency. If they won't give you a vice-presidency, they don't really want you. You have a future with us.'

"I go to John Bell and say, 'I talked to some people, and I think I should be offered a vice-presidency.' John Bell's eyes got as big as dinner plates. He said, 'For Christ's sake, I'm not a vice-president.' That was that with the job. Whatever DeVira said, I believed.

"I stayed until 1970 when I left to become 'world-wide' advertising director for Bernie Cornfield of Geneva, Switzerland, for the *International Business Digest*. He hustled this youngster right out of his socks. I was making four thousand dollars a month, cash, until the U.S. government came and said, 'Mr. Cornfield will no longer be working in this country.' And then Bernie died.

"DeVira called me one day and took me to lunch," said Mike. "He asked if I would consider taking back my old job. I would have died to get back, it was in my blood so deep. I missed it so much. He gave me my job back for eighteen thousand dollars a year.

"I carried one hundred and six pages of advertising one year, and De-Vira carried one hundred and eleven and was the manager to boot," said Mike. "I tell my kids this story. I've told them a hundred times. I was coming back from Syracuse one time and that was a long loop. I'd go to Buffalo and Toronto and Rochester, calling on French's Mustard and Kodak and Crossman's Arms. I was driving the New York Freeway, and I was so tired I could hardly stay awake. If Joe Horan were alive he'd tell you the story.

"DeVira always said, 'Make the last call, no matter how tired you are.' So I stopped by this old state building in Albany before they built the new government complex. I called on Joe Horan," said Mike. "I pitched him about New York State advertising in *Southern Living*. I can visualize him sitting there, that long face of his. And, finally, he said, 'I'll give it a test. I'll run some third-of-a-page ads, and if we get the response you say we'll get, we'll advertise on a regular basis.' By God, the first ad he ran got four thousand responses. Horan called me up," said Mike, "and he said, 'What did you do, call all your subscribers and tell them to call here?' Later in New Orleans, at the DATO meeting, he said, 'We are running a four-color schedule with you.' That sale made me as happy as any sale I've ever made in my life, and Joe and I were friends for a long, long time. I tell my kids, 'No matter how tired you are, make that last call.' "

Fitzgerald said, "I always wanted to move South. Roger McGuire came up to New York to see me. I always loved him and respected him and thought he was a wonderful man, but I didn't really understand why until I was older and could appreciate his accomplishments and his style. He instilled in all of us a sense of decency, a sense of commitment to the magazine. He never browbeat you. He wore the white hat and DeVira wore the black hat.

"McGuire took me to breakfast at the old Sheraton Park Hotel at 38th and Park Avenue. He said, 'I don't know how grown up you've become. Do you think you're pretty well grown up now?' I said, 'I think so.' He said, 'Can you handle responsibility?' I said, 'I think so.' Roger had told Mike Silver from McKinney-Silver, 'He drinks too much, he's too wild, he's too social.' And Mike said to him, 'Are you running a summer camp or a magazine? If you want him to sell advertising, he'll sell advertising.' He offered me the job as Atlanta manager, and I took it *for the exact same salary as I was making in New York.*

"McGuire told me my money would go twice as far in Atlanta," said

Fitzgerald. "It wasn't until I moved down there that I found out the fallacy of that deal. I was on top of the ever-loving world. I worked so hard those first couple of years. All of us did. We carried some three hundred pages. Harold Chambliss and Don Cunningham and Rick Rush, with his wide ties and lime green suits, and Don Martin, who I advised not to put his bonus money into real estate—me, the wise investor—but he did and kept on putting it there, and years later he had a party that DeVira went to. DeVira told me, 'I go to this kid's house, a kid who couldn't write a letter but could sell advertising, and some guy in a uniform comes to the door. I figure the Salvation Army is making some kind of collection. But it's this here Martin's doorman.' Martin became absolutely wealthy and is a hilariously good fellow."

Mike recalled from his days as the Atlanta manager: "I was going to get a company car. I wanted an Oldsmobile instead of a Ford. A gunmetal gray Oldsmobile. I called Britt Butler to tell him. He asked me, 'How much does it weigh?' I shook my head, I said, 'I have no idea. I never weighed an Oldsmobile.' Britt said, 'Emory's figured out a way that we can determine how much gas it's going to use by how much it weighs.' I said, 'Oh, this is wonderful.' Britt said, 'You have to buy a Ford. It's under thirty-two hundred pounds. The Oldsmobile is forty-two hundred. Only executives drive Oldsmobiles.' I got my revenge," said Fitzgerald. "I ordered four thousand dollars worth of furniture to go in my office. Britt called me up and almost died. He said, 'Even Emory Cunningham doesn't have an aromatic dispenser.'

"My relationship with Emory?" said Mike. "None. None. At a managers meeting, right after we opened the new building, we were sitting in that all-glass room, and Emory was telling us about the architect Henri Jova, and then we got started in the meeting. Emory took exception to something about selling a particular account, and I said, 'Well, Emory, that may be true from your perspective, but you've really never sold consumer advertising space.' And it was about eighty degrees outside, and the air conditioning was on inside, and suddenly the heat kicked in. I said to myself, 'I think I've made a mistake.' Emory never let go of that for three days.

"We went out to play tennis that night, and DeVira and I were playing Roger McGuire and somebody, and Roger came up to me and said, 'I don't want to necessarily give you advice, but I think you made a bad mistake today, and take my word for it, *I know.*' I apologized to Emory (who, of course, helped sell millons of dollars in consumer advertising in his day in Chicago), but it never did work."

Fitzgerald thought about what he'd said for a minute and amended: "I'd come into Birmingham as the Atlanta manager, and the office was doing so well, and he would treat us really well. I'd have to say we had a good relationship, and Emory, at that time, was good for the magazine. He was president, and he looked like a president."

Fitzgerald was to leave the magazine one last time. "I was making thirty-three thousand as eastern manager," said Mike. "Jim said if I played my cards right, I'd become advertising director. Meredith called me, very secretly, and offered me a fifty-six- or fifty-eight-thousand package, with a big expense account and a lot of perks. I had a new bride. I thought about it, and they sweetened the pot with a country club membership. I was so damn nervous telling Jimmy I was leaving. He was pretty good about it. He was barely making that at the time." So Mike left for good, and ultimately hooked up with his own advertising rep partnership in Atlanta, which has flourished.

Fitzgerald lifted his glass and said, "I can recall people asking me what made *Southern Living* the great magazine that it was. And I say, unabashedly, that there were three people who made the magazine: Jim DeVira, Jerry Jehle, and Gary McCalla. And the rest was icing on the cake. I really feel that. I mean I sold it. I loved it. I knew it. Jehle sold business in Detroit that had no business running in that magazine. I was down in Florida recently with Gene Richmond, who was ad manager at Jeep for years, and with Chrysler. He's now advertising director of the Citrus Commission. Gene said Jehle would come in 'with all these percentages, how many Jeeps, Oldsmobiles, Chrysler New Yorkers were sold in the South, how Southerners loved big cars. And I bought the magazine,' said Gene. 'I really had no business buying it. There were no numbers then to back up *Southern Living*. I bought it because I liked and respected Jehle so much.'

"What else can I say about DeVira?" said Fitzgerald. "And McCalla ran the damn magazine."

"I just kept it in the road," said McCalla. "Not in the center of the road but between the ditches."

Mike said, "I always thought of you, Logue, more on the selling end of it, hanging out on the streets with us pitching the magazine, than of you as an editor."

"That was me, the song and dance man," said Logue.

"Speaking of song and dance, did either of you see the Broadway play *Ain't Misbehavin'*?" asked Mike. "Well, they asked the guy who was playing Fats Waller: 'Fats, how do you do it? What do you do each night for the audience?' Fats said: 'I've got a very simple formula. I find out what they want, I find out how they want it, and I give it to them *just that way.*'

"And that was the true secret of *Southern Living*," said Fitzgerald, and the three of them raised their glasses to that and to the old times, long gone, Godamighty.

17

From Jericho to Armageddon

This chapter will not begin to tell the complete history of the book division, Oxmoor House. That is a book in itself. Or maybe it's a soap opera.

It began, like *Southern Living*, under the most improbable leadership. Bob Haney was named to direct Oxmoor House in 1970. Like Red Youngsteadt, Haney had been responsible for the physical production of *Progressive Farmer* magazine. Like Red, his tenure was a brief one.

As previously explored, the cookbook *Southern Living: Our Best Recipes* was an instant success in 1970, thanks to the formidable Lena Sturges with a lot of help from Betty Ann Jones, the first staff member at Oxmoor House.

But Haney was an inveterate pipe smoker, and that habit helped get the best of him. He began selling metallic pipes in the magazines. In those days, McCalla and Logue also affected pipes. They lit one of Oxmoor's pipes, and it *melted* in the ashtray. The pipe caper proved to be a burnout. Then Oxmoor House began to sell tool kits by direct mail, and that proved a double disaster. A great number of customers failed to pay for the kits, which was awkward for the bottom line. And a greater number of customers found them to be horrendously ineffective. The wrenches would bend in your bare hand.

Oxmoor House had its first casualty. Haney was out. And in came Les Adams, sporting a small mustache and a lively ambition. He had been vice-president and sales manager of Oxmoor Press, The Progressive Farmer's printing company.

Adams was bright, very bright. He had a degree in English from the University of North Carolina and a masters in English from Columbia, and had earned a law degree from Cumberland College—even editing the *Law Review*—while working full-time for Oxmoor Press. Adams was a self-taught pianist who could knock out an acceptable *Rhapsody in Blue*, not Gershwin's easiest tune. He was a delightful, mercurial guy, with a short fuse that was liable to ignite at the onset of any crisis, a shortage of which never existed at Oxmoor House.

Adams' legal career had been brief but colorful. It consisted of one case. He was appointed to represent an accused felon, "Big Red." It seems Big Red and his girlfriend were booming down the road with the Highway Patrol in hot pursuit. Gradually Big Red's pickup truck coasted to a stop . . . out of gas. As the patrolman leaned down to put the arm on Big Red, his girlfriend pulled a double-barreled shotgun from the rack behind her and stuck it between the patrolman's eyes and pulled both triggers. *Nothing*! "Damn you, Big Red," she said, "out of gas and out of shells!"

Adams thought there had to be a more promising future in publishing books. He was right. But crime itself was hardly a more precarious occupation than book publishing.

"The Southern Living Homemakers' Cookbook Library" had been thrown together without testing a single recipe, by packagers Millard Fuller and his partner Morris Dees, now famous for running the Southern Poverty Law Center in Montgomery. Fuller is equally famous for founding Habitat for Humanity in Americus, Georgia. The "Library" helped fuel Oxmoor House's existence for the next several years, until those flawed books were mercifully laid to rest.

The direct mail package that inflicted the "Homemakers' Library" on innocent subscribers began: "Run lickity-split to your mailbox." They should have been running in the opposite direction. The Progressive Farmer Company management knew the books were flawed and the recipes untested, but took the profits anyway. Some of the worst, most confusing recipes were ultimately replaced, and some photographs upgraded, but the venture was not the company's finest hour.

Oxmoor House was surviving, but was hardly known in America.

Enter *Jericho*, which proved to be one of the most successful art books published in this country.

Logue stepped into McCalla's office one day in the early seventies. He was sitting behind a huge open book, nothing but the top of his head showing.

"Don't let it fall on you," said Logue, "or we'll be looking for a new American Indian editor. What is it?"

McCalla gathered his strength and held the heavy book higher. The jacket was a watercolor painting of three cowboys on horseback in a desert landscape, under the title: *Peter McIntyre's West*. Published, of course, by Sunset Books of California.

McCalla and Logue looked at each other with a knowing grin. The *Sunset* boys were good for one more idea that could be lifted.

Les Adams was a quick read if there has ever been one. He took one look at *McIntyre's West*. He didn't like the idea; he loved it. He decided on the spot that he would look for a painter, and Logue would look for a writer, to capture the American South.

Adams somehow found his way to the Plum-Nelly Art Show, which is "plum out of Georgia and nelly in North Carolina." He was looking for the work of Hubert Shuptrine, a little-known artist from Chattanooga, Tennessee. Shuptrine's work was more than a bit reminiscent of Andrew Wyeth's, whose agent also lived in Chattanooga and who had befriended Hubert and his agent-brother, Jim. Hubert was in Wyeth's league as a craftsman, painting old barns, and apple trees in the winter landscape, and old boats among the reeds, but he did not have Wyeth's original vision of his own little world. Shuptrine's stuff was openly literal and nostalgic rather than interpretive and dispassionate. More importantly, *every* Shuptrine painting had been sold before the Plum-Nelly Art Show opened. Adams had found his man.

A couple of years earlier Logue had dropped a letter to the *Atlantic Monthly* to inquire if the James Dickey whose poem "Looking for the Buckhead Boys" it had published was the same James Dickey with whom he once played tennis at Bitsy Grant Center in Atlanta. It was ol' Jim, all right. One day they'd finished playing and Dickey said he was quitting his lucrative job writing jingles for Coca-Cola.

"What are you gonna do?" asked Logue.

"I'm going to be a poet," said Dickey.

"Damn if I'm buying the tennis balls, with what Furman Bisher pays me," kidded Logue, who until that moment had no idea Dickey was a poet.

In 1970, Dickey had published something else, his first novel, *Deliverance*, and it had swept the country and been translated into a powerful motion picture for which he wrote the screenplay. He was a hot property. Dickey looked at Shuptrine's paintings and agreed to write the text.

Adams and Logue loved Hubert's painting of an old black fisherman in his rowboat as the image for the jacket of the book. Dick Benson, the company's intrepid direct-mail consultant, thought the South would hate a black man on the cover. Benson knew the mail; he didn't know beans about the South. Now they needed a title.

Logue worked up a list of over fifty possible titles, including a first suggestion, "The South Beheld," which sounded faintly biblical but was just off the top of his head. He flew to Columbia, South Carolina, rang Dickey's doorbell, and said, "I ain't leavin' until we have a title."

They tried it for two days, cold sober. Then one night they tried it the other way. They were sitting on Dickey's back deck, looking over Lake Katherine, having exhausted their efforts with his long African blowgun against a target mounted on a tree, talking about this and that and the other. "We need a title with the power of a novel," said Logue.

Suddenly Dickey said the word *Jericho*. All got quiet over Lake Katherine.

Dickey disappeared inside his house to look up the word in his biblical concordance. Jericho, the ancient city in Palestine, was perhaps the oldest city in the world. Also, in the modern vernacular, especially among blacks, it carried the connotation of *freedom*. It was The Word. And with it, they joined the first phrase on Logue's original list to make: *Jericho: The South Beheld*.

Logue's old friend Dickey liked the idea that he didn't have to refer to any of the paintings in his text, but could write his own impressionistic prose poems. The old black fisherman did catch Dickey's fancy, and this is what he wrote:

> In the waters of Jericho, where we have come in a long flash-
>   straight
> line, the Black fisherman still pulls at his heavy boat, pulls out
>   where the view expands: where he can see more and more of
> Jericho. He pulls one pull all the way from the heart, pulls again
>   from the loins, and then slacks the oars

and drifts. His net goes down. Above him, we take on the slow,
    mist-feathery slant of gulls,
and begin to call. On the desolation of
waters there is our cry, and the fisherman from East Jericho
leans over and feels in his palm the weight of all life
in his net, and we, mainly the weight of lived-on
land, and the people of the land at random.
They all seem to add up to something,
for their movement has been intimate,
like the movement of association and
inevitability caught in a net. But what is the meaning? We cannot
know that; we can only move along.

In the company of such words, Shuptrine's images took on a weight
they never before had, and readers felt it without knowing why.

Les Adams put into play his inventive instincts for the jugular, and the
book-selling world never beheld a more popular title for an art book.

McCalla added fuel to the bonfire of interest by publishing Logue's
story on Shuptrine's quest to capture the South in paintings, and his interview with Dickey about his life's work, which has since been reprinted in
at least one scholarly book.

At a book signing at Rich's in Atlanta, hundreds of people lined up,
buying over two thousand books at forty dollars each, and some of them
had shopping carts to carry off six or more copies. Dickey looked over
the crowd from under his safari hat and said, "We done set down in the
cream jug."

Indeed. Dickey took his show on the road, publicizing the book, and
he was quite marvelous, somewhat to the distress of Shuptrine, who felt
he was the painter and deserved most of the limelight.

At the big book and author luncheon in Nashville, Dickey was introduced by John Seigenthaler, then editor of the *Nashville Tennessean*, who
said his ninety-year-old mama had cautioned him to keep his introduction short, as she couldn't wait to hear James Dickey. Dickey, his eyes
shifting wickedly, promptly read his poem "The Sheep Child," told by a
half-sheep and half-human fetus in a laboratory test-tube. Dickey said
the poem had been criticized "but never faulted for originality of point
of view." He then read from his poem "Adultery." But first he quoted a
New York taxi driver who once asked him: "Young fellow, do you have
a mistress?" "He was the last person to call me 'Young fellow,' " said

Dickey. "I said 'No.' He said, 'You will. But don't do it. *Her brother always needs an operation.*' "

"How did you like that, Mama?" asked Seigenthaler.

"I loved it," said his ninety-year-old mama.

So it went on the promotion tour. The book, published in 1974, sold over one hundred thousand copies. It won the Carey Thomas Award, much prized within the publishing industry. Over the years, Dickey went on to write three more art books for Oxmoor House: *The Wayfarer*, with photographer William Bake; *Southern Light*, with photographer James Valentine; and the truly classic *God's Images*, with artist Marvin Hayes.

"I say Les Adams was mercurial," said Logue. "I can't think of a more apt description: changeable, volatile, quick-witted. We started out to publish an art book of wildlife with Hayes, who did wonderful animals in demanding egg tempera on masonite. Somewhere along the way, Adams switched the project to reproducing, in black-and-white etchings, the great stories of the Bible.

"Hayes grew up in Texas and played football at Texas A&M for Bear Bryant, and made it on the art scene in New York City against impossible odds. He took on the challenge of capturing the best-known stories in all Judeo-Christian tradition in new and timeless images. Rather amazingly, representatives of the big religious denominations actually *endorsed* the book. And the Louvre and the Metropolitan Museum of New York both accepted original sets of the etchings into their permanent collections. And Dickey took just as great a risk as Hayes in retelling these biblical stories in his own voice, the stories of Moses and Job and David and Christ himself. He told the story of Saul and David from the point of view of the dark spirit in Saul. The book was a critical success and a modest financial success.

"Jim never missed a deadline or let us down even once," said Logue. "He used to say, 'Mark Twain was the first person to write literature on the typewriter, and I am the first to write it on the Dictaphone.' Lord Jim never suffered from lack of self-confidence."

Oxmoor itself was to suffer. "The terrible success of *Jericho* went to our collective heads," said Logue, who had moved over from *Southern Living* to become editor-in-chief of Oxmoor in 1974. "If we could make such a success of one art book, think what we could do with three or four, was our thinking. What we could do was to lose a bit over a million dollars about 1976. A book, *Fabric Decorating*, came flooding back after we mailed it out. It wouldn't have been so awkward except that we printed about a quarter million of them.

"We had tested two direct-mail packages. One made it clear this was a sewing book. The other package did not," said Logue. "The test package that quietly omitted it was a sewing book drew a much bigger response. So we mailed that one, which was less than wise. The women who ordered it thought they were getting a pure decorating book, not a sewing book. Back it came in rivers of returns.

"We also printed a huge quantity of *My Son Joe*, the life of quarterback Joe Namath as told by his mother, a caper I got us into. We sold twenty-five or thirty thousand, which would have been respectable, except that we printed seventy-five thousand."

Oxmoor House threw a gigantic party for the Namath book at the American Booksellers Association convention, which happened to be held that year in Manhattan. "We were on the thirty-second floor of the hotel," said Logue. "We had hundreds of people jammed into our party suite, plus Namath and his three brothers. Now the NFL is a tough outfit, but nothing compared to the Namath brothers from Beaver Falls, Pennsylvania, when they'd been too deeply into the grape. They got into some kind of blood argument and disappeared into the bedroom behind a locked door. Out came incredible noises of crashing furniture. Now at that time Namath was with the New York Jets and was the most valuable commodity in pro football. Luckily we had hired a guard, Mr. Moon, who stood about six feet five, and weighed about two-eighty.

"Adams said, 'Mr. Moon, I think you better go in there and settle things down.' Mr. Moon knocked open the locked door and grabbed the Namath brothers by their necks. Two of them were about to hold a third out of the thirty-second-floor window. The king-sized bed was flattened to the floor. A huge mirror was smashed into tiny smithereens, scattered everywhere. No piece of furniture in the room was left intact. Joe Namath himself emerged and joined his girlfriend of the moment with a big smile on his face, as if he'd just scored on the Chicago Bears."

In the midst of impending disaster, Oxmoor published some of its finest visual titles. *A Southern Album* featured timeless photographs from life in the South over the last century. Most of the images had never been published and were searched out among private and public collections by Irwin Glusker, who also designed the book, which itself has become a collectible. The images were paired with excerpts from works of the South's greatest writers, from Capote to Faulkner to Welty. Ann Harvey, a young professor at Samford University, did so thorough a job researching excerpts from these writers that Logue and Adams hired her, and she became a formidable editor at Oxmoor House.

Classic Lines represented the work of Richard Stone Reeves, of Oldwick, New Jersey, who was considered the greatest living painter of thoroughbred racehorses. Tony New York art galleries cut the paintings out of the book and sold them individually as prints for more than the sixty-seven-dollar price of the book. The text was by the English turf writer Patrick Robinson, an unsinkable character who once covered the Mediterranean for the *London Daily Express* and was a big drinking buddy with Richard Burton. To prove it, he could get Burton on the phone and have him recite from *Hamlet* in his native Gaelic. Robinson's life is an adventure novel too daring for this rather discreet memoir.

Classic Lines these days is routinely advertised in *Blood Horse* for several thousand dollars for a single copy. Oxmoor went on to do two other art books with Reeves: *Decade of Champions* and *Legends*, both of which are also collectors' items. By the mid-1970s, Oxmoor was losing its anatomy but was certainly building in value for its book buyers.

This was true in the production of Oxmoor's "Southern Classics Library," leather-bound volumes of the South's greatest books: *Absalom, Absalom!*, *To Kill a Mockingbird*, *Gone With the Wind*, *Look Homeward Angel*, *Let Us Now Praise Famous Men*, *The Heart Is a Lonely Hunter*, etc., with outstanding commentaries on each book. The leather and paper and design of these books has given them an enduring value, while costing Oxmoor House an arm and a leg. "One of the company's finest hours," said Logue.

The Progressive Farmer Company, however, frowned on Oxmoor House losing more than a million bucks, since the whole company was only making about three million at the time. Les Adams had been reporting directly to Emory Cunningham. Emory got advance notice of all publishing and direct mail plans, so Oxmoor's bold intentions were no secret to management. It was only the disastrous results that were so unacceptable.

Throwing up his hands in frustration, Cunningham turned the responsibility for Oxmoor House over to Chief Financial Officer Vernon Owens, who didn't know anything about book publishing but understood the bottom line in all its manifestations. He made things exceedingly hot for Adams, walking him through every nuance of Oxmoor's press runs and direct mail efforts. Adams was also directed to all but disband the Oxmoor House staff, retaining only a skeleton crew to keep the imprint alive. Logue was told to dismiss most of the editors, and it was a painful process.

Logue is quick to agree that he should have been a calming influence on Adams' ambitious, even reckless, publishing program. "Instead, adding me to the Oxmoor mix was like pouring gasoline on a brush fire," said Logue. "The two of us together needed a keeper. But, Lord, it was fun."

Logue had his own bonus plan cancelled by Cunningham, and was dispatched back to *Southern Living*, joining Philip Morris as an executive editor, a happy combination. He did keep his title of editor-in-chief of Oxmoor House, though all publishing had been suspended.

"McCalla didn't have to take me back, and I had a job offer in Atlanta, but I never have been much of a quitter," said Logue. "I thought at the time that Emory's treatment of myself was absolutely fair and correct. And I'm glad ol' McCalla took me back. They were in a bit of a jam, as Pirtle and Crawford had just quit the Travel Department. And I hoped Oxmoor House could rise from the ashes."

Enter one of the major figures in this book, Don Logan. Actually Logan had joined the company in 1970, taking over its computer fulfillment division, Akra Data. Which had been in a state of arrested collapse. He got there the way Bill Capps did, by answering an ad. At the time he was working for Shell Oil in Houston and going to school part-time, working on his doctorate in topology.

McCalla and Logue could not begin to explain *topology*, which the dictionary defines as "the study of those properties of geometric forms that remain invariant under certain transformations, such as bending or stretching." Logan, sitting in his huge office on the thirty-fourth floor of the Time-Life Building, said, "There's not a practical application for topology that man has ever discovered."

"I believe it," said Logue, who once flunked trigonometry.

Logan would probably IQ at about 180 to 200. "If you add me and McCalla together, you get one Logan," said Logue, "and you have to double me to get one McCalla."

For all his smarts, Logan had a gift for people. And for turning a buck. He was also once an athlete, having played a mean brand of basketball in high school in North Alabama. But Logan didn't have any hobbies. What he liked was work. It is now wonderfully funny to Logue and to Southern Progress Vice-President Jeanetta Keller that Logan is president of the company that owns *People* magazine, and that the only Madonna he is aware of who ever existed is the one in the New Testament. "He thinks R.E.M. is something that goes on a car," said Logue.

Logan grew up near Hartselle in North Alabama, studied mathematics at Auburn, and then took a master's degree at Clemson before joining Shell in Houston. "I decided I didn't really want to be a Ph.D," said Logan. "I liked working for Shell. It's a great company. But everything at Shell and NASA, where I worked as a co-op student at Auburn, moved about as slow as molasses on a cold morning in February.

"I happened to pick up a Birmingham newspaper," he said. "There was an ad for a data processing manager. It sounded kind of interesting. I called the number, and Vernon Owens answered."

Logan said that all his experience had been on the scientific side of computers. "I didn't know beans about mailing lists or commercial applications." He flew to Birmingham and met with Owens, who reluctantly agreed also to fly Logan's wife, Sandy, to Birmingham.

Owens offered Logan the job at about thirteen thousand dollars. Logan pried out an extra thousand, which was no mean feat dealing with the tight-fisted Owens, who never actually introduced Logan to the Akra Data staff. And Logan neglected to ask where he would be working, or exactly what he would be doing, or whom he would report to. (Vernon Owens, he discovered.) He finally found Akra Data at 7th Avenue South and 24th Street. The place was a low-rent zoo. It had been operated as a separate company so that it wouldn't come under the mailers' union.

Finally Billy Smith, a good and somewhat zany guy who worked for Akra Data but who had his own company that served Akra Data in the same office—it's too complicated to explain—came up to Logan and said he would "help him get started."

"I don't have any idea what my job is," said Logan. "Do any of these people work for me?"

"All of 'em," said Smith.

"We had two junior programmers," remembered Logan. "One was an ex-inspector for the state food department, going around inspecting restaurants, and the other had gone to trade school to learn programming. We had about twenty women doing the keypunch work for data entry. The company didn't trust us to open the mail with checks and cash in it."

Logan's office was the thing of legends. "They had sheetrocked the walls up to only about six feet seven inches," he said. "I needed some bookshelves, so they just nailed these flimsy metal shelves to the wall and painted around them, leaving about a two-inch, unpainted gap around each shelf. I thought, boy, what have I hooked up with here? You guys had it made over on 19th Street; compared to where we were, it looked like heaven.

"We were pretty primitive," he said. "We had an old RCA Spectrum 70/35 computer, and I think they went out of business about three days after we finally dumped it." He said it took about forty hours to do a main run on *Progressive Farmer*, turning out all the mailing labels and renewal notices. "We almost never had a run without the machine crashing, and having to start over from scratch, and we had two runs a month," said Logan. "We'd have to be there twenty-four hours around the clock on a run."

Logan ultimately brought in an IBM computer with a more reliable printer, and added and trained people "who knew what they were doing, so I didn't have to stay all night. Somebody else had to, which was a big improvement."

Akra Data was soon doing fulfillment for Oxmoor House, as well as *Progressive Farmer* and *Southern Living*. And Oxmoor hit the skids in 1976. "The big debate going around was whether the company should be in the book business," said Logan. "I don't know how I got pulled into the meetings. I guess it was because we had developed a fulfillment system for books and knew something about marketing them, more than most people around. I got pulled into meetings where the discussion was going on: Should we keep Oxmoor alive?

"Actually, Oxmoor lost well *over* a million dollars that year [1976]," said Logan. "All of it wasn't reported, because of returns we had to eat the following year. I think company profits in 1975 were only slightly over three million dollars. Compared to the company's size, Oxmoor's loss was huge. Les Adams was still there, and he was reporting to Vernon. Emory was going to let Vernon and Les try and figure out how to fix this thing."

Logan said, "I was called into a meeting with Emory and Vernon and Les. I don't know exactly why I was there. I wasn't on that management level. Les left to do something, and Emory suggested we 'close Oxmoor down.' He was saying, 'Maybe we made a mistake, and maybe we shouldn't be in the book business, because very few successful magazine publishers are successful in the book business.' And that is still true," said Logan.

"But Vernon really wanted to work with Les for a little while," said

Don, "and he thought maybe they could turn it around. Emory had just given him the responsibility for Oxmoor, and he didn't want to be the guy to shut it down without even trying to do something. I give Vernon credit for not shutting down Oxmoor House," said Logan.

"What did you advise Emory?" asked Logue.

"I said, 'I think we ought to continue on, try a little longer.' "

"Why did you think that?"

"If you looked at what had happened," said Logan, "if you pulled out three or four big mistakes, the results really weren't all that bad. And it seemed to me if you built on the successes and minimized the failures, you would be okay, which I later learned is what everybody would like to do in the book business and few can do."

"Publish the winners and don't publish the losers," said Logue. "Like the stock market: buy only those stocks going up."

"Yeah," said Logan. "Well, after a few months, Les decided he would leave, and as I remember, the memo that went out said: 'Les is going to leave and get rich.' "

"Which is exactly what he did," said Logue, "and God bless him." Adams started his own company, publishing leather-bound volumes of medical classics, such as *Gray's Anatomy*, and he ultimately sold the company for a not-so-modest fortune, and has since been fly-fishing his way around the world, undoubtedly without a thought of Oxmoor House or "Big Red."

Logan began to divide his time between Akra Data and Oxmoor House, but "I was told by Emory and Vernon that I was not going to move permanently to Oxmoor House," said Logan. "They told me it was a temporary assignment. They brought in this one guy, a production director at some company here in New York, whom they almost hired to run Oxmoor. Emory valued Dick Benson's opinion on a lot of things in those days, especially about direct marketing, which Oxmoor House was built around. Asked about my running Oxmoor, Benson told him, 'That's the dumbest idea I've ever heard. Nobody from the computer side ever went over to marketing, they don't know anything about marketing.' And Benson told me—he wouldn't say anything he wouldn't say to me, this was early 1977—he said I should stay in the computer center."

Logue said, "I don't think there is a room large enough to hold the great ideas that made our company successful that our consultant Mr. Benson wasn't *against*. Not to mention some of the quirky ideas he was *for*. Capps once had McCalla and me in a meeting with Benson, who was bound and determined *Southern Living* should put out a thirteenth issue each year. He went on and on about it. *Family Circle* was doing fifteen issues, *Woman's Day* was doing eighteen issues, or some such numbers. McCalla didn't open his mouth and didn't budge; he was fighting in those early days to get out twelve winning issues."

"I always referred to these proposed extra issues as 'moonlies,' " said McCalla.

"And *Southern Living* still doesn't put out a thirteenth issue," said Logue, "and those two other magazines have suffered all manner of trouble. Finally, I said, 'I believe what we have here is an inexhaustible supply of Mr. Benson's opinion.' I thought he was going to hit me with his cane."

ABA, the booksellers' convention, was being held in Atlanta in 1977. Logan went over to represent the dormant Oxmoor House. And McCalla went over to talk to Logan, who was staying in the Peachtree Plaza Hotel.

"We had a lengthy, fairly intense conversation," said Logan.

"Yeah, in the lobby of the Plaza Hotel until about four o'clock in the morning," said McCalla, laughing. "We stayed so late the hookers kept trying to pick us up, until I said to them, 'How do you know we're not house detectives?' "

McCalla used his considerable influence to convince Logan to take over Oxmoor House. He was preaching to the choir; Logan already wanted the job. He told McCalla if he didn't move over to Oxmoor House, he would probably leave the company "sometime fairly soon," because he'd done what he could do with the computer division.

"I was convinced you could make Oxmoor work," said Don, "if you thought of yourself more in the direct marketing business, as opposed to being a book publisher. Then you could start looking for winning projects. And you could still layer in the fun books, the visual books that Logue loved. Gary and I talked about the terrible relationship that existed between Oxmoor House and *Southern Living*. Oxmoor being so antagonistic, not wanting anything to do with the magazine, wanting to go its own way, rather than enlist the resources and skills and knowledge at *Southern Living*.

"We talked about how to break down those walls," said Logan, "how to get the Foods Editors, the test-kitchen people working on cookbooks. If it hadn't been for that long conversation with Gary, and Gary's going back to Emory the next Monday, I might never have gotten the job."

McCalla said, "I left Atlanta that Sunday to go home for my daughter's birthday. I planned to go back to ABA Monday. But I decided to stay around, and I went in to see Emory the first thing Monday morning.

"I told Emory, 'Hell, I think it would be easier to find somebody else to run the computer division than to find somebody else to run the book division,' " said McCalla, " 'I mean, somebody who understands what we are doing.' Emory said, 'I'll think about that.' And he said, 'I appreciate your opinion.' "

Logan met with Emory within the week, and the deed was done.

Without introducing any new books, just by judicious management, Logan cut Oxmoor's losses in half the first year, and eliminated the losses entirely by the end of the second year. And it was in the third year, 1979, that Oxmoor, under Logan's leadership, introduced *Southern Living Annual Recipes*, which insured the survival, and the triumph, of the book division. You've read the story of that venture in Chapter 10. Oxmoor House still sells more than one million copies a year of *Annual Recipes*. In 1980, Oxmoor House moved from the small cottage off Shades Creek Parkway to the 500 Building off Highway 280, where the book division built its own first test kitchens. It gave Logue much satisfaction to return to Oxmoor House as full-time editor-in-chief, with bonus.

Postal rates climbed ever upward. And it was obvious by the 1980s that Oxmoor House could no longer sell a single title in the mail profitably. Not even a cookbook. Annuals became the stuff of survival. As mentioned earlier, each year the book buyer is notified that she will be sent the new annual title unless she declines the offer, saving the costly chore of rounding up all new buyers from among the random millions of potential customers.

The second big breakthrough in annual books, as described in Chapter 10, was the title *Cooking Light*, which has a following of several hundred thousand buyers a year. It was originally made up entirely of new recipes, but now includes all the recipes that have appeared in the past year in *Cooking Light* magazine. Oxmoor House, like Fats Waller, gives it to you whichever way you want it.

One low profile title, *Award Winning Quilts*, published in 1974, lay hidden on the Oxmoor House backlist for years. Years later it was tested in the mail on a whim and proved very popular with book buyers. It then opened up to Oxmoor House the new but exceedingly expensive world of the crafts book.

Mary Johnson, known as "Sunshine" for her smarts and her irrepressible personality, joined the Oxmoor staff and produced a number of crafts books, including *NatureCrafts*. These books were beautiful and moderately popular and costly to construct. Free-lance fees would drift into accounting months after the books had been printed. Don Logan held his breath on each title until Oxmoor got its money back.

The company bought *Decorating and Craft Ideas* from the Tandy Corporation in 1975. Mary Johnson eventually moved over to edit that ill-fated magazine, and Candace Conard, Carey Hinds's ace recruit, took over responsibility for editing Oxmoor's crafts books.

One day Logan called Logue into his office. "We've got to get out of this crafts book business," he said. "They are expensive to produce. We have high returns. One of these days we are going to get killed."

"I'll talk to Candace," said Logue, "see what kind of commitments we have."

Logue cornered Candace. He didn't tell her the idea was to get out of crafts books. He said, "How many crafts projects have you got lined up?"

She counted them, "Seven."

"How many contracts have we signed?"

"None."

Not the answer Logue was looking for. "If you could only publish two of them, which two would you choose?" She thought about it. Then told him.

"I'm going to tell Logan we are committed to those two books," said Logue. "Hold off on the other five." Candace agreed, somewhat puzzled.

Logue stretched the truth to Logan. "Hey, Candace says we are committed to two of the crafts books. She's holding off on five others." Logan agreed.

One of the two crafts manuscripts, thank Candace Conard and the fates, was a book titled *Lap Quilting*, by Georgia Bonesteel, who had made her reputation hosting a quilting program for North Carolina Public Television. It sold 150,000 copies the first year. Georgia Bonesteel has gone on to make a not-so-modest fortune in Oxmoor House crafts books. And crafts books have gone on to outsell cookbooks at Oxmoor House. Included among those crafts is the enormously successful annual *Christmas with Southern Living*, and there has been a great variety of other successful Christmas titles.

Oxmoor House has never suffered a shortage of creative talent. Sisters-in-law Carol and Charlotte Hagood, with their quiet intellectuality, could be considered in their editing as the "Brontë sisters" of American crafts. Linda Wright helped nurture into print the famously successful crafts books by Georgia Bonesteel and has launched many other crafts titles since. Senior Editor Olivia Wells, who once edited *Annual Recipes*, now manages all editorial services for Oxmoor House. She is famous for the talented young editors she has hired and had spirited away by various of the company's magazines. Kay Clarke has made a reputation for herself as a supreme photostylist, working with the talented Jim Bathie and other photographers. Oxmoor's books, like the company's magazines, live on the excellence of their visual appeal. The talented Susan Payne moved over from *Southern Living* to run Oxmoor's food empire, first edited by Betty Ann Jones and then by the tenacious Ann Harvey.

Employees of New York publishers change jobs with each passing season. Not so at Oxmoor House, where loyalty is not an old-fashioned word. Judy Burlage has starred in marketing since the early 1980s, as has Chloe Fraser in accounting. Cindy Cooper has endowed numerous Oxmoor books with her design touch. Joan Denman survived the production and marketing battles to retire and take a leisurely trip up the Amazon River. What's a few freshwater piranhas compared to the book wars? For years Jerry Higdon coaxed all Oxmoor House books into print while bleeding orange and white for his Tennessee Volunteers. Tommy Carlisle rose through the financial ranks at Oxmoor, ultimately moving to Little Rock to take over responsibility for the highly profitable acquisition *Leisure Arts*.

"The career of Steve Logan is one of my favorite stories," said Logue. "He worked his way through school as a part-time photographer/artist for Oxmoor House. Then he worked his way through law school. And somehow he managed to stay fit as a drill instructor. Steve wasn't exactly sure where to set up his law practice. Oxmoor House said, 'While you're looking, stay where you are. You can practice out of your office and still free-lance for us.' Did any other publisher have a lawyer-photographer-artist on the part-time payroll? Finally, we said, 'Steve, you're too nice a guy to be a lawyer. You have a better career here at Oxmoor House.' "

Steve went on to become a vice-president, heading up Oxmoor's research and development for new books and direct mail properties. And now he is heading up Southern Progress's move into commercial television.

Dianne Mooney, once an editorial assistant, is now vice-president for development, not only for Oxmoor House but for the entire company. She found the two unpublished young authors of Oxmoor's sexy 1996 title *How to Cook for Your Man and Still Want to Look at Him Naked.* The title created quite a sensation at ABA, as did the male model, wearing an apron and very little else, who was hawking the book in the Oxmoor booth. Mooney helped launch Oxmoor into the world of the celebrity title with the best-selling *Bubba Gump Shrimp Co. Cookbook*, in collaboration with Paramount Pictures and Logue's old pal Winston Groom, who created *Forrest Gump*. The shrimp book wound up on the *New York Times* best-seller list.

Mooney has orchestrated a number of ventures between major advertisers and Southern Progress, including publishing a quarterly magazine for the food company Healthy Choice. The magazine is titled *Choices for Living Happier and Healthier.* Not to mention, more profitably for Southern Progress.

A planning session at Biscayne Bay, Florida, led by Mooney in collaboration with senior officers under Logan, helped plunge Oxmoor House into the profitable world of the three-ring binder continuity program, especially for crafts.

Mooney's former role as VP Promotions for Oxmoor House was taken over by her one-time assistant Lane Schmitt. Schmitt not only has shown a genius for the direct mail, she knows the lyrics to more songs from the sixties and seventies than even Johnny McIntosh, assuring herself perpetual tenure so that she can lead the singing at Oxmoor House beach parties. In fact, she has sung her way on to the Southern Progress management team.

Logue was always happiest plunging Oxmoor House into some costly visual book, of which he counted on Logan to figure out a way to sell enough copies to keep them from being killed. "I always felt these books caught the beauty and the culture of the South and helped strengthen our publishing franchise," said Logue. "That's my official justification. And a true one. But, damn, they were fun to publish.

"We ran across a photographer, William A. Bake, who lived in Boone, North Carolina, and taught at Appalachian State," said Logue. "He specialized in timeless photographs of the landscape. He'd hike for days and wait for hours to strike a winter image in a spot in the mountains so isolated only park rangers might have seen it. Bake was agreeable to a book.

"We needed a writer," said Logue. "So I contacted James J. Kilpatrick, who first gained popularity (or enmity, according to your politics) for his hard-line conservative columns in the nation's newspapers. Later his Sunday columns took up arms against those who would violate his beloved

English language. Jack has known the South from his youth in Oklahoma and understands it and loves it, but offers no false apologies for its short-comings.

"He was agreeable to a book," said Logue, "until we mailed him our typical Oxmoor House contract, which called for the publisher to have the final say regarding 'form and content.' " Jack fired back (to para-phrase him): *Hell, no. After twenty years of the study of orthography, I'll not turn my work over to some tin-eared copy editor.* To paraphrase Logue's reply: *I'm not offering this amount of money for purposes of subverting your language. If you will put your name on it, we will pub-lish it.*

Jack, for all his bombast, proved to be a very sweet guy. The manu-script arrived with a one-word plea: "Help." It didn't need any.

The book, *The American South: Four Seasons of the Land,* was as suc-cessful as it was beautiful. It inspired a sequel, *Towns and Cities,* which was equally handsome but less successful, proving that people love any mountain or river more than someone else's town or city.

The Amon Carter Museum in Fort Worth, Texas, had been featured in *Southern Living* many times, beginning with Logue's story in 1968. Always the emphasis had been on its collection of Western art. But the museum, under the direction of Mitchell A. Wilder, had begun collecting classic American photography as early as 1961, with the donation of a Dorothea Lange photograph of cowboy artist Charles M. Russell. By 1980 the museum owned more than 120,000 prints and negatives of the leading nineteenth- and twentieth-century American photographers, in-cluding Berenice Abbott, Ansel Adams, Margaret Bourke-White, Imo-gene Cunningham, Thomas Eakins, Walker Evans, Laura Gilpin, etc.

Drawing on the Amon Carter collection, Oxmoor House brought out *Masterworks of American Photography,* with a brilliant text by the young curator of photographs, Martha A. Sandweiss. With its customary attention to excellence, Oxmoor printed the black-and-white book on a four-color press so as to capture the tone values in each separate print. It was no best seller, but it was among the distinguished American books published in 1980.

Logue and Logan found themselves on the road in Texas, checking into a hotel room in Dallas. In the room was a copy of the hotel chain's in-house magazine. On the cover was a tranquil painting of sailing boats in a harbor. The artist was Ray Ellis. The painting appealed to both of them.

Logue had heard of Ellis, who lived in Savannah, but had never before seen any of his work. He dropped down to Savannah to check him out. Ellis had once owned his own advertising agency in the East and had placed ads in *Progressive Farmer*. He'd finally taken the plunge as a full-time artist, specializing in marine watercolors. He had a true gift. A show of his in New York, "A Tang of Weather," had drawn a flattering review in the *New York Times*. A number of his paintings were owned by significant museums. He also had a knack for the popular image. His paintings were collected from Martha's Vineyard to Savannah.

Ellis, who can complete a complex painting in a couple of hours, was keen to do a book. They needed a writer. Logue and Logan found themselves back in Texas, sitting in Joe Garcia's Mexican Restaurant in Fort Worth. Logue banged his fist on the table, tilting their large margaritas dangerously. "Let's get Cronkite," he said. "He's a big sailor. I saw a show about him and his boat on public television." "Sure," said a skeptical Logan.

Logue knocked out a letter to Walter Cronkite. Sorry. He was too busy. Thanks anyway. "I made a mistake," said Logue. "I didn't mention anything about payment. I checked with Logan. He could arrange anything. I spent two days writing Cronkite again. You can almost never turn a guy around after he says no. I wrote him that I had neglected to mention payment. That I knew he was from Scandinavian stock. I said it was traditional among the Vikings that when one of them died, they put his body on his boat and shoved it out to sea. Did he currently have the boat he wanted to be put to sea on? We would build him that boat.

"I got this phone call," said Logue, "Cronkite clearing his million-dollar throat. Were we serious? We were. Three books later the boat was his."

South by Southeast came out in 1983. It was a smash hit at fifty dollars a shot, and a bargain at that. Ray put tears in the eyes of those who had lost their hearts to the South's Atlantic coast. Cronkite knocked out his own anecdotal text on his old portable typewriter, and it was a fine read. Walter and Ray had actually met on the tennis court on Martha's Vineyard, and now they became buddies, which meant they competed on the book promotion tour to see who could tell the best bawdy stories. "Cronkite in a one-sided tell-off," said Logue.

After the success of the first book, Cronkite and Ellis collaborated on *North by Northeast* and *WestWind*, the latter named by longtime Oxmoor Art Director Bob Nance, who designed all three of the elegant art books, as he did William Bake's two books and many others. Bob has since retired to his beloved Auburn, Alabama, and free-lances, as does his talented artist-wife, Faith. Karen Irons edited *South by Southeast* with her velvet fist, and Candace Conard edited the other two Cronkite-Ellis books.

Oxmoor hosted grand parties in Los Angeles and San Francisco and New York, promoting *WestWind*. In L.A., many of the highest-profile Hollywood moguls showed up to press the flesh with Lord Cronkite.

"We've pushed some famous people at Oxmoor," said Logue, "but never anybody like Cronkite. He couldn't take two steps on a public street without somebody speaking to him as if he was a member of the family. He loved it. He loved to tell about taking a cab to the New Orleans airport, on the old road before the four-lane highway. And the cab got stuck in traffic. And he had to get out and walk across a plank over a little ditch to a small, working-class house and knock on the door. And a middle-aged housewife, in her housecleaning gear, opened the door and stood speechless. 'I know, madam, it's me,' said Cronkite, 'but could I please use your bathroom?' Logue loved to imagine her husband coming home from a long week driving a big eighteen-wheeler across the country and she saying to him, 'You can't believe who used our toilet while you were gone.'

"One more Cronkite story," said Logue. "We were sitting at a large, round table in Commander's Palace, the great New Orleans restaurant, and the woman owner was making a big fuss over Cronkite. His wife, Betsy, could only shake her head and whisper, 'Look at Walter. He's loving it. He dreams that he will die with a seventeen-year-old girl on a seventy-foot yacht. But he's gonna die on a seventeen-foot boat with a seventy-year-old woman.' "

Anchored off the dock of Walter's home on Martha's Vineyard is the *Wyntje III*, a beautiful sailing memory of the three books and the good times had selling them. And Ray Ellis and his vibrant wife, Teddie, have built a comfortable home of their own on Martha's Vineyard, proving that some of the riches from the sea have been caught on canvas.

In one day and one night in Savannah, Oxmoor's great trade sales manager, Fred Burk, pulled off a sale of almost two thousand copies of *South by Southeast*. Burk was a gentleman's gentleman, a Princeton man from Philadelphia. He had been vice-president and on the board of J. B. Lippincott when it was a great publishing house. He made Harper Lee's *To Kill a Mockingbird* the No. 1 best-selling, best-loved book of its time.

He would go to ABA and know more booksellers and book buyers than any ten people there. He would flip his hair off his forehead in a lifelong gesture and calm the most tempestuous customer that ill circumstances could set loose. Now if Fred fell into the firewater, he could be a handful. But everybody loved him too much to hold it against him.

Happily, Burk survived the purge when Oxmoor House faltered. Don Logan loves to tell how the very literal Vernon Owens, trying to get a grip on the ever-elusive book business, kept pressing Burk to assure him exactly how many copies of a particular book he would sell in bookstores. Burk tried to explain that it was impossible to know. Owens wouldn't hear of that answer. "Finally," said Don, "Fred told him, "We are going to sell *one copy*. And *I* am going to buy it.' "

Burk retired and moved back to Philadelphia to look after his aged mother, and died all too soon thereafter. American booksellers have not produced a classier gentleman.

"We can't talk about all the memorable books at Oxmoor House," said Logue, "but we can't *not* talk about *Southerners: Portrait of a People*. It was done as sort of a celebration for the company's one-hundredth anniversary. In fact, a number of the images were published in a special hundredth-anniversary issue of *Progressive Farmer* that I enjoyed working on. Our old friend Irwin Glusker looked into archives, every public and private collection he could get his hands on, to select the photographs representing life in the last century in the American South. Some of the most memorable images came from the files of *Progressive Farmer* magazine. Famous faces and anonymous faces. This book comes as near to capturing the Southern experience in images as any book that has ever been published," said Logue.

Oxmoor had to thank, and to pay, Charles Kuralt and novelist Mark Childress for the text, which is equal to the images. The words are definitely Kuralt's. But he was so busy criss-crossing America for his television show that he could not sit down at the word processor. So, Oxmoor House dispatched Childress with a tape recorder to travel with Kuralt and tape his memories of growing up, his favorite family stories, his most enduring recollections, which in their honesty spoke to all Southerners. Kuralt, from his years of scripted and unscripted television, had the gift of speaking in polished sentences. The images and narrative wear exceedingly well. Arranged and edited by Childress, this book too is a collector's item. And Childress was bankrolled to write another novel.

18

Comings and Goings

In 1981 Emory Cunningham called in Logue and asked him to become Creative Director of the company, working with each of the magazine editors to help introduce new and innovative subject matter or new ways of handling traditional subject matter. But he would have no authority over the editors, who would continue to report to Emory.

Logue didn't want to do it. It was too precarious a position—to have responsibility without authority. He said to Don Logan, "Look, Oxmoor House is flourishing. We have great independence to publish whatever we believe in. We have a terrific thing going here. I don't want the creative job."

Logan was not persuaded. He wanted Logue to take it. Sitting in his thirty-fourth-floor office all these years later, he laughed. "We wanted somebody in management to keep Emory off our backs. To take the heat. That's what you did."

And very possibly Logan wanted someone on the second floor to help prepare the way for his own move into corporate management.

So Logue became Creative Director even while holding on to his role as editor-in-chief of Oxmoor House. "Oddly enough, the job worked out okay," he said. "McCalla at *Southern Living* and Tom Curl and Jack

Odle at *Progressive Farmer*, and whoever happened to be editing *Southern Accents* after we bought it and *Cooking Light* after we started it, knew I wasn't after their jobs. I was friends with most of the editors of the magazines. I got a kick out of working with them. Helping *P.F.* improve its cover selection process, helping *Southern Living* consider bonus stories that it could publish, helping decide just what should be the format of *Cooking Light* and of *Decorating & Craft Ideas*, and now and then doing a critique for the various staffs. And still giving editorial presentations to advertising agencies in Detroit and Chicago and New York and L.A. It was fun, to tell the truth. And I don't think I did too much damage."

As the 1980s came to pass, neither Logue nor McCalla realized that Cunningham was thinking seriously about selling the company. Eugene Butler and the other major stockholders were old men. When they died their families would have to sell their stock to pay their inheritance taxes, and the company would be cast into play with little influence as to its ultimate ownership. Emory himself was approaching retirement age. Any potential buyer would want a logical successor to the CEO in place.

In 1983, Emory moved Logan to management as vice-president of corporate development. He hit the ground taking the title seriously. By the next year he had been named executive vice-president.

Jeanetta Keller, whom Emory hired from the University of Montevallo in 1985 as director of public relations, swears that Logan and Logue ignored her for months. "They wouldn't take me to lunch. They didn't trust me," she enjoys saying.

"Yeah," said Logue, "we thought she was going to be the house flack. With no opinions. No agenda. No willingness to take a tough stand. I think the last two people who were that wrong about anything were president and vice-president of the Flat Earth Society. And you couldn't believe how many lunches it has cost us since."

"Ha," said Keller. In truth, she became Logan's right arm, and later, being vice-president in charge of human resources and employee benefits, she accomplished more things for employees than anyone in that role in the history of the company. She has recently swapped assignments, taking on editorial responsibility for all the company magazines. "Ha," said Logue, "now she gets to work with the true crazies."

One of Logan's first responsibilities was *Decorating & Crafts Ideas*, which had continued as a small-niche magazine, modestly profitable. Logan determined that only with a change of identity would it become a major profit center. He led its makeover into a general-interest magazine, *Creative Ideas*, still with a crafts emphasis. Logue was all for the makeover, which proved disastrous. But he did warn Logan, "Careful of this *DCI*. A number of careers have gone down the tube over it, including Roger McGuire's."

"There is one big difference, in my situation," said Logan, ever the artful dodger.

"What's that?"

"I still have responsibility for Oxmoor House."

The old subscribers to *DCI* missed their ticky-tacky crafts, and the new, very sophisticated *Creative Ideas* didn't catch on with advertisers or general-interest readers, and soon passed out of the company's ownership.

"I learned that when you go from specific subject matter to general subject matter in a magazine, you had better be careful," Logan said. "Changing the name of the magazine was also a big mistake." Unlike Roger McGuire, Logan lived to fight another day.

This is as good a spot as any to take reluctant leave of McGuire, one of the true gentlemen and founders of *Southern Living*. With the purchase of *Decorating & Craft Ideas*, Roger took it over, giving up his role on *Southern Living*, which was an awful mistake.

At various times, both Roger and Emory said they thought *DCI* had "as much potential as *Southern Living*." McCalla, who functioned as editorial director of *DCI* for two years, in addition to his editorship of *S.L.*, had a one-word reply, "Bullshit!" McCalla was not one to spiff up an opinion.

McGuire also accepted responsibility for several other dubious company ventures, including Sunland Plans (a system for selling subscriptions to some 250 magazines through schools and other organizations), Ag Response (a system to serve buyers of Akra Data's farm list), and Progressive Farmer Insurance Service (which employed a number of insurance agents, selling especially to farmers). None of these enterprises any longer exists, and were doomed from the start, no matter who was responsible for them.

McGuire suffered a serious case of adult-onset diabetes. He was unable to work for a number of months. When he did come back he asked for a new publishing role, representing the company's magazines both within the industry and outside it. He did not want to hit the airways and the sidewalks hustling advertising, as he had done since the late 1940s. No man ever had more friends, within the publishing industry and outside of it. But management did not look favorably on his request. The one significant vote in management, of course, belonged to his longtime friend Emory Cunningham.

Roger determined to retire from the company and seek a new challenge in life. He owned 1 percent of Southern Progress and could afford to do it. Emory remembered one day Roger came to him and said, " 'I need just a little more stock, and I could be listed among the 1 percent owners.' And I helped him get it," said Emory.

It was appropriate that Roger be one of the owners listed on the mastheads of the company magazines for the landmark work that he had done over his career. As it happens, it was Roger who came up with the name "Southern Progress" when it was determined that "The Progressive Farmer Company" no longer represented the real identity of the company.

Cunningham, looking back on the sad time of McGuire's departure, said, "I tried to figure out a way Roger could stay with Southern Progress. But Roger came in on a Monday, and he and Pat had been talking all weekend, and he had decided he was going to resign and they were going to leave Birmingham. They ultimately moved to Asheville, North Carolina, where they had a good life. I think Roger did the right thing leaving."

But at the time he left, Roger's old friend was not prepared to let him go into his new life with the company's unqualified blessing. Company management demanded that McGuire sell back his stock at a price he believed to be far below its true value, saying he had not fulfilled his professional obligations. McGuire hired his next-door neighbor, a formidable lawyer. And the company did not elect to sue him.

The company would have been hard pressed to present witnesses who could or would testify that Roger McGuire had not fulfilled his professional obligations.

Roger and Pat did settle in Asheville, where they made a considerable impact on the small city, especially on the renaissance of its downtown. When McGuire died in 1994, the city of Asheville mourned the loss of an adopted son. And his old colleagues at Southern Progress knew they "would smile again, but they wouldn't be young again," as one of Jack Kennedy's old Navy buddies said when the president was killed.

* * *

"Emory gave me *DCI*, and I kept Oxmoor," Logan said, "but we really didn't talk much, because he wasn't interested in developing new things. That's when the idea for *Cooking Light* magazine came along. [Came along to Logan.] We started it without an editor or publisher. Marty Spector functioned as advertising director. We had two people selling ads, and I made a lot of sales calls with them. We never had as much as five million dollars invested accumulative in *Cooking Light*. About its fourth year it had a positive cash flow, and by the next year it made a profit."

Logan said, "We were trying to buy *Southern Accents*, and had been for some time. We wanted an upscale magazine of the South. That's when we started *Southern Living Classics*." After only a couple of issues of *Classics*, under Editor John Floyd, the Atlanta owners of *Accents* agreed to sell the magazine to Southern Progress. Emory had been negotiating with *Accents'* publishers for some years, but Logan and Jim Nelson handled the surprise acquisition while Cunningham was on a Time, Inc., trip to China.

When Logan left Oxmoor House, he left it in the charge of his protégé, Tom Angelillo, as vice-president and general manager. Tom was a tall, slim young man who still played full-court basketball, as in his undergraduate days at Washington and Lee. He also worshiped at the shrine of the Brooklyn aka Los Angeles Dodgers, having caught the fervor as a young boy in Cherry Hill, New Jersey. The morning after a Dodger shutout was always a wonderful time to hit Angelillo with a new idea.

Angelillo was always immaculately dressed and his office more shipshape than the desk of the chief of staff of the U.S. Navy. He unconsciously reflected the gentlemanly qualities of the men who had led Southern Progress since 1886. And he loved Logan like a brother.

Angelillo pushed for several years for Oxmoor House to buy a growing crafts publisher in Little Rock, Arkansas, by the name of Leisure Arts. He finally got his way in 1992, and the acquisition has proved to be a highly profitable one for both publishing companies, Leisure Arts specializing in retail and Oxmoor House in direct mail.

In the great tradition of the company, a young woman from Leeds, Alabama, Nancy Fitzgerald Wyatt—graduate of Auburn University, of course—worked her way through the art departments of several Southern Progress magazines, winding up on the editorial staff of Oxmoor House. Nancy had the eye of an artist, a great love of crafts, and a high tolerance for the sometimes Queen Bees of the crafts world whose work found favor under her guidance. Nancy ultimately followed Logue as only the second editor-in-chief of Oxmoor. The company has been so much a part of Nancy's life that she even was married on the mezzanine of the new building on Lakeshore Drive. You never saw a more beautiful bride. And Oxmoor House remains in sure editorial hands, though not as many rowdies have been seen hanging around the offices since Logue took his leave.

19

Finale

In May 1985, Southern Progress was sold to Time, Inc.

"It's ironic," said McCalla, "while they were selling us, our editors, who did not own company stock, were producing some of our all-time best issues. It was a vintage year, 1985. I guess you could say it was the best year of our lives. At least it was for some.

"The purchase of Southern Progress," McCalla said, "set a market value on what we had done in building *Southern Living*. I guess you could say that we had earned our keep, but no one really told us that.

"By the time Time, Inc., bought us," McCalla said, "we were working on the June and July issues and the whole year's magazines had long been planned, even photographed for the most part. Looking back at those issues, they represented one of our greatest years."

McCalla wandered nostalgically through the magazines of 1985. Particularly memorable in January was Philip Morris's "Home to Mount Vernon," photographed by John O'Hagan. It was the first of the "Southern Places" series, later expanded into one of Oxmoor Houses's finest art books. March featured San Antonio. "It's always been one of my favorite cities in America," said McCalla. "I tell everyone my church is the eighteenth-century Mission San Jose. I first saw it almost fifty years ago.

I was there when San Antonio had the big snowfall in the 1980s and wandered through the grounds almost alone that snowy New Year's. Mission San José seems like the soul of the Southwest to me."

Bruce Roberts shot a striking aerial view of Hilton Head Island in April, looking down on the lighthouse at Harbor Town, with a notable essay by Dianne Young on the island whose coming of age almost exactly duplicates the rise of *Southern Living*. The same issue carried Mark Childress's "Southern Journal" piece "At the Pond with Grandmother." McCalla said, "One more reason that year was such a high point in the magazine's history."

"The Garden Department, under John Floyd, really hit its stride about this time," McCalla said. "You could publish a book on the four-color spreads that have opened the garden section." Steve Bender and photographer Van Chaplin featured "Old Roses Find New Friends" in May. Old friend Geoffrey Norman wrote of "A Reunion in West Feliciana" in June, with tour de force images by Roberts. The descendants of Alexander and Ann Sterling gather at the home place, Wakefield Plantation, in Louisiana every fifty years, a classic subject for *Southern Living*. Margaret Agnew produced "Summer Suppers" in July, fifty-two sumptuous pages.

Harry Middleton wrote one of his finest pieces in August, on the Civil War battlefield Shiloh: "Shiloh, Biblical word thought to mean place of peace, became a field of death and honor over two days in April, 1862." Harry was to leave the magazine and die a young man of much promise. The September cover by Roberts looked down into a valley from the Blue Ridge Parkway as the parkway turned fifty years old. Logue produced his nineteenth All-South College Football section, naturally picking Auburn third and the two Oklahoma teams second and seventh. Bo Jackson was the big noise on the All-South squad, and he went on to win the Heisman Trophy as the best college player of the year.

Charles Walton captured all manner of nuts and fruits on the October cover for "Time for the Taste of Autumn," Deborah Lowery and Beverly Morrow collaborating on the words and images. McCalla loved "The Small Town Experience" in November. "It was a great survey piece," he said, "of elegant accommodations, fine dining, and unusual shops in the small towns of Franklin, Tennessee; Covington, Louisiana; Abbeville, South Carolina; Salado, Texas; and Middleburg, Virginia. We spread the joy around in large and small places, one of the secrets of our success."

Finally, December and "our famous cookie cover," said McCalla, "at least it was famous in Southern kitchens. I think we narrowed the story down to eighteen recipes and baked each one in volume. We had enough cookies to feed the entire building. I still think it is probably the best Christmas cover we ever published. Everyone participated. But the main crew working on it were Kaye Adams, Deborah Lowery, photographer Charles Walton, and stylist Beverly Morrow, with Jean Liles orchestrating everything, of course. Oh, it was a vintage year," McCalla said, closing the bound volume of 1985.

The day the company was sold, Logue and Logan went to lunch at Mauby's, where many a Southern Progress question had been raised or settled among the predictably good eats. Logan said the deed would be done that afternoon; they would be sold to Time, Inc.

"Well, Don," Logue said, "it won't happen this year, or next year, or probably the year after. But you will be moving to New York. Those guys know you weren't standing behind the door when they handed out the brains. But as soon as they really get to know you, you'll be headed to the big city."

"Oh, no," said Logan. "Not me. They've got hundreds of guys up there smarter than me. They don't need me. I'm happy right here in Birmingham." And no doubt he was. For the time being.

Department heads gathered around the long conference table, and Emory Cunningham said a deal had been worked out with Time, Inc., to buy the company for $480 million. Logue and McCalla couldn't keep from smiling at each other. This was the same company that was doing $9 million in gross business when *Southern Living* was launched. Emory said that though a price had been agreed on, if the people in the room didn't want the sale to go through, he would call it off.

Now that would have been a scene. And who would have explained to the primary owner, Mr. Butler, that he wasn't about to be $100 million richer after all?

Logan looked on the entire transaction with an unsentimental, absolutely practical eye. He said, "We will keep our independence as long as we grow profits. The day we stop growing, there will be somebody at the door from the Harvard Business School."

There were no dissenters in the room. Whereupon Emory called in Time, Inc., President Dick Monroe—likable, casual in his signature trousers with no belt—who said all the right things: they didn't want to change the company, which was brilliantly run; they only wanted to help grow it.

A really funny thing happened. He and Time, Inc., lived up to their word.

And Cunningham said his very prophetic thing: "Maybe we will change them more than they will change us."

The literal selling of the company at the law offices of Bradley, Arant, was like a scene out of a more benign *Godfather* movie, as the stockholders of the old farm publishing company gathered to pick up checks undreamed of in their most outlandish fantasies. Older employees and retirees of The Progressive Farmer Company, who had worked all their lives for modest wages, were thanking the fates for those lean years when they were paid in company stock rather than in hard wages.

Subscribers and friends of the company worried openly that the "Yankees" would subvert their beloved *Southern Living* and perhaps jettison the century-old *Progressive Farmer*, whose own editors put hot questions to Dick Monroe about their place in so formidable a publishing empire. Monroe talked until he was hoarse at a *P.F.* editorial meeting, assuring the editors that their spot in the company was secure.

In an effort to insure the company's best chance at independence, Cunningham named Logan as the next president of the company. And Time, Inc., agreed to the appointment.

It was not an easy transition for Cunningham. He had held the powers of the president's office in his two hands since 1968. Emory said, "In selling the company, one of my concerns was who they might send down here to run it when I retired. Part of the deal was that I could choose my own successor. I really struggled with that one. If Roger McGuire hadn't developed that disease, I probably would have made him the president. Jim DeVira was there, and some people wanted him as president. But to take what we had, and organize it, and do the things that had to be done, I thought Don Logan would be the best."

Emory Cunningham's name disappeared off the masthead of the October, 1987, issue of *Southern Living*. It was a landmark absence. Gone was the name of the man who named *Southern Living*, and whose energy and patience and ability to convince the Old Guard to risk everything had made the launching of the magazine possible. And in January of 2000, Emory died after a long, heroic bout with cancer. He left as many friends as he did major accomplishments.

Logan moved into Emory's corner office as Chief Executive Officer of Southern Progress in August, 1987. And from the moment he sat down he was a very popular president. He never reserved his own parking place in the company lot. Those who had worked directly for him knew he would be in the office before the sun had a grip on the sky. Half the impromptu planning sessions they would have with Logan over the years would be breakfast sessions, in the early, single-digit hours.

Emory spent his last months supervising the construction of the new Southern Progress building, a couple of miles up Lakeshore Drive, south of Birmingham. The company had persuaded Samford University to sell thirty-five wooded acres adjacent to the campus.

"Jim Nelson deserves a lot of credit," Emory said. "He had to relocate families in four or five houses and a church. I knew I wasn't going to be working inside the new building, so I left the inside to others. I concentrated on the exterior, the siting, the staggered parking decks. I didn't want a high-rise parking deck. We had big arguments about that."

Emory worked with his old friend and architect Henri Jova to create a splendid stone-and-glass building of 150,000 square feet that was fitted into the trees as if it had grown up among them. The building straddled the great ravine, in which the three descending ponds were ultimately created that flowed into the one-acre lake, upon which a pair of wood ducks had recently mated and set about raising a family.

Under Logan's leadership, the *Southern Living* franchise was extended in many directions. Special issues evolved for "*Southern Living* House Plans," "Family Vacations," a "Garden Guide," "Holidays," etc. Logan nurtured the idea of quarterly state magazines within the main *Southern Living*, and *Carolina Living, People & Places* was successfully launched, to be followed by similar efforts in Tennessee, Georgia, and eventually Texas.

Cooking Light flourished, reaching one million subscribers. Oxmoor House passed *Southern Living* as the most profitable arm of the company. Profits reached unanticipated heights. Company morale was even higher. The purchase of Southern Progress was proving to be one of the best investments in the history of American publishing.

Of course, not every venture was a success. Southern Progress acquired a failing Southern magazine in Little Rock and turned it into *Southpoint* magazine, under the razor-sharp editorship of John Huey, from *Fortune* magazine by way of the *Wall Street Journal*. It was one-half business magazine and one-half general-interest magazine, with some dazzling writing—including a wonderful excerpt from the book *Barbarians at the Gate*, one of the co-authors of which was an editor of *Southpoint*, John Helyar. But the magazine was still searching for its heart and soul (not to mention its readership and advertising support) when Logan stopped it dead after five issues and about five million dollars.

"It hurt," said Logue, who served as editorial director. "I still don't know if it failed us or we failed it. McCalla called it right in the beginning. He said it wouldn't work. But the magazine was just beginning to find its way. It had a sharp edge that frightened many in the company. I liked that best about it. But I agree with Logan that nothing in the world is tougher than turning a magazine from something it was into something it has never been. The entire caper should make a case study someday in somebody's business school. John Huey has gone on to make a magnificent job of editing *Fortune* magazine."

Logan also named Nancy Woodhull, of *USA Today*, as editor-in-chief of Southern Progress. Logue said, "She was bright. And tough. And energetic. And held an inspiring *Southern Living* editorial meeting at the University of Mississippi in Oxford. But her style, honed in the brass-knucks world of women's issues, just didn't find favor at Southern Progress. To be fair, Nancy didn't pretend to be somebody she wasn't to get the job. She left the same 'right-on' person she had been when she came." She left to form her own consulting company, and made quite a success of it until she died after a very brief illness. "I thought she was an unlikely fit for Southern Progress," Logue said. "But I liked her. I'm amazed that some people were afraid of her. They should have spent a few years on the *Atlanta Journal* working for Furman Bisher."

The progress at Southern Progress did not go unnoticed in New York. One day in June, 1992, Logue's wife, Helen, who prefers to wake up at the ungodly hour of 5 A.M., stuck her head in the door and tossed the *Wall Street Journal* on the bed, saying, "Your buddy is headed to New York." Logue did not open his eyes, answering, "So, they finally offered him The Job."

McCalla was sitting in his home office, a rare thing at 2 P.M., when Bert O'Neal called. Bert had given up the camera to become a vice-president of Merrill Lynch, and McCalla's broker. "Are you sitting down?" asked Bert. "Your old boss Don Logan is going to Time, Inc., as president." McCalla was not really surprised.

By 1994, Logan was president and CEO of all of Time, Inc. And he was extending their magazine franchises in all directions. Cunningham's prophecy had come to pass; Birmingham's influence had swept over Manhattan.

Jim Nelson stepped from the financial arm of Southern Progress to the office of CEO. He occupied the role only a brief time and was moved to California and then to New York, where he works again with Logan. Nelson's lasting impact was the construction of an annex of seventy-three thousand square feet and the marvelous atrium connecting it to the main building. Nelson concentrated on the exterior design of the annex, and Tom Angelillo helped map out the interior. Aesthetically, the annex has proven the equal of the original building itself.

One action by Nelson was not popular with the company. He abolished Tom Curl's job as editor-in-chief of Southern Progress. After a twenty-year career on *Progressive Farmer* and then *Southern Living*, Tom had been appointed by Logan to succeed Woodhull.

"Emory sent Tom to be my managing editor when he thought I needed help after I got back from Brookwood," said McCalla. McCalla's thirty-day tour at Brookwood allowed him to drop his old pal, Jack Daniel's, for life. He said it was not half as tough as giving up cigarettes. And giving up cigarettes probably saved his life when he underwent his second round of heart bypass surgery. McCalla's doctors were amazed at the power of his recovery.

Logue said, "In truth, McCalla has helped an untold number of people follow in his path. Even as we were writing this book, he would sometimes be up at 1 A.M. on the Internet, encouraging some dancer to stay sober in Manhattan, or a farmer in Australia."

"I resented Tom Curl at first," McCalla said. "But I grew to like him. And respect him. He was smart and a hard worker. And a genuine fellow. I think he learned you could get the job done and not be so uptight." Curl, a proud Texas A&M grad, and Nelson, an Arkansas farm boy, didn't march in step. But shortly after Tom joined another publisher in the Midwest, he was promoted to president, confirming his old colleagues' opinions of his ability.

Tom Angelillo took over Nelson's office as CEO in August, 1994. He became the second president not to have a reserved parking place and not to need one. Not even Logan himself was a more popular CEO. Or a bolder one.

Angelillo first left Bruce Aiken in charge of Oxmoor House, then brought him over as his executive vice-president. Johnny McIntosh moved up from marketing to run Oxmoor House but recently moved into magazine circulation.

In 1996, Angelillo presided over the purchase of *Weight-Watchers* magazine, and prepared to launch a new national magazine in 1997,

Coastal Living. Logue had offered the idea for such a magazine for six or seven years. Angelillo didn't stop with the idea; he appointed Burton Craig of the Atlanta office as publisher and Katherine Pearson as editor of *Coastal Living*. She got it rolling with a circulation approaching a half million, and turned it over to Michael Carlton, an excellent writer and a skilled teacher of writing.

"Ah, *these* are the days," said Logue, envying Carlton and the young lions at their work at *Coastal Living*.

After almost twenty-two years as editor of *Southern Living*, Gary E. McCalla from Amber, Oklahoma, had had enough. "When you get a little bored, when you feel you might be repeating yourself, it's time to hang it up," McCalla said. "I wonder how long it will be before another editor of *Southern Living* lasts twenty-two years?"

The senior editors of the magazine staff collaborated on the editor's page, "Life at *Southern Living*," the month McCalla left. They wrote such lines as: "Anyone who has met Gary knows he is down to earth. . . . He liked his garden staff to be out digging in the dirt. . . . For McCalla, it meant a big, sometimes unruly crowd competing for space in the magazine. . . . A strong visual editor. . . . He presided over the Test Kitchens with an iron wit and a knowing palate. . . . He always wanted it to be fun."

"Amen," said Logue.

The company threw a mighty party at a local country club. The good times flowed. It might have been fun night at an editorial conference on some island off the South's Atlantic Coast. McCalla looked back on the years and said, "Hell, let's do it again."

The unshockable McCalla was shocked into speechlessness when the company off-loaded a two-year-old thoroughbred racehorse: Four Mile Penny, by Rambler Red, out of Fair Penny by Cutlass. They handed him the bridle and wished them both Godspeed.

McCalla put the filly and other stable mates to work on racetracks across the South until he'd had all the fun he could afford. The next summer, Four Mile Penny "broke her maiden" at River Downs in Cincinnati. Four months later, on a frozen track at Turfway Park in Northern Kentucky, Penny won her second and last race. She paid $254 to win (on a $2 bet). McCalla was pouring a floor for a barn that day and forgot that she was running. He did not have even a $2 bet on her. Somewhere Walt Osborne must have been smiling.

These days McCalla is still working the barns and fences and the meadows on his thirty-five-acre farm south of Birmingham, living the good life with Barbara, and keeping in touch with the folks in Oklahoma and especially his American Indian heritage.

One of McCalla's own men, Dr. John Floyd, was named editor of *Southern Living.* "I couldn't be more pleased," McCalla said. "John rescued the Garden Department after it wandered in the wilderness all those years. He's one of our own. He's smart. He understands the South and, most importantly, its differences. He also understands business. That'll help him."

Floyd promoted a strong staff of executive editors: Carlton, before he was stolen by *Coastal Living*; Eleanor Griffin, a whirlwind of creative ideas; and Kaye Adams, ruler of the magazine's all-important food empire.

Time whipped past. In July, 1991, John Logue retired. The company turned the Highland Bar and Grill into a loud roast. They even had a "fashion show" of his infamous golf shirts and suspenders. Kuralt and Cronkite and Dickey and Willie Morris and Childress and Ray Ellis told lies on a videotape. And Logue found himself speechless when they handed him two tickets to Scotland, to play the Old Course at St. Andrews and see the British Open Golf Tournament. Logue can't remember one damn thing he said that evening. But he thought, "McCalla was right. Let's do it again. Let's invade Manhattan with a tray of slides and a song and dance. Let's eat a platter of fried smelt at Joe Muir's and swap lies with old buddies building the 'Detroit Iron,' as they love to call their American cars. Let's have one last brawl of a color pick at *Southern Living*, with McCalla, still the unbeaten and untied welterweight champion, challenging the room for 'What else you got?' Let's deal one more hand of draw poker at 2 A.M. at the advertising sales meeting. Let's put an outrageous amount of the company's money in one more glittering art book, with an old drinking buddy to write the words. Let's hire some kid selling his clothes to get back from Europe. Let's do it all . . . one more time . . . again."

But time moves unconscionably on.

Logue and his wife, Helen, live in Birmingham and at their beach house on the Alabama coast, and he writes "Morris and Sullivan" mystery novels, including the latest one with Dell publishing, set at the 1995 U.S. Open: *On Par with Murder.*

"You see, McCalla, I had to get in one plug," said Logue.

"Don't think I wasn't expecting it," McCalla said.

"This book is over, and we forgot everything," Logue said.

"Oh, God, yes," said McCalla, "in twenty-two years, we published fifty-eight thousand total pages of *Southern Living*, and we haven't touched on one in five hundred."

"All the scandals we left out," Logue said.

"Well, we were part of most them," McCalla said.

"The time in the funky sixties when Lena Sturges went to the Kentucky Derby and stood in the rain in the infield with all the college 'flower children,' " said Logue, "and one of the guys had too much beer and didn't want to leave the shelter of the long plastic sheet over their heads to find a restroom and unzipped his pants and started doing his business, and Sturges whacked him in the most vital spot imaginable with her umbrella. Oh, I would have paid all the money we lost on the horse we bet on to have seen that action."

"If Lena had been there, they wouldn't have had a Woodstock," said McCalla. "I forgot the night Pete Fountain drove me ninety miles an hour through the French Quarter to my hotel."

"Good thing that was in your drinking days," said Logue.

"Remember the time Bill Capps took the vibrator ad that McGuire had accepted to Emory, and Emory killed it on the press," said McCalla, laughing, "and at the next advertising sales meeting, I gave McGuire the 'Advertising Decency Award,' and presented him with a gilded vibrator, vibrating on a gilded board."

"We have a picture of that somewhere," said Logue.

"But I don't think it's going to make this book," said McCalla. "Anything serious we ought to close with? I think our editor has the hook out."

"Yes," Logue said, "we forgot the best 'Southern Journal' we ever published, 'Firelight and Steel,' by Howard Bahr, who at the time ran the Faulkner Library in Oxford, Mississippi. He wrote about working in a switchyard on the L&N railroad, long years ago. What he wrote, Old Man, is what we would like to say and are unable to . . . about all those years at *Southern Living* now receding into time:

" 'On Winter nights, when the yard lay like a slab of cold iron in the darkness, the switchmen would make a fire. They would scour the empty flatcars for pallet lumber, and now and then pull a loose pine stump off the cars bound up from Florida. In the last of twilight the pin-puller would lay the fire by the number three switch and touch it off with a fuse. There it would burn, far into the night, to warm the hands of men to whom a missed handhold meant injury or death, and to diminish, even by that much, the awful darkness of the yard.

"'. . . So I lingered in the circle of light, among those men whose faces and voices I should never forget, while around us the inexorable Century raced on. And in time I began to understand the secret of the fire and what it meant: that it was not just a fire, not just an evanescent pile of old lumber and stumps to warm the night and pass away. Like the talk itself the fire was a continuum, a symbol of those things in men which do not change because they cannot, because we will not let them. Because they are all we have to anchor us in a life where trains are forever leaving in the dark.'"

The poet said, "We are all moving in the same direction. It's just that we are taking separate exits."

Exit McCalla.

Exit Logue.

Index